The Project

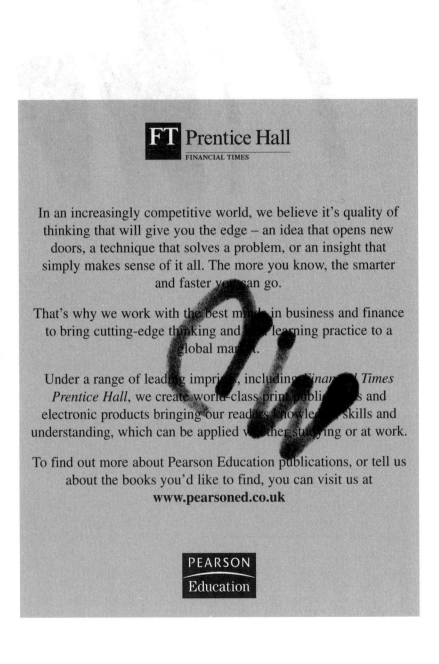

FT Prentice Hall

FINANCIAL TIMES

In an increasingly competitive world, we believe it's quality of thinking that will give you the edge – an idea that opens new doors, a technique that solves a problem, or an insight that simply makes sense of it all. The more you know, the smarter and faster you can go.

That's why we work with the best minds in business and finance to bring cutting-edge thinking and best learning practice to a global market.

Under a range of leading imprints, including *Financial Times Prentice Hall*, we create world-class print publications and electronic products bringing our readers knowledge, skills and understanding, which can be applied whether studying or at work.

To find out more about Pearson Education publications, or tell us about the books you'd like to find, you can visit us at **www.pearsoned.co.uk**

PEARSON
Education

The Project Manager

Mastering the art of delivery

Richard Newton

Prentice Hall

FINANCIAL TIMES

An imprint of **Pearson Education**

Harlow, England • London • New York • Boston • San Francisco • Toronto
Sydney • Tokyo • Singapore • Hong Kong • Seoul • Taipei • New Delhi
Cape Town • Madrid • Mexico City • Amsterdam • Munich • Paris • Milan

PEARSON EDUCATION LIMITED

Edinburgh Gate
Harlow CM20 2JE
Tel: +44 (0)1279 623623
Fax: +44 (0)1279 431059
Website: www.pearsoned.co.uk

First published in Great Britain in 2005

ISBN-13: 978-0-273-70173-6

British Library Cataloguing-in-Publication Data
A catalogue record for this book is available from the British Library

Library of Congress Cataloging-in-Publication Data
Newton, Richard, 1964 —
  The project manager : mastering the art of delivery / Richard Newton.
    p. cm.
  Includes index.
  ISBN 0-273-70173-8 (alk. paper)
  1. Project management. 2. Leadership. I. Title.
  HD69.P75N496 2005
  658.4'04—dc22

                                                                        2005040030

10 9 8 7 6 5
09 08

Typeset in Galliard with Frutiger by 70
Printed and bound by Ashford Colour Press Ltd, Gosport, Hampshire

The Publisher's policy is to use paper manufactured from sustainable forests

Contents

Preface

I HAVE BEEN INVOLVED IN PROJECTS for about twenty years. Starting as a project team member, I have made the transition through being a project manager of various hues, to running teams of project managers, finally to being a project customer and a sponsor. It has had its ups and downs – but overall it has been great fun. I enjoy tremendously the challenge of complex delivery.

As part of this fun I have been responsible for work to improve various organisations' delivery and implementation skills. Doing this I have recruited and built teams, set up and arranged training, read and shared the contents of lots of books, and sought outside consultants to help. I have seen project managers gradually become more accredited with industry-recognised qualifications. And yet I have not fundamentally seen a real shift in reliable delivery skills. Perhaps the standards and my expectations have kept on rising, perhaps the projects are getting harder – or maybe something is wrong!

I put this at least partially down to three things. Firstly, whenever I look at books, attend courses and talk to project management trainers almost the whole time they refer to what I call the 'mechanics' of project management. By mechanics I mean the processes, systems and tools that form the core body of knowledge of project management. What I have realised is that these mechanics are important, but they are not the only factor in ensuring successful delivery. There is a range of other skills and competencies required in addition. In fact, when I have watched really successful project managers I have seen that though they may understand and use the mechanics well – it is not the differentiating factor that makes them successful. Yet rarely does anyone look at these differentiating factors. Most of these factors are about the person who is the project manager more than the specific variant of project management approach used. Secondly, when I look at books on project management they are often poorly targeted. They can be overly simple and really only of interest to absolute beginners or people outside of the project management profession. Alternatively, they reflect hugely complex and intense approaches which are probably fine when you are working on a multi-billion pound defence procurement programme, but are of little practical use to the average project manager in a normal organisation working on a typically scaled project. Finally, when project managers are taught and successfully understand how to implement the standard project management mechanics they are not always taught why they are important, and how the various components come together as a whole. And yet without this understanding it is impossible to fully apply good judgement in their use and adaptation to the situation – which is essential to successful delivery.

I have sought out a book that is targeted at the majority of project managers who manage complex, key business projects without thousands of staff for several years. I have searched for a volume that spells out the difference between the average and the really good project manager. I have looked for a text to explain project management in a holistic form. And I have not found it – all I have found is frustration!

So, after failing in my searches I decided to write my own book. This is a personal view, I make no claim that it is an exhaustive study of the subject – but I believe it will add great value to most project managers big or small. This is the project manager's guide to delivery. It is called *The Project Manager* because it focuses on the person managing the project before thinking about tools and processes.

Richard Newton
January 2005

Introduction

The secret art

HOW DO YOU CONSISTENTLY MANAGE complex projects successfully?

There are people who are very successful at running projects. They have a track record in continuously meeting the objectives of complicated developments. When brought into conversation, and if they are being open, they will often query why people value what they do so highly. Not because the things delivered in projects are not highly valuable but because they think what they do is not that difficult. A regular comment is 'it's really just common sense isn't it'. They work hard, but they do not get into that maniacal stress and overload that is often a feature of less well-run projects. They seem to be calmly in control. On the other hand there is a huge number of people, including many project managers, for whom delivery of projects is at best a hard fought struggle and at worst a complete mystery. A secret art that they have not mastered. They somehow do not have the same type of common sense referred to by their more successful peers. So what is this black magic that is so simple to some and yet impossibly hard to others?

It's time to share some of the secrets.

Why read this book?

Project management is a skill set greatly in demand within both the public and private sectors. A skill set that a few decades ago would probably not have been formally recognised in any consistent way. Now it exists internationally both as an established profession in its own right, and as a competence that forms a part of many managers' general toolkit of capabilities. The demand for experienced project management professionals is a reflection of its success.

And yet for all its success and demand, there is something wrong. Ask a cross-section of managers in any large organisation do they have absolute, or even high confidence in their organisation's ability to deliver projects and you will get a resounding no. There have been countless studies of the low percentage of projects that are delivered to time and budget, or the high percentage that are late or even never completed, and the figures are usually depressing. For all the processes, training and methodologies there is a gap between the hype and expectations and the practical experience. And yet in contrast to this, most organisations have, or know of a few people, 'safe pairs of hands', who can consistently manage to deliver exceptional projects to time and budget. What causes this gap, and what is it that these individual safe pairs of hands do that is different?

> So what is this black magic that is so simple to some and yet impossibly hard to others?

To many people outside the project management profession it can seem at one extreme an almost mystically valuable black art and at the other a set of bureaucratic pomposity. At times the latter can be true, but project management is not magic and it is of tremendous value when well applied. The problem actually lies with those last three words of the previous sentence 'when well applied'. Applying things well is hard enough, but on top of this there is little common consensus in the case of project management about what good application looks like.

At one level good application can be seen as the use of a quality project management approach. The profession is supported by a set of processes and methodologies which attempt to define 'how' to run a project. However, ask an experienced project manager what makes a good project manager and they will rarely mention understanding of the formal methodologies. The open secret among project managers is that good project management is about how you work, interact and communicate with people. So where can you start?

The place to start is with some definitions. There are many definitions of what a project is, and what project managers do. And even if you never intend to manage a project in your life it is essential for every manager to at least know the meaning and purpose of project management. You are most likely in any business career to find yourself involved in or needing a project – having at least rudimentary project terminology is therefore useful. This book is not a glossary of terms, but in Chapter 1 the basic definitions are reviewed. This is mainly to give context to the rest of the text, and to provide a minimum common level of knowledge to build from.

Once some definitions are in place you can start to learn more about project management practice. In becoming a recognised profession, with commonly defined processes and working methods (such as PRINCE), associated widely recognised accreditations (such as PRINCE 2 practitioner), and even professional institutions to belong to (such as the Association of Project Managers) there has been much work put into defining good project management practice. The development of systematic methods has been of significant value in raising the standards and giving consistency in the approach of project managers. This defined approach can be referenced on many training courses and in literally hundreds of textbooks. They are variable in quality, but there are excellent reference texts and trainers out there. The aim of this book is not to add to these processes and methodologies, although they are referred to as necessary.

So if this book does set out to define project management roles, processes or methodologies – what is its purpose? It is a reference book, a set of observations from my personal experiences of what differentiates the great project manager from the merely average. This is not a normal project management primer – there are many excellent books and courses that can teach you the ABC of project management. It answers the question: what is it that you need to do to be a *consistently* good project manager?

The reason you should read this book is that it provides a set of experience-based lessons to help you consistently deliver results. If you are a project manager, someone who has project managers on your team, or someone who recruits project management staff it will provide you with a valuable addition to your core skills.

It is fair to ask at this point – what is my qualification to do this? It is simply that I have worked as everything from a junior project manager to a senior programme director within companies and internationally renowned consultancies. I have successfully delivered everything from consultancy projects with budgets of a few tens of thousands through to major programmes launching new products and business changes with budgets in the hundreds of millions. I have also learnt from the experiences of recovering messed-up projects and messing up a few of my own. I have run project management teams, have taught and coached project managers, have employed both permanent and contract project managers. I have operated up to director level in large companies as the customer or sponsors of projects being run by project managers. I have been involved in the development of delivery methodologies and project management approaches for consultancies. I have set up project management teams and project management centres of excellence in large companies. I have built competency-based assessment and standard career definitions for project management teams. In doing this I have worked extensively in the UK, mainland Europe – including France, Italy and Germany, the USA, and Australia. During this time I have deliberately observed and noted my impressions as well as managed delivery. What I have mainly observed is that even with the strengths of good process and training the difference between the results achieved by an average and the consistently good project manager are huge. Yet when I have analysed the reasons for this difference, as I have now been doing for a number of years, they are not so complex, and do not usually come down to basic project management knowledge. This book defines what those differentiating factors are. They are not a black art!

Will this book help you? It is true that some people are born to be project managers and intuitively know what to do, in the same way that some people are born to be accountants, lawyers or successful entrepreneurs. Yet all of these people, at least the really good ones, are willing to pick up lessons here and there – and there will be some valuable lessons here for you if you are lucky enough to be in this category. Then there is the much larger group of people who have the ability to be good or even great in their chosen profession but need a little guidance on the way. This book will help you too if you are in this category. Finally, there are project managers who feel that it is time for them to step up the project management ladder, make that move from junior to senior, cross the chasm from managing projects to managing programmes, or simply move from occasional project management roles to being a full-time project manager. That step will be assisted by this book.

The primary hypothesis of this book is that learning the core project management processes and following good standard project management practice is an important skill for a project manager, but that there is a host of hard and soft skills that are needed in addition. Taking that hypothesis, this book defines what those things are. Some of them are really good practice for any manager, others are specific to this profession.

This book does not contain a tick list or a process. Tick lists and processes are great when you get started, but as things get more complex they do not provide everything a project manager needs. In fact, at the extreme, over strenuous application of project management processes can be detrimental as it can make something that is best done with skill and experienced-based judgement into an unproductive mechanical application of bureaucracy. You will not find too much mention of terms like 'Gantt', 'PERT' and 'critical path analysis'. There is no talk of risk assessment methodologies or earned value analysis. There is little reference to the design of management forms, or how best to structure timesheets. It is not that these things do not have value, a good project manager has a wide toolkit of such capabilities that he or she often applies. It is simply that there are hundreds of good books, courses and people you can refer to to understand these elements. What is frequently missing is the thing that says, 'So, ok, now you know all the processes. You have read all the books, done the courses and even implemented them on live projects. You have seen their value, and sometimes the difficulty of actually implementing them. But so have many other equally qualified project managers. And yet among this group are some who constantly deliver results and some who struggle. Why is this? Well, here it is.

It is aimed at the experienced project manager, but will have lessons for and be of interest to the novice too. The sooner these are learnt the sooner you will be on your way to being a great project manager. What you will find is that many of these lessons appear simple, straightforward, perhaps even obvious. Maybe, but like common sense, they do not actually appear to be in common usage.

A brief word on job titles

We seem to have entered an age of what I call job title escalation. We have all seen the term 'consultant' move from being used by top doctors and specialists to being used by all and sundry. We have watched as the job title director migrates from being reserved for people on the board to becoming an attribute of the senior middle manager. We have looked at the organisation chart for financial services companies where everyone seems to be a VP. This phenomenon is equally true when it comes to

> We seem to have entered an age of what I call job title escalation

being a project manager. There are project coordinators, project managers, project directors, programme managers, programme directors and portfolio managers to name a few. Next to these titles may be a qualifying adjective like junior, senior, associate, executive and so on. To add to this complexity there are also professional project managers whose job title and permanent role is to be a project manager, and there are people who, for a period of time, take up the role of project manager while holding down a different job and having a different job title.

For the sake of sanity I will bundle this lot under the title 'project manager'. A project manager comprises a recognised professional skill set and is a job title that can be held with pride by those who really know what it means.

This makes life easy for me in writing this text, but obviously hides much detail about various levels of skills. There is, nevertheless, some considerable value in the different role titles in some situations, and there can, for example, be a significant difference between a true programme manager and a junior project manager. But I do not intend to go into that in detail, as it will not help with the content or focus of this book. In practice I always take the job title of any individual with a pinch of salt. To use an old expression – the proof of the pudding is in the eating – and the same is true of the various types of project manager. Sometimes the titles reflect real skills and experience, occasionally a formal difference in role, and there are, as I intimated above, separate methodologies for programme managers in addition to those for project managers. However, all too often these different job titles are simply a reflection of over-inflated egos and positioning within organisational hierarchies. This unfortunately has had the effect of devaluing the titles and leads people to seek ever grander, and in some cases ridiculous titles. Bring on the senior executive consulting programme director!

To avoid any risk of bias I have intermittently swapped between the pronouns 'he' and 'she' throughout the book.

Work-streams, projects, programmes and portfolios

As well as having a hierarchy of job titles, the project world has a hierarchy of chunks of project work. A component of a specific project with a particular focus may be called a work-stream or work-package; a large or complex project, or a set of interrelated projects may be called a programme (or for the USA, program); many projects together, whether related or unrelated but within some common area of responsibility may be called a portfolio. In Chapter 1 I will define a project, but I am not going to spend any time defining the other terms. The categorisation of projects of different scales, or the sub-categorisation of components of a project into chunks of work can occasionally be useful. (Although often this categorisation is applied in a bogus or over-emphasised manner.)

I avoid the distinction in this book as it is about better project management – to me this is about managing better not necessarily bigger. Whatever the scale of the projects you manage you can do it better. If this was a general text on being a good manager I would not differentiate between a team leader, a manager and a department head – the principles of good management are the same. The skills here will help you to manage bigger projects and programmes if that is what is important to you

> Whatever the scale of the projects you manage you can do it better

– but they will also help you to manage your work-stream better. So, for now, forget the hierarchy – I will focus simply on the principles of great project management.

A short overview of the contents

The contents of this book are structured to achieve two results. Firstly, it is written so you can read it easily from end to end. It is not an overly long book, but it is packed with value. Whether you diligently sit down and read it in one session, go through a little every night before you go to bed, or use it to fill your commuting time you will find it easy to consume. Secondly, it is written so that you can call upon specific parts of its advice in an easy manner. Carry it around with you and use it on a daily basis. At the end of the book (page 232) a quick reference guide provides a chapter-by-chapter summary of key points for easy future reference.

The book is divided into twelve chapters. Each can be read on its own or in sequence. In the following table I note the chapters and have tried to give them a priority rating out of 3 (3 being the highest priority). You will get the most benefit from reading the whole book in the order it is written, but if you are short of time and must prioritise, start with those chapters with the highest priority rating. (The ratings for Chapters 5, 7 and 10 are a reflection of how important these topics are to this book, rather than how absolutely important they are.)

Chapter	Title	Overview of chapter contents	Rating
1	Some basics	Review of basic terminology – project, project manager, customer, success.	1
2	Listening and talking	Core communication skills for project managers – the basis of good project management.	3
3	What actually is your project?	Really understanding what is wanted from the project you are delivering.	3
4	Some key traits	Personality traits needed by the project manager.	3
5	Getting your project started	Setting up your project taking account of practical realities. You understand the theory, but what does it all mean in practice?	2
6	Personal styles	Personal styles to avoid and to encourage in project managers.	2
7	Managing your project	A rapid overview of the mechanics of managing your project.	2
8	The team	How to manage your project team and get the best from them.	3
9	The limits of knowledge	Tasks project managers regularly get involved in that they should really avoid.	2
10	The mechanics of project management	Project management process basics that get forgotten.	2
11	Knowing when to say 'no'	When and how to avoid involvement in a project.	1
12	Closing thoughts	Round up for the book.	2
	Quick reference guide – summary contents	Chapter-by-chapter summary of key points for easy future reference.	2

The structural logic of the book is as follows: I start by defining its objective and key terminology (Introduction and Chapter 1), then there are two interwoven threads. The first takes the reader through a project lifecycle, what must be done at each stage, and the tools you have to manage (Chapters 1, 3, 5, 7, 8 and 10). In these I put project management processes in context and provide some practical and implementable advice. In parallel with this I weave a description of the human side of project management that is core to success but that is normally forgotten about (Chapters 2, 4, 6, 8, 9 and 11). I finish with my closing thoughts (Chapter 12) and the Quick reference guide.

For each topic I start by identifying the issues associated with it. Where possible I provide good practical answers and approaches to these issues. In some situations there are no single answers – and here I provide a framework of questions for the reader to use to work out an answer in the specific context he or she is working in. It is an intelligent guide to project management that does not say it is a purely mechanistic topic, but is one that requires the project manager to think and make judgement-based decisions.

1

Some basics

Key lesson

You must understand and be able to define the key terms used within your project. This must include a clear definition of your role as the project manager, a definition of the customer, and a common understanding of success for your project.

AN ASSUMPTION ABOUT READERS of this book is that you are not only interested in project management, but that you may already know something or even quite a lot about it. However, as a starting point, and to ensure we are working from the same 'knowledge set' it is worth having a common definition of some basic concepts. The starting point for us is to have a common view of – what is a project? and what is a project manager? (If you know all about these things then you can feel free to skip the first two sub-sections of this chapter.)

As well as ensuring that you can follow and absorb the contents of the book it is important to be able to define these terms – you will regularly need to use them yourself on projects, and when communicating about projects. Being able to define these terms easily when required shows competence – struggling to define them looks like incompetence.

Having defined what a project is and what a project manager does it is next sensible to think about who drives you to do a project. The reason a project is undertaken is because someone or some group of people want it done and want something achieved. This person or people are the customers. The next sub-section quickly runs through the concept of a customer for a project. This not so simple or clear cut as project managers often think and 'who is the customer?' is a good question to keep asking yourself when running a project.

With these basic definitions understood, and given that one of the core aims of this book is to articulate the differentiating factors between the average and the really successful project manager you had better also have a view of what success means in this context. This is discussed in the fourth and final sub-section of the chapter. Even if you think you are an expert it is worth running through this sub-section.

All the definitions given in this section are my own.

What is a project?
What is project management?

A project is essentially a way of working, a way of organising people, and a way to manage tasks. It is a style of coordinating and managing work. What differentiates it from other styles of management is that it is totally focused on a specific outcome, and when this outcome is achieved the project ceases to be necessary and the project is stopped. Contrast this, say, with running a production line, or managing some company operations – these are tasks that run continuously and have no one single end point.

A project starts at a defined point of time, ends at a specific point in time, and is complete when the outcome (normally as agreed at the beginning of the project, and normally defined in terms of specific tangible deliverables) is

> What differentiates it from other styles of management is that it is totally focused on a specific outcome

complete. Typically, there are limited resources, most commonly money and people's time, to deliver the outcome. When the outcome is delivered something will have changed. Although different projects may have some common features, each project is unique, with a specific one-off set of activities.

Project management is a formal discipline that has been developed to manage projects. A wide range of activities can benefit from project management, whether it be building a ship; constructing a house; developing an IT system; designing, building and launching a new product; or running a cost reduction exercise. The types of skills necessary to perform each of these activities vary immensely, but they can all be delivered by a project and managed by the project management approach. They all meet the criteria of having a clear and definable outcome – or result.

Project management tools, techniques and processes can be an extremely powerful means of achieving a desired outcome, or in project manager parlance of 'delivering'. I have a very strong faith in the capability of this approach, but it does have its limits. These are useful to understand – it helps to scope the boundaries of projects. Great as this approach is for achieving a specific set of deliverables, it is not a helpful technique if it is applied to continuous activities such as running a railway line, or a production plant. I have experience of project mindsets being applied to operational situations and in all cases the results have been sub-optimal.

What is a project manager?

A project manager is a person who has the responsibility for delivering all the components of a project. This can be a full-time job, or a role in a given situation. The work a project manager does varies from project to project, but in essence the project manager is responsible for scoping out the work (see Chapters 2 and 3); planning it and determining what resources are required (see Chapter 5); getting the resources allocated (see Chapter 5); and then managing the completion of the tasks required and ensuring any problems or issues that may cause the completion of tasks to be delayed or stopped are resolved (see Chapter 7). A project manager works according to a project management approach (see Chapter 10). (In addition a project manager needs to apply a set of communications and people skills – as discussed in Chapters 2, 4, 6 and 8.)

Sometimes there can be hierarchies of project managers. Each project manager then has a specific area of the project he or she is fully responsible for, and they in turn report to a more senior project manager – often called a programme manager. As we have discussed in the Introduction the job titles and scope of roles can vary, but the fundamental responsibilities of the job do not. (Arguably there is more to being a programme manager than simply being a more senior project manager, but the details do not matter in this context.) If you are working in a situation in which there are multiple project managers you must be able to define your own specific role – the best way to do this is to be able to show which part of a project plan you are responsible for managing, and which deliverables you are responsible for ensuring are delivered.

A professional project manager is someone whose full-time job is to be a project manager and who is usually trained in project management processes and tools. This can be differentiated from someone who takes the role of a project manager on a specific project, but who normally fulfils a different function.

The key point is that for any one scoped piece of work the project manager is the one person fully responsible for its delivery.

Who are projects for?

Every project is done for someone, or some group of people. These are the customers. At first glance this seems a simple concept, and theoretically it is. The relationship between a project manager and their customer should be clear and explicit, although in practice it can be obscure and full of various levels of intrigue and politics (I do not exaggerate). Unless there is a specific need to differentiate between various customer groups for simplicity's sake throughout the rest of this book I shall generally refer to the person or group of people a project is done for as 'the customer'. However, as a project manager you do need to understand fully the concept of customer in each and every project you are involved in.

> The relationship between a project manager and their customer should be clear and explicit

My definition of a customer is someone who has any of the following three characteristics:

1 She will legitimately put requirements upon the project.

2 She will enjoy the benefits of the project once it is complete.

3 She has a formal role in judging the success of a project once it is complete.

It is critical for the project manager to understand that:

◆ The customer has requirements which must be understood as these are the basis for the project to be delivered against.

◆ There is often more than one customer.

◆ Different customers or customer groups may have different (and potentially conflicting) requirements and measures of success.

◆ The project needs to have a common set of requirements documented and agreed with the customer(s), noting those which must be considered and those which can be ignored.

◆ The customer's views and needs may change through the life of the project.

So far what I have stated is elementary. In reality though the ability to identify and understand the needs of varied customer groups is a complex subject in its own right. For most projects the customer can be broken down into various categories, and all have some interest in its being undertaken. The most common categories are:

◆ The sponsor.

◆ The financer.

◆ The beneficiary.

◆ The end user.

◆ The end customer.

◆ The stakeholders (which is really a broader group than just customers).

(These groups are defined and described in some detail in Chapter 2.)

When you start a project it is worth thinking through each of these categories of customer and determining whether they exist, and, if you need to, to interact with them and manage their input to the project. Ideally there is a single person who acts as the overriding customer, or customer representative on a project. This person is often the project sponsor and they are critically important to a project's success – but it is a foolhardy project manager who assumes that the sponsor really represents all requirements and does not review these other groupings, even informally, when kicking a project off. The dangers of not understanding fully who has requirements on a project are essentially:

◆ Incomplete or incorrect requirements – and hence the project does not deliver all that is required.

◆ Unsatisfied customers – which can result in a lack of support or even active obstruction during the life of a project. It can also result in the project manager not being seen and treated at the end of a project as a successful manager.

◆ Poor understanding of success – customers may assess success in many ways, unless you understand these your project may well fail. (This is described in more detail below.)

What is success?

If this book is to lay out a debate about what makes a successful project manager I had better define what success is. Without this baseline it is possible to argue forever about whether the factors I have described in this book are really the basis for success, without agreeing this, success can become like beauty – its measure being in the eye of the beholder.

I need to start therefore, like a good project manager, by scoping out what I mean by success in this context. Every individual has their own definition of success. Whether that be to have a great family life, hold down a good job, be able to retire at 45, have a new Porsche on your drive, or to feel spiritually fulfilled on a daily basis. These are about 'personal success', and, as this is not a self-help manual, I am not intending to say too much about this beyond the few words in the next sub-section. In this book, when I talk about success I generally mean success in terms of what constitutes *project success*. If I am the customer, sponsor, stakeholder, or person paying for a project, how do I define project success?

Personal success as a project manager

There is an almost infinite number of ways of defining personal success, but these definitions lie beyond the remit of this text. However, in the limited context of the career of a project manager how would he or she define success? Typically, to a project manager the definition of success is to have project success and to such an extent that they are able to go on to run other projects and are sought after to run the projects of their choice. What makes such projects worth doing to any individual typically falls into one or more of three categories:

◆ **The project content** – personal success driven by the ability to choose the projects working in the most interesting areas. Some project managers are driven by the desire to manage projects which relate to specific areas such as new technology, organisational change, or in particular industries or geographic locations.

◆ **The project complexity** – this relates to either the riskiness of the project, or the fact that the project is working in novel areas. Some project managers specialise in intellectually complex projects, or those that have a high risk or need recovering from seemingly intractable problems.

◆ **The project scale** – the size of the project or programme. There is a significant difference between running a £50k, 50-man/day project and a £500m, 500-man/year programme and it requires a variety of more advanced skills.

All of these are valid and interesting options for project managers, and in many cases it is a combination of these factors that excites or interests project managers. The key point I would make to any project manager is that the ability to select between the types of project you are involved in as a project manager will be driven over time by people's expectations and experiences of your delivery of projects. In other words your personal success is directly related to your perceived project success.

> Your personal success is directly related to your perceived project success

Project success

Every project will have a set of things that can be used to measure success. These may be formally laid out as critical success factors, or may simply be implied between the project manager and whoever is driving or sponsoring the project. In fact, one of the first tasks, and key skills, of a good project manager running a well-run project is to get clarity around the explicit success factors and tease out the implicit or hidden ones. In some projects the results will be a simple set of deliverables, in others they may be a very complex set of interrelated factors. In some cases these may even be contradictory leaving the project manager to perform a balancing act trading off one against the other.

The theory is that at the end of a project the person who wanted it done can simply compare what she or he has been given with the success criteria and decide whether a successful outcome has been achieved. Every project manager balances this against a list of caveats and reasons that can limit the ability to achieve the successful outcome (for example: this is enough money and time for the project as long as nothing changes; or, I will get it done as long as I get these resources; or, the end results will be achieved as long as this risk does not occur).

Unless it is a very simple, or very clear cut project, the absolute measure of success can be hard. However, in simple terms all types of success measures can be boiled down into the three high-level categories:

◆ **Deliver the deliverables** – this may seem blindingly obvious, and for many projects, especially the non-complex ones success is simply the achievement of the deliverables planned at the start of the work. Such deliverables will take many shapes and may be documents, IT systems, other technology and infrastructure, buildings, or, more subtly, some kind of business change. The list of possible deliverables is endless – a project and project structure can be used to deliver almost anything.

◆ **Achievement of associated benefits** – typically someone or an organisation who has initiated a project wanted the deliverables for some reason that gives them benefits. A common business example would be to deliver a new IT system, which in turn results in the benefit of lower costs or higher quality somewhere else in the business. So using this example success is then measured by checking that the lower costs and higher quality has been achieved.

(I will discuss this last point more in Chapter 10, but in brief it is worth pointing out that there are three problems with knowing exactly what benefits have been achieved. Firstly, they are often difficult to measure. Secondly, it is usually difficult to be sure that it was the project that delivered them and not some other change. Finally, they typically only arise after the project has been completed and the project manager is working on something else. But I will ignore this for now and assume that they can be measured.)

Hence success can be measured first against a pile of deliverables, and a stack of achieved benefits. But success is not simply a matter of delivering deliverables and achieving business benefits, there is a specific caveat: they must be delivered within the time and cost agreed at the outset of the project, and to the agreed scope and quality. It is no good delivering deliverables and achieving benefits if the cost is too high (or more generally the amount of resources used was too high), it took too long, the quality is not good enough or the end results are somehow less than originally perceived or planned.

But assuming success is achieved. We have got to the end of the project. We did not spend all the money or use up all the time. The deliverables are wonderful and the benefits are now rolling in. Is that enough? Well almost, but not quite. There is one more factor:

◆ **Customer satisfaction** – this is the third category of success measures, associated to the deliverables and benefits, but not synonymous with them. Every project has a customer of one form or another. This may simply be the person asking for, or paying for a project. Or it may be a host of people with a complex set of relationships. Understanding who the various stakeholders in projects are is a skill project managers should acquire and the degree of success will depend on these people being happy with the outcome of the project. Some project managers may baulk at this final category, on the basis that it is not often specified as an explicit requirement of the project and may simplistically be seen as an outcome of providing the customer with the deliverables originally requested and achieving the follow-on business benefits. Another reason for discounting it is that it is often intangible and difficult to measure. These things are true – but then no-one ever said being successful was easy. Success is more complex than handing over deliverables and waiting for benefits to roll in. Being truly successful is not always about doing simply what you were asked to do. If a project manager wants to be successful he or she must not only be successful in their own eyes but also in the eyes of their customers. Happiness, satisfaction or delight on the customer's behalf is core to being a successful project manager.

So, if that is what success is what is a successful project manager? It is simply someone who consistently completes projects and meets these three goals: he gets the deliverables completed and handed over, he sees the business benefits arising, and he leaves the customers with smiles on their faces. If you can do this consistently, then you have every right to feel you are good – and I can pretty much guarantee you still stay in demand.

(As a final note, in the remaining chapters I will show how this is not always absolutely true as the key to success is really about meeting *expectations* about deliverables, benefits and satisfaction. This is related to achieving it, but subtly different, as expectations can be managed to change! This too is part of the project manager's art that will be discussed in the following chapters.)

2

Listening and talking

The most important chapter in the book

> ### Key lesson
>
> Think about, plan and execute your communications with care, effort and impact. Your communications must be based on an understanding of your customer that goes beyond the requirements specification and sharing periodic reports. Your communications with the project team must go beyond sharing the project plan and having sporadic updates.

IF YOU ARE JUST GETTING STARTED in your career as a project manager and are taking time to learn the trade then this chapter is a very good place to begin. Alternatively if you are an experienced and very busy project manager with only the time to read one chapter of the book, read this one. The other chapters all have valuable insights that will improve your project management and it would be a shame not to read them now you have a copy of this book – but this chapter contains the essence. All else is about advancing skills and finesse, this is about getting the basics right.

Although the topics in this chapter are rarely covered in any project management course they can be considered as even more fundamental than learning the various disciplines and processes that make up a project manager's toolkit. They may be missed because they are obvious, or because they are thought of as rudimentary rather than fundamental. My experience is that the communication skills I describe are the core differentiator between great project managers and the average, and yet are rarely analysed or taught in the specific context of managing projects.

This chapter aims to make you think about whom you should communicate with, what you need to listen to, and how you should respond. It does have some specific answers, but it also poses questions that you need to answer yourself, and which may have different answers in different situations. It is focused as much on how you communicate as what you communicate – as to be successful you not only need to communicate the right information you need to do it in the right way. If you only take one lesson away from this chapter it should be to think about, plan and execute your communications with care, effort and impact. Do not forget it because it seems so self-evident.

The chapter is broken into three sections. I first look at understanding the audience you are meant to communicate with, I then look at the things you need to listen to from your customer, and finally I cover the key communication skills a project manager should possess. Some of project management concepts that involve communications will not be dealt with in detail until later chapters – but I have decided to cover communications first as it is the framework that underpins and surrounds everything else. Without adequate communication skills you will never succeed.

Your audience – who you must listen and talk to

Key lesson

Identify and assess your audience's information needs. Identify who is your customer and plan your interaction with them.

This section briefly looks at who you need to communicate with and why. All too frequently project managers regard communications as a painful overhead and not as the core task that it is. 'I am so busy talking to people that I do not have time to get on with my day job', is a familiar complaint that misses the point that talking to people is *the* central part of a project manager's workload.

In most situations either we communicate with whoever we intuitively feel we need to communicate with, or we respond to a specific stimulus to talk. We do not often sit down and independently ask ourselves – so who is it that I need to be in dialogue with now? It is true that much of good communications needs to be intuitive to project managers, and any good project manager will have built up from experience mental triggers to begin communications when starting out on a new piece of work. You may even be now thinking – isn't it obvious who I need to talk to? The purpose of this section is not to confirm what is already clear to you, but to make you think and plan your communications explicitly. The truth is that intuition is usually at best incomplete, and at worst flawed – and some key communications will be missed if you wait for external triggers. You need to plan them out. Frequently project managers rely too heavily on their reflexes. Good project managers are often great instinctive communicators, but they also plan through and make sure they have covered all their bases when it comes to communications. On a big project thinking through and planning who to communicate with is a worthwhile use of significant amounts of project management time.

> Thinking through and planning who to communicate with is a worthwhile use of significant amounts of project management time

The dangers of not adequately identifying your audience are a risk to the project. If you do not enter into dialogue with all the people you need to, the level of risk will increase. Risk that you will miss the point that a customer wants you to understand. Risk that you will not be told something you need to know. Risk that you will miss out some vital task in your plans. Risk that your customer will want to change something and you will remain unaware. Risk that some group of people you have not spoken to will actively oppose your work. The list is endless. The misunderstanding of what is wanted and what is happening, and the incomplete explanation of what you want, and what should be happening lies at the core of most project failures.

So let us start by considering what basic groups of people you need to communicate with. All project managers have a set of people they must talk to in both informal and formal ways on a regular basis. This audience can be split into three broad categories:

1   People directly involved in the project – this can be the project team, but will also include suppliers and other third parties responsible for delivery and delivery-related activities.

2   Customers of the project – the person or group of people for whom a project is being delivered.

3   Other stakeholders – a wide group that can include anyone else impacted by, or able to impact the outcome of the project.

Next, let us briefly think through – who are these people, how important is each of these three groups we have identified, and what must the project manager consider in each case?

The project team

The main day-to-day communications of the project manager will be with the project team. It should not need to be said, but without these the project will not even get off the starting blocks. As far as the team goes the project manager obviously needs to communicate with them to explain what needs to be done, and to direct their work. In addition the project manager needs to:

◆ Explain and continually update understanding on the plan and scope as they change through the life of the project.

◆ Provide specific instructions as to which tasks are to be performed by which team members.

◆ Motivate the team to complete their work in an effective and efficient manner.

◆ Understand the team member's progress relative to the plan.

◆ Support the team to keep progress going.

◆ Understand issues and risks as they arise.

◆ Understand the team and personal dynamics so any management intervention that is required can be planned and implemented.

◆ Listen to the team, as they are often a source of critical information, good ideas and suggestions.

In doing this the project manager must learn to understand what information is relevant to the project team, and what approach to communicating with them is best.

Who is on the project team is probably obvious, but think through who else needs to be brought into your regular communications process. Do you have any third party suppliers delivering key activities into the project? Do you have any specialists who only contribute for short periods to the project? Groups like this need to be directed as much as any core project team members.

Unless you can be sure that everyone on the project knows everything they need to to do their work, and to do the correct work, then more communication is required.

Customers

In business the phrase 'the customer is king' has become such a well-worn mantra that it rarely needs saying, and when it is said it feels like a cliché. As we discussed in Chapter 1 all projects have a customer, and yet rare is the project manager who really thinks in terms of a customer–supplier relationship. How customer focused are you when managing your projects? There is usually a gap between the theory of customer focus on projects and the reality. One reason for this gap is that it is often taken for granted that the project is customer focused as the customer has normally defined and documented some requirements. The other reason is that the whole concept of 'the customer' can be complex on a major project.

Unless you are continuously and consciously focused on your customer's needs and achieving them (or at least managing expectations about them), customer satisfaction will decline and your project will not be the 100% success that it might be. This is not only about giving good news or doing only what the customer wants, but also having an open trusting relationship in which you have empathy for and understanding of their needs.

The customer can be broken down into several distinct categories:

◆ **The sponsor** – the role of the sponsor varies from project to project.
Most project managers know them as the person they must send their
periodic status reports to. The sponsor should be the person driving the
work, acting as the senior interface point for the project manager. This
person may or may not be the beneficiary of the work, but is often
ultimately accountable for its completion. He or she will direct the
project manager and act on a day-to-day basis as if they were the
primary customer. The relationship with the sponsor should be two-
way, they need to direct the project manager, but he or she is also a

resource the project manager can call on for help. An example might be a project to build a new production line for a company. In this case the sponsor may well be the operations director – she is the person who is accountable for ensuring there is enough production capacity and so will sponsor a project to build the new production line. She will provide the overall scope for the work, and will help resolve problems the project manager cannot sort out on his own.

◆ **The financer** – the person paying for the project. This is quite often the sponsor, but in some organisations it may be someone different, with more or less interest in the outcome of the work. For a major programme of work, it may, for example, be the finance director. The finance director (FD) needs to be kept on board as he or she may be able to cut the flow of funds at any time, but otherwise may have limited interest in the work. In the example of the project to deliver a new production line the FD will be very interested in how much it costs and that it is completed, but unlike the operations director, normally will not be too interested in the daily details of the project's progress.

◆ **The beneficiary** – the person or group who will realise the benefits from the project if and when they are achieved. This may be the sponsor, but can be quite a different set of people. While on a day-to-day basis they may have limited involvement and interest in a project, if the beneficiaries are not satisfied with the end results the project will not have succeeded. In the case of a company building a new production line to expand capacity, the beneficiaries are really the company's owners who will receive greater profits as a result. If the new production line does not deliver the profits expected they will be unhappy and will take appropriate action.

◆ **The end user** – the person who will end up using the deliverables from the project. For many projects these are the staff of the organisation involved. These people are not really the beneficiaries as they do not personally benefit from the results, but if they are unhappy or unable to use the deliverables the project will not be a full success. In the example given the end users are the people who work in the production plant. They are customers who need to be considered as any production facility must be usable by the staff involved.

◆ **The end customer** – the final customer. For example, a different project may be delivering a new product to a supermarket chain. From the project's perspective, during the life of the project the supermarket chain is the customer. However, the supermarket is doing this in turn to sell to its customers – the end customer. Do these people matter? Typically, on a day-to-day basis on a project, individually they do not. But they do matter to the overall project's success: if the end customers do not like the supermarket's new product they will not buy it, and the project will have been a failure. Their views and needs must be understood, either directly or indirectly through a specialist like a marketing department.

Project managers do need to talk and listen to the relevant members of the customer community on a regular basis. The relevant customer in any specific situation will vary and you must take time to work out which customer is appropriate.

Overall, the project manager therefore has to:

◆ **Identify who the customers are** – when you think through the list above you can see that this is not necessarily as straightforward as it might trivially seem to be. Go through the list above for every project you are involved in and make sure you know how critical these groups are to the success of your project.

◆ **Identify relative criticality and importance** – not all customers are as important as others: you have limited time and you will not be able to communicate fully with everyone. Do not use this as an excuse for poor customer management, but you will have to focus the majority of your time on the most important.

◆ **Determine what information is relevant to them** – each of these customer groups has different information needs. A financer will typically be worried about how much you have spent relative to how far through the project you are, the end customer will be more concerned with how the end result matches their needs.

◆ **Determine what is the best timing, media and approach to use in passing information** – some customer groups will need very regular, perhaps even daily communications. Others will be quite satisfied with more infrequent information. I have seen very successful projects having only quarterly brief communications to certain customer groups. Some need very detailed reports, others simple one-line e-mails.

◆ **Determine what you need in return from the customer** – information flow is a two-way process. Project managers often dump information on their customers without thinking what they can get in return –

whether this is some more requirements or a commitment to do something that will help the project or project manager.

I talk more about each of these later in the chapter.

Stakeholders

I introduced the concept of stakeholders in the previous chapter. The importance of these stakeholder groups varies immensely from project to project. On small projects, or those with deliverables that have impact in a limited domain, they can largely be forgotten. At the other extreme with large business-change programmes, or things that have a significant impact on large numbers of people such as a major road building programme communicating with stakeholders may be one of the main tasks on the programme. As far as the stakeholders are concerned the project manager needs to:

◆ **Identify who the stakeholders are** – who can impact or is impacted by the project?

◆ **Assess their relevance to the project** – are they only marginally relevant, or is their support critical to the project?

◆ **Target those with significant impact on the project's success** – anyone who can stop you delivering is likely to need to be managed.

◆ **Target those significantly impacted by the project's outcome** – should this be a goal of the project. For example, on a project to build a new road there may be a large number of people affected by the road. Some positively with faster journey times, some negatively by suddenly finding themselves living by a noisy road. These people may not be able to impact the project's success and so you may feel you can ignore them. Your sponsor may still require you to take their views into account and to minimise the impact upon them. Taking people with you is often a success factor for large projects.

I discuss stakeholder identification and management processes in more detail in Chapter 10.

Listening – learning to understand what the customer wants

> ## Key lesson
>
> There is much more to understanding your customer's needs than is written in the requirement specification. As project manager you must understand all the requirements at a high level, and specifically understand fully the scope of the project. Real understanding requires a constant two-way dialogue.

It will seem clear to most project managers that to deliver a project successfully you have to start by knowing what your customer wants. After all, it is self-evident – if you do not know what the customer wants you would not start on a project. Without understanding what the customer wants how would you know what to do? Without understanding what the customer wants would it be worth even considering starting a project? Logically the answer to these questions is 'no', but in practice it often happens that a project starts without fully understanding customer needs. It happens for a number of reasons, such as:

◆ **The customer does not know what they want** – or to put it more accurately they know they want something, but they do not really know what it is. I have frequently seen even senior executives coming up with the answer 'we need a project', without knowing quite what question it is trying to answer.

> I am sure I have even met a few senior executives who believed in telepathy!

◆ **The customer cannot define what they want** – they know roughly what they want but need help in expressing it in a useful format. Communicating what is wanted in an unambiguous way is often hard. Don't you ever find yourself being quite clear about your need for something but having difficulty communicating this to others?

◆ **The customer thinks that you understand what he wants** – without needing to explain it. This is very common for inhouse project managers who can be faced with line managers who think by common experience with day-to-day issues nothing ever needs to be fully explained. I am sure I have even met a few senior executives who believed in telepathy!

◆ **The customer's thinking about what they want is not stable** – they are quite clear about what they want until they see it starting to form at which point they decide they need something else. This something else may be a minor tweak on the original idea or it can be substantially different. (There are some specific development techniques such as prototyping to help resolve this type of problem.)

◆ **The customer is impatient for results** – to some people work such as collecting requirements and planning out activities seems like wasted time – and they want to get on with achieving tangible results. Although with any degree of thinking this is obviously nonsense it is a common viewpoint.

It is worth being prepared for the fact that you may find yourself in any of these situations, and also being explicitly aware of them when you do find yourself there. In fact, the most productive mindset to take is to assume that the customer does not exactly know what he wants and needs some help getting it scoped out. The project will not be a success unless at some stage, and preferably reasonably early on, the requirements and reason for the project are commonly shared and understood.

Requirements exist in various forms, whether it is an architectural plan for a building, a requirements specification document for an IT project, or a bill of materials for a complex procurement project. Whatever format the requirements exist in, they are the basis for the output of the project.

Approaches to collecting requirements, especially in technology-led work, have evolved over time. Initial structured approaches relied on completing a full and detailed requirements capture at the start of the project. No development was done until all the requirements were complete. Such approaches have been given the general title of 'waterfall' as they require full completion of a step of a project in its entirety before cascading onto the next step in uni-directional processes through the life of the project. Like a flow of water the project only progresses in one direction. The alternatives are many, but they can be lumped together under the title of 'iterative' development approaches. These rely on enough requirements being captured before moving onto the next step when some deliverable, or a prototype is produced which in turn generates more thinking on the requirements and hence an iteration back into requirements capture. Such iterative approaches may flow between requirements capture and delivery several times before completion. The different approaches suit different types of project and different technologies. However, the overall point is that whatever the approach towards requirements capture and whatever the development approach, requirements are at the core.

What the customer wants is normally encompassed within a number of key documents on a project and depending on the industry or organisation in which the project is being carried out these documents may have different names. The size, level of detail and richness of these documents is usually a function of the scale of the project and complexity of the deliverables. What can be said in generic terms is that there are several essentials the project manager needs to know before she can say she understands what the customer wants. They are:

◆ **The scope of the project** – defining what counts as 'inside' and equally important what counts as 'outside' the project. This is usually held in some kind of project definition or brief.

◆ **The measures of success** – defining the things that can be measured at the end of a project to see if success has been achieved. This is usually also held in some kind of project brief.

◆ **The detailed requirements** – defining all the particular things the customer wants from the project. This is normally held in a specific document, typically referred to as the requirements specification or requirements catalogue. Development of detailed requirements can often be a stage of the project rather than a prerequisite of the project.

Teasing out, refining, documenting and checking requirements is a skill in its own right. On more complex projects this is not even the role of the project manager, but is a specialist skill set typically called 'business analysis' (this is discussed more in Chapter 9). However, even if doing all the detailed requirements capture is not the job of the project manager, she does need to be sure that it is complete. In addition, the task of capturing some particular sorts of requirements – 'scoping requirements' – is specifically the role of the project manager. (This is outlined more fully below.) Another way to look at it is that scoping is really the last step before the project can begin – requirements capture is normally an activity during the project's lifetime.

Any basic course in project management will teach that project managers need to collect and document what the customer wants in one way or another, and will stress the importance of understanding scope. Many project managers carry template project scoping and project definition documents around with them. They start each project by essentially filling in the blanks. This can be both effective and efficient. The problem comes not in knowing what to capture in general, but in understanding how to go about capturing it and the ability to judge when sufficient detail is available and when more is needed. All too often project managers are guilty of not putting enough effort into this process of understanding customer needs, and taking what is initially said to them at face value.

> It is your customer's project, not yours

Although there are specific times when listening is critically important, listening to understand the customer is something that project managers need to learn to do throughout the life of a project. Without writing a treatise on business analysis, there are six key lessons for the project manager when it comes to understanding customer needs:

◆ **Make assumptions explicit** – minimise the number of assumptions, and, if you must assume, get the assumptions clear and shared.

◆ **Derive a clear understanding of scope** – and make sure you can write it down in words meaningful to both you and your customer. If you cannot write the scope down you probably do not fully understand it, and will almost certainly have difficulty communicating the scope to other team members.

◆ **Make sure you understand the customer requirements and how they relate to the project you are running** – expect differences of opinion over requirements between different customers, and put in place some mechanism for resolving them.

◆ **Keep checking and enhancing your understanding** – things change and being sure last week is not the same as being sure today.

◆ **Understanding the customer** – this is not simply about understanding the things documented in the requirements' specification.

◆ **It is your customer's project, not yours** – the attitude you take to your customer's input is important.

Let's think about each of these in turn.

Listening lesson 1 – Make assumptions explicit

The golden rule is: check your understanding, do not assume anything.

Managing assumptions is a core project management activity that is often forgotten. In every conversation and communication there are lots of imbedded ideas and implicit information. However, there is absolutely no guarantee that what is clearly implied within the words of one person is also clearly implied in the understanding or interpretation of those words by the person listening. This becomes especially true when people are firmly lodged within an organisational culture (I'm sure you will have been involved in those 'why do you do it this way – because we always have' conversations), or when specialists in one field or another talk to each other passing what is very clear information to one another, but is not clear to anyone without their background. What you need to do as a project manager is to make these assumptions clear – at the very least other people in the project need to know them. In addition they must be checked as often they may undermine the project as they are not always true.

Poor understanding of assumptions is one of the major sources of risk on projects. (In Chapter 4 I look at when it is reasonable to make assumptions, and in Chapter 10 I describe more about the process of managing assumptions.)

Whenever you are collecting information on the project keep asking yourself the questions 'are there any assumptions within that statement?' and 'that does not make sense unless something else is assumed . . . what is it?' – and if it seems that these are valid questions then ask the person to make the assumptions explicit.

Listening lesson 2 – Understand the scope

Detailed requirements capture is best done by a trained business analyst, and as this book is not a primer in business analysis I will not go through everything business analysts must do. However, there is some key information which it is the responsibility of the project manager to capture, refine, understand and document. This is what I will call 'scoping requirements'. They are the requirements which define the fundamental shape, size, purpose and range of the project and are critical to understanding what the customer really wants.

Understanding scope is the first thing a project manager must start to do when appointed to a project. For a project manager a full understanding of what is within, and almost as important what is not within, the scope of a project is essential. An inability to understand and communicate the scope of a project is as close to a cardinal sin as it is possible to get in project management.

When you have talked with your customer to understand a project's scope, the next thing to do is to write it down. The reason for writing it down is firstly obvious – because it means it will not get forgotten and it can easily be shared. Also important is that the practice of writing down the scope in a coherent manner is a good test of whether you really understand it or not. If you cannot write it down you probably do not fully understand it, and will almost certainly have difficulty communicating it to other team members.

Understanding the scope of a project is so fundamental I have broken it into a separate chapter. Chapter 3 expands on this subject and defines a set of key questions that you can use to be sure that you have really scoped out the project.

Listening lesson 3 – Understand customer requirements and how they convert into a project

The whole of this section of the chapter has been about listening to customers and prompting them with the right questions at the right time. When you have done this you will have a full set of customer requirements. The next thing you have to do is to convert these into a project. That is what project managers do.

That sounds straightforward. In doing this you need to have a good grasp of what the requirements are, why the requirements exist, and how this converts into a project plan. Without this understanding you will have difficulty shaping and running the project, and you will find it very difficult to manage a team – the team will need their work explained and put in context.

The test for you is:

◆ Do you have an overall grasp on the customer requirements, and how they relate together to give the overall customer solution?

◆ Do you understand why the customer has included these requirements?

◆ Do you understand how these requirements will translate into blocks of work that the project will deliver?

◆ Do you understand how these blocks of work hang together?

◆ Can you visualise and explain this?

The answer to all of these questions must be 'yes'. This is not a demand that you memorise and understand each and every line of the requirements specification, and each and every line of every plan within your project. It is a demand though that you have a logical understanding of how it all comes together and when you look at every major activity within the project you know why it is being done and what the impact of it failing will be. (I always read the whole requirements specification, even if it is often long and tedious. I do this to ensure I understand what will be required in the project and to make sure there are no surprises hidden away in the details.)

Without this knowledge you cannot plan, manage or deliver the project. If you are on a project and you cannot answer 'yes' to each of the questions above – do some more work so you can answer 'yes' (or find someone else to run it). In practice on a project with any complexity you will be reliant on other specialists to build components of the plan for each specialist area. However, you still must integrate the components into the overall plan, and you own and are accountable for that plan.

When requirements are captured expect differences of opinion both about what requirements there are, and what the relative importance of them is. Only the very simplest of projects clearly have one customer who gives all requirements and therefore you must have some mechanism for agreeing what counts legitimately as a requirement. This can be as simple as the sponsor having the decision, or can entail setting up a requirements committee which can resolve any requirements conflicts. Make this mechanism as simple as possible – or else you risk never completing the requirements capture stage of a project. (People can generate and discuss requirements for ever. One of your early tasks is to get control over this process and see that it is completed in a timely fashion.)

Listening lesson 4 – Keep checking

The first point I noted here in capturing requirements was to assume nothing. Once you have documented requirements and agreed them with the customer assuming they will never change is a poor assumption. Regularly go back to the customer and check the basic scoping requirements; when key decisions are being made based on these that will alter or shape major parts of the project, test them with your customer. Being posed with a question of the format 'we are doing x, because of your requirement y' is a powerful way for people to be forced to see the implications of their requirements and from that to decide whether they really were true and if they need to change.

Do not simply do this once, keep checking with the customer. You should be constantly vigilant to the question yourself – have requirements changed, have assumptions changed? All good projects have a change control process which can be used when requirements change to manage the assessment and impact of that change upon the project and to get agreement to that when it happens. However, the change control process is merely a mechanism to handle the change, it will not generate the changes itself.

At this stage some project managers may well be thinking 'but I don't want changes'. A project without changes is a more straightforward thing to deliver than one that keeps changing. That is true, and one key reason why it is worth putting in the effort to get the requirements as right as possible up front. But however comprehensive the requirements capture, however long you spend in conversation with your customer on your scoping requirements, people are fallible, people cannot predict the future with any accuracy, and even the most senior customer is not in control of or aware of everything. A project that successfully delivers yesterday's needs cannot be guaranteed to be considered a success today. Make sure it is controlled – but be open to change.

Listening lesson 5 – Customer needs go beyond requirements specification

Remember that no matter how good your requirements capture process – it will not capture all of your customer needs. Your customer will have needs about the way you work with her, the style of interaction you adopt and various other factors. We are all imperfect, we work in a political and social world that has needs beyond pure functional requirements, and finally we are all human and how we interact is important to us. It is your job as a project manager not just to see that the project delivers the requirements specified, but also that it does so in a way that is acceptable to the customer.

Listening lesson 6 – Remember it's not your project

As project manager your job is to ensure the project meets its objectives – but in the end it is not your project. You are the agent of your customer, and this must be reflected in the way you listen to your customer, think about the project, and in your behaviour. The high level guidance is that your customer owns the 'what' of the project, and you own the 'how'. In this situation 'what' refers to the scope and requirements; 'how' to the way in which it is managed and delivered.

This does not mean you should not have views, or even be opinionated – but you must know who has the last say in what situation. A constructive relationship is one in which you can challenge the customer about require-ments, but the choices are hers; similarly she may challenge you about how you plan to deliver the project, but the final choice is yours.

Two good examples of where this is often forgotten are with defining requirements and with changes to scope. Project managers must avoid the temptation to add or remove requirements that seem obvious to them; if you think something is missing or should not be included advise your customer, but let her make the decision. With customer-driven changes the problem can be more insidious. Project managers often develop an attachment to a project and a passion to complete it, and can resent it when people try to change things that make their lives more complex. It is worth remembering that the project does not exist for the project manager's benefit, and as long as the customer understands the impact of a change – it's her decision to make.

The project belongs to the customer and the customer needs to know how it is going and has the right to change it or stop it when they want to. When you listen to your customer, listen openly, hear what they say, by all means debate and challenge their needs, questions and suggestions – but don't forget who has the last say.

Communicating with your audience

Key lesson

Talk, talk and talk again – the weekly report will not do it all. Practise and learn the seventeen communication lessons to ensure you communicate fully and continuously with your customer and project team.

So, you have now got a great and comprehensive set of requirements that everyone on the project understands. You know that there are a few assump-

Talk, talk and talk again

tions, but they are clear and explicit and you know what will happen if they turn out to be false. You have also put in place efficient mechanisms for regularly going back to your customer and checking that nothing has changed. The project is up and running and things are starting to happen.

Project management does not operate in a black box. Even when you know everything that you do you need to go back and talk to the customer and talk continuously with the project team. One of the absolute fundamental differences between the good and the great project manager is often the amount of regular communications.

It should be obvious why you need to communicate with your project team. Given that you have a documented scope and set of requirements it may be less obvious why you need to talk to your customer. Rather than shrugging this point off as being too simple it really is worth putting yourself in your customer's shoes as it drives understanding and the opportunity for comprehensive empathetic engagement.

The key reasons you need to communicate with your customer throughout the life of the project are:

◆ It's not usually your money you are spending or your resource you are using – and resource owners have a right to understand how things are going and if resources are being used well. In most organisations, resources of one form or another are scarce or limited, and it is worth remembering as a project manager that people have the option of allocating them elsewhere at any time. The most common resources of money and people's time can easily be shifted to other work and managers must make an active and ongoing choice to allocate them to a project. For a project to continue to be a success it needs continuing access to resources. Managers will only continue to allocate people if they see it is worthwhile and it is working. You not only need to deliver results, you need to be seen to be delivering them – and to do this you must tell your customers!

◆ Success as a project manager requires trust. You do not have an inalienable right to be trusted and it is not automatically achieved – trust must be gained and you can improve on trust by good regular communications. If you disappear for six months telling your customer you will come back when everything is done you are likely to find that your customer is not impressed and does not believe you (and he or she should not accept this).

◆ Things change and you need to talk them through; you cannot assume that changes you need to make whether it is cost, time, resource usage, scope or whatever else will be acceptable to customers. On the other hand you also cannot assume that the customer will not want to make changes himself. The world customers operate in is dynamic – even though a few weeks ago your project may have been their number one priority, it may not be today.

◆ You may need or want the customer or sponsor of a project to do something for you. Passing things up or along the management chain, done in a constructive manner can be an extremely powerful way of getting things done.

◆ We are all human – and human beings like to be talked to, and base their judgements of others largely on their interactions. This sounds trite, but a project manager who diligently hides in a corner while managing a project is less likely to be seen as a safe pair of hands. This may be unfair – but it is human nature.

◆ It's good to have to report on progress – it keeps project managers on their toes! Be honest with yourself – don't you work harder when someone is measuring your performance?

The basic mechanism for a project manager's communications is usually some form of regular reporting, be it weekly or monthly (though in some cases daily or quarterly). The rest of this section will describe how while this is essential, it is not enough on its own. There are seventeen additional communication lessons the project manager should learn. They are structured into three main groupings:

1 Your planning and approach to communications (lessons 1–4).

2 The style and method of communications (lessons 5–13).

3 Rules to underpin all communications (lessons 14–17).

So what are the seventeen core communication lessons?

Lessons 1–4: Your planning and approach to communications

Communication lesson 1 – Plan your schedule of communications

Your approach to communications will ideally come across as confident, relaxed and natural – but this does not mean it should not be planned. Communications must be planned on a project like any other task. For a small project this can be very simple, on a large programme with many people on it you may even have a dedicated communications planning team. In this context the word 'plan' means not only the formal plan you create, document and manage to as a project manager, but also the mental rules and guidelines you develop, think about and structure your day-to-day interactions around.

Your communications may include a variety of people, but should centre on your three key audiences:

◆ The project team. Plan regular meetings to assess progress, discuss issues, risks and changes, and also agree what the team will focus on for the next time period (do not leave this to everyone's individual interpretation of the plan). Agree a schedule and format of regular reports and/or meetings.

◆ Customer reporting. There are two primary groups to consider at the very least – the sponsor for ongoing updates and support, and the end users in preparation for the results of the project. Agree meetings and reports as required.

◆ Stakeholders – as part of your ongoing stakeholder management.

(In Chapter 9 I discuss the limits of project manager communications and the situations in which you may need some support from professional specialists in communications.)

Commence your communications planning by thinking about the objectives of any interactions, and then think about the actual message and approach to communicating. And remember communications is not only about providing information and messages – it is also about building relationships.

There is no generic communications plan – it will vary from some informal thoughts on the smallest and simplest of projects, through to a complex piece of work on a major change project. Generically though your communication plan should be made up from three main components:

◆ Tasks within the project plan – there will be some major communications deliverables and events that should be built into your project plan. These are mainly presentations and actions based around key milestones in your project. The specific events depend on the scale and type of project. Typical examples for a larger project include a mobilisation event, customer presentations related to acceptance of deliverables, and stakeholder events to prepare for the impact of the project launch. For complex programmes there may be a separate communications work package made up of multiple tasks. (See lessons 2, 3 and 17 below.)

◆ Guidelines and rules for project team members – for small projects all communications will be the responsibility of the project manager. As projects become larger this may become impractical. It is good practice then to outline what regular communications are to be made, by whom and in what format. So, for example, the project manager may hold responsibility for monthly sponsor updates, but other customer groups may be updated by other project members. For large programmes such guidelines will need to be formally documented as a part of the communications plan. (See lessons 2, 7, 10, 11 and 13 below.)

◆ Ongoing communication approaches for the project manager – these are typically the dynamic and undocumented thoughts of the project manager. I include in this approaches such as deciding to hold regular casual conversations with project team members. Because there is a constantly changing informal combination of proactive strategies and reactive tactics does not mean they should not be thought through. Great project managers look at communications as a holistic set of activities to support achieving the goals of the project. (See lessons 4, 11, 13, 15 and 16 below.)

Communication lesson 2 – Accept regular reporting as part of the job

To start your communications plan it is easiest to begin by thinking about the cycle of regular reports you will make and meetings you will hold as a project manager. Such regular interactions form the basis for a factual understanding of status, which is essential to determining what management action is required on a project. There are many options and formats. In practice, my experience is that a weekly report is essential for the project sponsor, supported by less frequent reports and meetings for other customer groups.

Many project managers complain about reporting on weekly or monthly cycles. You must accept that reporting is a core component of your work – and if it is difficult, you are not on top of your project. Once a weekly report has been created, the updates required for the following week should be easy. Try to manage the reporting overhead with standard formats and devise a format that suits as many audiences as possible.

In terms of your main weekly status report, it should at least provide:

◆ A very clear statement of status – are you ahead, behind or on track? Ideally this is covered unambiguously in the first few lines of the report.

◆ A simple description of any major issues that are affecting progress, what is being done about them, and when they will be resolved.

◆ A simple description of any new risks, or changes to risk status, that the audience for this report needs to be aware of.

◆ Finally, to specify anything you need in return from the report's audience (for example decisions, resources, help with issue resolution, etc.).

Keep such reports very simple and short – if people need more detail then they can come and talk to you. Very complex weekly reports risk people not bothering to read them, and the really important information being lost in too much detail (it is worrying how often I have seen status updates, read them, received lots of little bits of information, but had no idea whether the project was OK or not). My ideal report is certainly no longer than one side of a sheet of paper.

Communication lesson 3 – Use formal presentations as appropriate

Next on your communication plan will be some formal presentations. Opinions vary as to whether presenting to people (probably using the ubiquitous MS PowerPoint slides) is actually an effective use of time. It is a part of modern business life – and whether it adds value or is just part of the cultural ritual of contemporary business, you will have to do it.

You cannot predict what presentations you will require on a project – sometimes during a project's life stakeholders will realise something is impacting them and ask for a presentation; perhaps customers will require an analysis of why a project is going wrong; perhaps project team members may need to understand more about some part of the project they are having difficulty with. So, leave some time for unplanned presentations, but start by planning the presentations you know will be required. Think about key times when you will have important information to report to customers and stakeholders. The basis for such a formal presentation schedule is your project's activity plan (see Chapter 5), so base presentation times around major milestones and critical events in the project.

The attitude to presentations must be to see them as part of the job. You should see them as an opportunity to shine rather than being the shadowy, unknown manager of the project. Project managers who make comments like 'I am doing so many presentations that I can't get on with my job' are failing to understand the critical importance of communicating. It *is* possible that a project team has to make too many presentations, if so, talk to your sponsor to reduce them. But, generally, complaining about presentations is missing the point. Presentations can be helpful to you and the project. Importantly, in the short run, they can provide an opportunity to get things that you need from your audience – use them to get support, decisions made, resources allocated, issues resolved, and risks accepted. Points to remember are:

◆ Communicate to suit your audience not to suit your process, existing templates, etc.

◆ Use different media wisely – slide presentations can be powerful, but can also bore people senseless.

◆ Think about what you and the project want from every presentation and include it in the presentation.

◆ Decide whether the material you are developing is only to be presented or will it be read as a standalone document. Some great presentations are almost impossible to understand without the presenter talking them through; similarly some great documents to read are impossible to present. If you need to achieve both plan it out carefully.

◆ If necessary press communication on your customer. If he does not want it, it is a good sign that he trusts you, but it may also mean he is not interested enough in the outcome and you may not be able to get him to do things what you want or need.

Communication lesson 4 – Use informal communications spontaneously and continuously

Finalise your communications plan by thinking about your informal communications. I am not saying you should actually plan out every little chat, but you should be consciously thinking about the balance between formal and informal communications. Informal communications score highly on a number of objectives – including building relationships and trust, finding out critical information quickly, and getting a variety of viewpoints when consensus does not exist. Because such communications are unofficial and relaxed does not mean they should not be deliberate. It's wonderful if you are one of those people who naturally network, know everything and everyone; but not everyone is, and even if you are a little thinking helps to ensure all bases are covered.

No matter how formal the environment or culture you work in, do not rely on formal presentations as your sole communications mechanism. Over-reliance on formal communications will result in a lack of real understanding and trust between a project manager and his audience. Informal communications – short chats, calls, coffee machine conversations and e-mails (though see lesson 11 on page 50) – are a critical part of your ongoing work. In addition, if you really dislike formal presentations you may reduce the need for them by doing more informal communications. The more often you call your key audience members, catch them by the coffee machine or ask them out for lunch or a drink the lighter your load on formal presentations will be.

Informal communications work well with certain customer groups, but are particularly important with your project team. The project manager who relies only on formal structured input is not likely to understand all the issues nor will he develop a good relationship with the project team. Simply walking around the project team once or twice a day, asking them how they are will bring all sorts of critical information to the surface, help to bond the project manager and project team, and, in a non-challenging way, can ensure the information being presented to you on progress and status rings true with what project team members are actually experiencing. It will also let you observe non-verbal communications to pick up information such as emotional states, which are essential to understand to optimally manage people.

> Informal communications are not just about telling people things, they are primarily about listening

Informal communications are not just about telling people things, they are primarily about listening. The best way to find out what is actually going on in a project is simply to go around and listen to project team members. Their comments must always be put in context and balanced with multiple views – but they are worth finding out. Informal communications are most effective when they manifest themselves as a dialogue. Dialogue is important not only because two-way information flow is essential, but also because it is the basis of building relationships.

Lessons 5–11: The style and method of communications

Communication lesson 5 – Use your audience's specialist language where appropriate

Most projects have specialists of one type or another, who each have their own jargon and communication tools. Additionally many organisations have a specialised language set because of the industrial sector they are in, the way they are organised, or because it is part of the organisation's culture. The ability to pick up and use the language of the various people involved in a project is critical for project managers. If you work in one company in one industry this is normally not a problem as your communications will naturally be studded with the local jargon. However, if you are a mobile, contract or consultant project manager jumping from company to company and industry to industry you must learn to pick up the language around you.

Do not consider local vocabulary as irritating jargon – anymore than if working in a foreign country you would consider the local language as irritating jargon. Jargon will have grown up for many reasons, and it can be an efficient way to communicate. Think of jargon as part of the environment you are working in – your job is to fit into it and not to expect it to fit with you.

Communication lesson 6 – Avoid too much project management jargon

Project managers, like other specialists, have their own jargon. Do not assume that other audiences understand it, or even need to understand it. This lesson is the opposite of needing to use the local jargon yourself. I have heard people questioning the difference between a project and a programme manager, or the difference between an issue and a risk too often. In my experience certain terms cause regular confusion, for example:

◆ Work breakdown structure and organisational breakdown structure (or even more obscure, WBS and OBS).

◆ PID, Requirements Spec., Technical Spec.

◆ Change request.

◆ Planning terms, e.g. PERT, Gantt, critical path, critical chain, earned value analysis.

◆ Project roles, e.g. project manager, programme manager, project director, project sponsor, project office manager.

In any project there may be many more terms that are not universally understood. If you do find yourself thinking about using these terms, my advice is:

◆ Ask yourself if the concept the term encapsulates is even required in the conversation you are having. (For example, the number of conversations in which you need to use the words WBS, PID or PERT should be quite limited!)

◆ If you do need to use such a term try to find common everyday language alternatives. (For example, a Gantt chart may be described to most audiences simply as a plan – the fact that there are other types of plan is normally irrelevant.)

◆ When you cannot find an alternative, explain the term before using it. (A term like 'critical path' is very useful but not intuitively obvious in its meaning – explain it, then use it. Even terms like 'issue' and 'risk' are not clear to all non-project managers.)

Communication lesson 7 – Clarify what you mean by risks

A key piece of information that needs to be communicated often on a project is the degree of risk. It can be difficult, not only to pass on the basic concept of risk, but for the person you are communicating with to understand the implications. I have seen lots of presentations to executives where the project manager lamely runs quickly through a risk register. It can come across as 'well here are the risks, but don't worry about them because I will manage them away and I have only presented them because I was asked to'. Either this is wrong and the risks really may derail the project, or, if true, they are minor risks and you probably need not have communicated them to the executives in the first place.

Communicate a full understanding of risks. Ensure that your customer understands that the work may actually fail, and not that they think that you are simply telling them that this is something you are managing. Start by checking that the term 'risk' is actually understood in the context of a project as opposed to its use in colloquial English.

Do expect them to ask what can be done about it (if they don't it may well be that they have assumed it is not a problem for them or that they did not appreciate the possible impact of the risk), and have an answer to this question.

In Chapter 10 I talk more about risk management and contingency plans.

Communication lesson 8 – Present complex information in a clear way

Many projects over time become complex; either because of the scale, or sometimes because of the nature of the content. A real skill is the ability to explain complex information and detail about a project in concise, easily understandable terms. This is especially important when talking to senior audiences.

Learn to differentiate between what is complex, what people need to understand, and detail. Very few people you will talk to need to know the detail about everything on the project, so don't waste your time and theirs by relating it. Tell them what is relevant and, if you don't know, ask them what is relevant to them. Similarly, complexity does not have to be explained in a complex way. (Chaos is complex, being an expert in chaos theory I'm sure is very complicated too, but some of the theories and specific algorithms for chaotic events are intellectually straightforward. It is possible to explain the fundamental concept in a few sentences – for most people this simple explanation is sufficient.)

When talking with people take the time and effort to explain difficult concepts and do not assume automatic understanding. Confirm their understanding, and prepare a further explanation if necessary. (However, although you should be prepared to explain complex ideas check first with your audience whether they understand them. If they do, don't continue with the explanation – move on to the next part of your presentation. People are easily irritated by having concepts explained to them that they already understand.)

Do not under-estimate what people may consider as complex concepts. For example, when talking to an engineering audience you may well patronise them if you talk about the need for a requirements specification. When talking to an executive audience you may not only need to do this, but also explain what a requirements specification is. I have been in many situations where the necessity for a require-ments specification had to be explained to senior board members. It is not that they were stupid; it was just outside of their experience. The best thing to do is to ask whether people are comfortable with concepts and, if they are, move on, if not, explain. If you are concerned that your audience may feel you are patronising them start with a statement like 'I often find teams do not understand this term'. Then at least they do not feel you are specifically assuming they are idiots!

_____

If you really do not know then ask

_____

Communication lesson 9 – Tailor communications to the audience

Different audiences require different styles of presentation – don't assume you can use the same set of slides for a project team meeting as you can for an executive meeting. Yes, you should re-use materials if you can, otherwise you may constantly be developing communications materials. Don't assume, however, that what works well for one group will automatically suit another.

There are hundreds of different possible audiences, but those to start thinking about are clearly:

◆ The project team and separate work package teams.

◆ Third party suppliers to the project.

◆ The project sponsor.

◆ The executive (sponsor's peers or bosses).

◆ Customers.

◆ End users.

◆ Resource owners.

◆ Other stakeholders.

The points to think about when presenting to these audiences are:

◆ **Why are you presenting to this audience?** Without understanding this, it is difficult to develop relevant communications. Very frequently people find themselves making presentations to audiences for less than totally clear reasons. (If you really do not know then ask whoever has set up the meeting what she would like covered. If you have set it up yourself you should know!)

◆ **What is relevant to this audience?** Many features of the project will not be relevant and the audience has limited time and patience.

◆ **How is it best to tell the audience this information?** In doing this you should consider what vocabulary you are using. Do technical or specialist words and concepts need to be explained?

◆ **What is the best media?** Is it formal or informal? Is it a presentation, an e-mail, a newsletter, a poster or something else?

◆ **What can you get out of this?** Different audiences can have different impacts on the project. For example, senior audiences can allocate more resources, a project team well motivated can do more work, etc.

Communication lesson 10 – Effectively communicate with senior audiences

One of the challenges to face new project managers is presenting to a senior or executive audience for the first time. A good presentation to a senior audience can make your life easy; a poor one can cause significant problems for a project. For a senior audience specifically it is therefore worth putting some real effort into thinking about:

◆ **What is relevant to this audience?** Many features of the project will not be and they have limited time and patience. A good starting point is to really challenge yourself – why are you presenting to this specific audience and what do they want from it? List the questions that your audience will be able to answer *after* your presentation and which they cannot answer beforehand. Typical examples of these questions are:

   – What is the current status?

   – What are the risks and issues?

   – What else do you think we should know?

   – Is there anything we can change to make it better/easier?

   – They typically will *not* be interested in things like the details of how your change control process works, or which version of MS Project you are using.

If you cannot identify what questions your presentation answers it is likely to be a failure. It is worth holding in mind what senior audiences are particularly looking for when projects are normally presented to them: confidence that you are in control of your work, and confidence that you are telling them the whole truth.

◆ **What are they feeling and thinking?** You cannot be a mind reader – no-one is, but everyone has some innate ability to feel what others are feeling and this is especially important with senior audiences. Try to get at least some feel for:

– What mood they are in. You do not always have the choice but try to save difficult messages for times when people are in good moods.

– What they are thinking as you present. They may be thinking 'this is interesting' or 'this is adding value', alternatively they may be thinking 'this is boring and why am I here?', or they may be irritated. Try to analyse what you are doing to create any negative sensation and adapt your style and content accordingly. I am not saying avoid tough messages, but if information you are presenting is optional and they are obviously bored cut it short.

◆ **How is it best to tell them this information?** There is no golden rule here other than tailor it to suit. Some executives love detail, others are 'big picture' people. Some like presentations and others like text. This is partly a function of personal bias, but it is also related to how expert the specific executives are with the subject you are presenting. It is best not to try to present high level overviews if the executive is an expert. You need to tailor your contents for this as well. It's easy when you know your audience well, but there will be many situations in which the audience is new or unfamiliar to you. If you do not know the audience and cannot get advice on their preferred style my general advice is to plan for a formal presentation – keep it at a reasonably high level, but be able to drill into detail if required. A good way to do this is to make a high level presentation with a set of appendices full of detail should you need to go into it.

◆ **Is this better done formally or informally? Is it better done as a group or on a one-to-one basis?** The reasons you may wish to talk to someone informally rather than formally come down to personal style, the content you are communicating and the degree of risk you bear in communicating to a group. For example, contentious, unproven data that is new is generally best presented informally on a one-to-one basis.

◆ **What can you get out of this?** Senior audiences are the ones that have the power to reassign more resources to your project, signoff changes, and accept risks. On top of this they are the ones who can help your career progress. (This is a perfectly reasonable way of thinking as long as it does not become obsessive or over-played.)

◆ **Is this contentious or run of the mill? Are there any major surprises?** When senior audiences are being asked to make key decisions or to support an approach, or, generally, when you need their support and it is not certain that you will get it, it may then be worth 'pre-selling' to them on an individual basis before presenting to them as a group. If you present a major contentious decision to a senior audience without warning, and without giving them the opportunity to think about it, they will often respond badly, feeling that you are 'rail-roading' them into a decision. I remember one specific project which was stopped because the project manager surprised a powerful executive with something he did not support. The problem was not that the executive did not agree with the approach being taken by the project manager, but that it caused him problems with his own boss (the CEO). If the executive had been pre-warned on a one-to-one basis he would have had time to gain support from his own boss, and tailor the message to suit, and possibly change the project a little to suit his needs. Having been surprised this executive then lost confidence in the project manager and removed his ongoing support. This effectively killed the project.

◆ **How does this group make decisions?** Some groups and cultures like decisions made in forum with much debate, others like them made beforehand with the group effectively rubber stamping an answer they have each already agreed to. Finally, most groups are not equal – there may be one or a few dominant individuals you need to ensure support you. Working out the dynamics and politics of decision making is a great skill for senior project managers. If, for example, there is one dominant decision maker try to get his or her agreement before you get the final sign off on a decision.

◆ **Plan your presentation.** Even if it is for an informal chat with a senior executive it is worth structuring your key points in your mind, and given that time with senior people is often restricted structure your thoughts so you can cover them quickly. I often have a set of five or six points on status, key issues, and any help I need, prepared and continuously updated in my head. I can then run through these if I bump into any senior executives in my daily travels around the office.

As you present you will get feedback from the executives. Some of this will be comments, criticism and questions, but some will be messages and ideas. Try and capture their suggestions, and, if necessary, take someone along to take notes for this purpose. Once you have completed the meeting you should analyse their ideas and either take them onboard or formally reject them. You may well need to involve your sponsor if rejecting someone's ideas. But there is nothing that irritates a senior audience more than to feel that their comments have been completely ignored.

The last point I will stress is do not obsessively worry about your most senior audiences. They can be perceptive and difficult, but they are often the most balanced and realistic in assessing risks and problems. Do not underestimate the danger of failure or receiving the raw end of their temper, but remember what can often be a topic for a heated argument for a middle manager is accepted with a nod from a senior executive if managed well.

Communication lesson 11 – Do not rely on e-mails

E-mail is a feature of modern business life and is a great support in managing projects. It provides an excellent productivity aid and has some good functionality. It is a superb way for communicating to large numbers of people simultaneously, for distributing documents, and for those occasions when asynchronous communications are needed, such as across time zones.

> I have seen well-meant jokes misread as insults

Project managers' lives would be considerably more difficult without e-mail. However, at times we all find them irritating – sometimes it is the sheer volume of e-mail and at other times it is their content.

I have not commented in detail on any other specific communications medium. I have picked e-mail as it is now so pervasive, is very powerful, and is quite dangerous! Most communication research shows that success in communications comes down to three components: the message you are giving (i.e. the words), your body language, and the tone of your voice. With e-mail you can only control the first. Missing out the other two makes it very easy to miscommunicate. There are other written media which potentially suffer from the same problem, but in my experience people tend to read reports for the words in them alone. When they read e-mails they interpret or assume a body language and tone to match, and I have seen well-meant jokes misread as insults. I am sure you have had similar experiences.

My advice on e-mail etiquette really comes down to four points:

◆ For one-to-one conversations always pick up the phone as a preference (if you cannot have a face-to-face meeting). Using e-mail to talk to one person when you can call them is really an abuse of technology.

◆ If you must use it think through your words carefully and avoid language that may be interpreted with an emotional tone you did not intend. Just because e-mail is easy to use is not an excuse for sloppy communications. I will often spend more time crafting an important e-mail than I do a presentation – precisely because I do not have the opportunity to amend it, or apply tone to my voice, once it is sent.

◆ Limit the number of people you copy an e-mail to. A long list of people's names after the 'cc:' smacks of political games. If people need to read it send it to them directly. If they do not – don't. Personally, I auto delete all e-mails copied to me. It may sound Draconian, but it saves me a lot of time and eventually people learn and only send me what is really relevant.

◆ Do not use the blind copy facility that is available on most e-mail systems. I have even insisted on it being disabled in teams I have been responsible for. No-one knows when you have used it except the recipient of the blind copy, but once people know you use it they will not trust you fully.

Communication lesson 12 – Be specific

The simple but fundamental lesson here is to avoid confusion, ambiguity and the opportunity for divergent responses by being specific in your language – and by cross-examining people when they use non-specific language with you. Words such as 'enough', 'sufficient', 'plenty', 'a little' should be avoided, especially in formal situations such as during requirements definition or when presenting status. You need to define and understand precisely how many, how much, how long.

Try always to be specific. It is better if you occasionally come across as a pedant than you miss the point or miscommunicate vital information.

Communication lesson 13 – Present key factual information in whole messages at discrete time intervals

Informal communications are best carried out in the style of ongoing dialogues. Any information passed can be partial or incomplete, and you can update and adapt it on a continuous basis as the dialogue evolves. This is the normal way for people to 'chat' – and it is an effective way for people to work together, build relationships, and manage ongoing dynamic communications.

Imagine for a moment though that you are not the project manager, but instead you are someone being updated on project status by the project manager. You don't want a chat – you want him to tell you the status. When he tells you the status you may have questions, but ideally once the update is over you have a full understanding of status. The information you have been told is complete and makes logical sense as a statement on status. You may then want to discuss it and its implications, or drive down to more detail – but preferably your understanding of status is comprehensive. Additionally, when he informs you of status you do not want him coming back in five minutes saying '. . . and another thing . . .', and five minutes later, '. . . and I meant to add . . .'. You expect it to be a whole message. Finally, you don't expect him to come back an hour later, or probably even a day later to tell you that it has all changed. Unless he has pre-warned you of something significant happening in that time frame which will alter status you probably only want an update a week or a month later. You want to be updated at regular time intervals.

There is a variety of key information for which informal dialogue is not a suitable mechanism for sharing in a project environment. Specifically, factual information such as project status, risks and issues, and instructions on what work needs to be done next. These need to be presented as complete pieces of information at discrete time intervals.

Why is this important? As intimated above, no-one wants to know half a risk, part of status, or a bit of the next activity you need to do. In these situations partial information is often meaningless, worse still it can transmit completely the wrong message, and it gives the impression that you do not really know what is going on. If you did – surely you would communicate the whole message. Finally, if you keep changing what you have said at short intervals of time it undermines trust in your competence. Your audience's thought process would be something like 'was what you said a little while ago true or not? If it was why do you need to change it? Why should I believe what you say now?' Status changes, but not significantly at very short intervals of time, unless you are out of control. This seems obvious, but very often project information is presented in incomplete segments. How often have you been updated by someone and felt that he or she has not really told you anything meaningful, or has left you suspicious because he or she keeps changing the information?

Completeness is relative to the level of detail that is appropriate for the audience you are communicating with. At the highest level a project status update needs to reflect whether you are on track or not, and whether you currently think you will stay on track. A simple statement 'we are on track, and currently expect to remain on track' is a complete message. At a slightly lower level a project status update may require a statement such as 'we are on track within expected tolerances, and expect to remain on track. There are two risks we are managing, and think unlikely now to occur, but if they do we will be late by six weeks'. This may be a complete message, as long as there are not other facts relevant to this level of detail. The skill here is determining what is actually relevant to a specific level of detail. That judgement is based on knowing your project and your audience's level of detail needs.

Lessons 14–17: Rules to underpin all communications

Communication lesson 14 – Tell the truth

Tell the truth. Avoid lying. There are situations in which telling the absolute truth is not productive, but these situations should be rare and avoided as far as possible. I am not saying that you should not tailor your message. If there is bad news, sweeten the pill, and choose your timing carefully. This is common sense and good people management. If you do find yourself being tempted to lie ask yourself what risk is involved – is it personal or is it project? If you get found out, which/who will suffer more: the project or you personally? (See Chapter 10 for a fuller discussion.)

If we ignore morals for a moment, the problem with non-trivial lies is that they will often come back to haunt you. You risk killing your relationship and feeling of trust with your manager, customer or other team member if they realise you have lied to them, or have even withheld information. If you do feel tempted to lie – ask yourself what is the chance they will find out anyway. Ask yourself what weaknesses you are trying to hide.

Another aspect of telling the truth is being open with the full truth. If we consider ourselves to be truthful and yet not open I believe that we are paying lip service to being truthful. There is a right and wrong time to impart a bad message – but it is best to assume that you will be doing it. Relevant information is not only that which is true, but also that which is complete and timely. This requires real openness with your customer.

Communication lesson 15 – Maintain only one version of the truth

There is nothing more frustrating to the customer of a project team than repeatedly getting different and contradictory information on status and risks, but it is quite common. I have regularly been the sponsor of projects where on talking to different members of the project team I get radically different interpretations of project status. There are many causes of this – some project members will only have partial information, some will have historic information that is now no longer true, others will interpret facts in a different light, and occasionally people will deliberately spread wrong information. This can cause significant loss of confidence in the project. In your life, if your car is in the garage and the receptionist tells you it will be ready at 5 o'clock, the engineer tells you there are major problems and it will probably be another two days, and the salesman tells you not to worry it will be sorted – how do you feel? When this occurs it is both frustrating and destroys your confidence in the garage. You have spoken to many people but you still do not know the truth with any degree of confidence, and tend to assume the worst.

To counter this you need to get the project team to communicate consistently 'one version of the truth':

◆ Regularly bring the project team together and discuss the project status so everyone has a common view. Agree with the team that anyone who really wants or needs a full status update should be directed to talk to the project manager.

◆ When critical activities are completed, or major issues occur, or are resolved, communicate this to the whole team so that no one is retailing past history to the outside world. A short e-mail is sufficient.

◆ Agree with sponsor and other customer groups who they should come to for status updates, and warn them that any other source will not have the full picture. When I am running projects I like to agree at the start of the project with my sponsor that he or she only comes to me for status information. Not because I am blocking them from talking to anyone in the team, but to ensure that when they are forming judgements on the project's status they have the full picture.

Communication lesson 16 – Obsessively manage expectations

The phrase 'manage expectations' could be the perfect project management mantra, and anyone working in project management circles will hear it all the time. But what in reality does it mean?

One of the critical success factors for project managers is to manage their customer's expectations throughout the life of a project. Like a good politician the project manager needs to ensure that what is delivered at the end is what the customer expects. This is quite a different thing from saying that what is delivered at the end is what was agreed upon at the start. Things change, even with the best risk management unforeseen events occur, customers change their minds which has an impact on timelines and costs. All project managers know about managing expectations

> If you surprise your customer you are not managing his expectations

in theory. Yet, as a customer, I have regularly been surprised by things going wrong without warning on projects being run by apparently competent project managers on numerous occasions. If you surprise your customer you are not managing his expectations.

I have seen many projects deliver a fraction of what was originally requested and yet been seen as a major success because the customer's expectations were properly and iteratively managed downwards as the project went forward. On the other hand, I have seen projects actually over-deliver against the original baseline but which have been greeted as a complete failure because the customer's expectations expanded without check as work progressed.

The best approach to managing expectations is to use the following easy instructions. These thoughts should be close to your heart at all times:

◆ Think through and be explicit with yourself about what sort of issues and risks you need to tell your customer about. This is partially about understanding your customer (does a 0.5% cost overrun matter to him, or does it need to be 5% or even 25% before he is bothered?), and understanding your own appetite for personal risk (do you think you can easily recover the situation without sponsor involvement?). There is a balance in involving your sponsor which I discuss more in Chapter 4. This balance must be considered when thinking about escalation (this is dealt with in detail later in the book, but escalation is calling upon more senior management for support, action or approval). In simple terms you should realise that if you escalate everything you are adding no value. Yet, on the other hand, if you escalate too late you will find an irritated sponsor – not only because it is irritating in its own right but because she in turn may need to manage upwards. She will have her own managers and will want the chance to manage the subsequent conversation with them. By surprising her you may have lost an opportunity for her to do something to help you.

◆ Try to gain an understanding of your sponsor's appetite for risk and information. Some sponsors like to have a micro understanding, others only want higher level information about issues and risks at regular scheduled meetings. My general rule is: if in doubt have an informal chat with the sponsor. At the start of the project ask the sponsor what her preferred style is – is she 'light touch', or does she want daily detailed updates? This simple question can avoid huge amounts of tension later on.

◆ Have a no surprises mindset. No one likes it when things go wrong, people like it less when no-one predicted things might go wrong, and they hate it when they learn very late that things have have gone wrong. If there is a major risk of derailment make sure the customer knows about it. Do not put your head in the sand and pretend it is not happening or hide it because you are afraid of your customer's temper. The longer you leave it the worse it will be (and you are in danger of converting an unpleasant conversation about problems on the project into significant personal risk). If something occurs that will make an impact on the project make sure the customer knows about it. Put yourself in your customer's shoes – it is far, far easier to deal with a known change in plans than suddenly have to deal with something unexpected. In your private life – would you rather a builder phone you up the night before your house is going to be re-roofed when the scaffolding is all around to say he is going to be a month late, or would you prefer him to ring you a month in advance and tell you he will be a month late? Would you rather know your plane was going to leave two days late when you arrive at the airport or a week in advance? Most people prefer the latter.

◆ When you are re-aligning expectations make them proportionate to where you are in the project. For example, with a few possible exceptions, it is inexcusable in my mind to say to customers one day before final delivery 'oh, by the way we will be a month late'. It may have been acceptable to warn them there was a risk of this happening a couple of months before the end, and perhaps to tell them it was going to happen a month in advance. Similarly with cost. You have failed to manage expectations if at the last progress report meeting you told your customer you had spent 10% of the budget and were 10% of the way through, but now without warning you are going to say you have spent 50% of the budget but are only 12% of the way through. You should at least have warned him of the risk of this occurring. Anything else is poor risk management and very sloppy project management.

◆ When you need to reset expectations do it in the customers' own language, and in a way in which they will understand the implications. Tell them the impact in measures they use (money, time, more people, fault rates, etc.). For example, project managers will often say 'there is a risk of x happening'. Customers often interpret this as you saying 'there is something that will cause me some pain, but I will deal with it'. If you want your customer to understand say more clearly that the impact of this risk is something like 'a 25% chance that you will need to spend an extra £100k – if you want to be certain the project will deliver you must hold a contingency budget'. Your customers will almost certainly not like this, but it is better they are forewarned than you simply start overspending the money. Make it clear that you will do your best, but that if the risk happens you may not be able to manage the impact away.

◆ Stick to the principle of 'one version of the truth' (communications lesson 15).

◆ Deliver on your promises. Every time you make a promise you are setting up an expectation with someone. The commonly held guideline of under-promise and then over-deliver is good guidance. Think of yourself as having a personal brand, and you want this brand to generate belief and confidence in yourself. For this to be true you need to live up to your promises. Nothing produces more poor expectations for the future than a track record of failing to keep promises in the past. *If you are not sure do not promise*, and when you are definitely unsure, definitely do not promise anything. (Avoid at all costs the tendency to promise to keep people happy – a promise should be built on a foundation of reality not wishful thinking.)

◆ When there is bad news to communicate, communicate it early. Ensure your customer never finds out bad news about your project from someone else or via the informal grapevine. This reduces trust and does not give confidence that you are in control.

Managing expectations is simply about understanding the status and risk in a project and matching this with timely and sufficient communications with your customer.

Communications lesson 17 – Communicate to deliver (don't deliver to communicate)

Throughout this chapter I have built up a picture of the communication skills that drive success in project management and tried to raise awareness of the critical importance of having and developing such skills. But don't fall into the trap of thinking that communication is a substitute for real delivery. Occasionally when we have not completed something we are all tempted to talk our way out of it with clever words – if we get away with it too often, talking rather than doing may become a habit.

Project management is about delivery, in the same way that football is about scoring goals. To make this happen you need to have good communication skills as delivery is built upon people interaction – and successful, productive interaction requires communication. It is the fundamental project management skill, but do not think that communication is a replacement for delivery, anymore than a footballer's dribbling skill is an alternative to scoring goals.

Don't be tempted to ameliorate poor progress with clever progress reports. Don't replace real progress milestones with communication events. Don't use talking as a proxy for action. Don't build your plans around your communications – build your communications around your delivery plans. Don't confuse setting up and having meetings with making progress. Keep on talking – and talk *as* you deliver.

If you do nothing but keep talking you may get away with it for a while, but you are not really achieving what you can. Communication is an essential support for delivery, some of your deliverables may include a communication element – but communication is not delivery.

3

What actually is your project?

THIS CHAPTER DEFINES A SIMPLE APPROACH to building a full understanding of what your project needs to be designed to achieve. This understanding I call scope. In some situations project managers define the word 'scope' much more tightly than this, but to me the most useful way to consider scope is the collection of information you need before you can go on to develop a meaningful activity and resource plan for your project. It is the basis for all your management of the project.

The importance of understanding scope

Key lesson

The foundation on which all good projects are built is a clear understanding of the scope. Without it a project manager will struggle to deliver successfully.

Once you have been chosen to work as project manager on a specific development defining the scope is where the real project management work starts. Defining the scope well requires great judgement – it must consist of all the information you reasonably might need to plan a project – but defining the scope cannot be an exercise that takes for ever. The scope needs to be concise and easily understandable – yet comprehensive and complete.

The importance of a good understanding of scope cannot be over-emphasised. The scope is the foundation stone upon which all further project management activities are built. The scope defines what is in and what is out of the project. Before you understand the scope you must not start to develop your project in any detail. Do not rush into developing solutions until you understand the scope.

As described in Chapter 2, scope is different from requirements. Requirements are the detailed and unambiguous definitions of what the final deliverables of a project must conform to. The scope is the instructions that enable you to build a good project plan in the first place – a part of which may be to do with requirements capture. The scope needs to be complete, but it is at a much higher level of detail than requirements. In addition, scope contains an understanding of factors that are important to the process of delivery of the project – but which have no relevance once the project is complete (for example, how your customer wants you to work on the project).

> **Before you understand the scope you must not start to develop your project in any detail**

For a project manager a full understanding of what is within, and, almost as important, what is not within the scope of a project is essential. An inability to understand and communicate the scope of a project is as close to a cardinal sin as it is possible to get in project management.

When you have talked with your customer and developed an understanding of a project's scope, the next thing to do is to write it down. The reason for writing it down is firstly obvious – it means it will not get forgotten and it can easily be shared. Also important is that the practice of writing down the scope in a coherent manner is a good test of whether you actually understand it or not. If you cannot write it down you probably do not fully understand it, and will almost certainly have difficulty communicating it to other team members.

The key scoping questions

Key lesson

The scope of a project can best be understood by going through a set of structured questions with your customer.

There are many ways to capture the scope of a project. Often project managers have a variety of template scoping documents which they complete. Others use their experience and intuition to collect the information that defines the scope. In either case collecting scoping information is about communicating with your customer – not about creativity on behalf of the project manager. Irrespective of the specific mechanism a project manager uses, underlying it must be a series of questions that the customer is asked.

The following sub-sections run through eight key and twelve subsidiary questions that you can use to ensure that you have really scoped out the project. It is acceptable to determine that the question is irrelevant in the specific context in which you are working, or to determine that you cannot answer it yet, and that in the early stages of the project you will undertake action to get an answer. However, in this situation you must accept that when you get the answer it may have an impact on your plans, and require you to change them. An inability to answer any of these questions adds to the project's risk.

In defining these questions I am not suggesting that in every situation you simply go through them one by one with your customer, though this is a valid approach that is viable in some situations. However, you must determine the best way in which to ask them in the environment and context of your project. At the end though you should be able to go through these questions and either answer them comprehensively, be clear they are irrelevant to your project, or understand you are working with a risk derived from incomplete information.

The questions are:

◆ What is the overall objective of the project?

◆ What are the deliverables?

- Are there deliverables required by the project which it is explicitly not responsible for?
- Are you working to deliver a finite set of deliverables or provide some business capability?
- Are you working to deliver a set of independent deliverables or an integrated end-to-end solution?
- How will the quality of deliverables be determined?

◆ Are you working to implement a specific solution, or to solve a problem?

- Are you responsible for the delivery of deliverables or for achieving the business benefits?

◆ How is the customer going to measure success at the end of the project?

◆ What, from the customer's viewpoint, can flex?

- Do you want predictability or speed?

◆ Are there any other constraints on the project?

- Are there any currently known issues, risks or opportunities?
- Are there any external considerations?

◆ How does your customer want to work with you?

- How will decisions be made on the project?
- How high is the project in your customer's overall priorities?
- Can your sponsor allocate all the resources the project requires or do other stakeholders need to be involved?
- Who can legitimately put requirements upon the project?

◆ Are there any implicit requirements, assumptions or needs that the customer has that are not defined in the scope or requirements documents?

Scoping question 1 – What is the overall objective of the project?

The aim of this question is to produce a simple statement, ideally one sentence, which encapsulates what the project sponsor wants to achieve. This statement provides both a framework in which you can operate and flesh out the remainder of the project, and also the base communication that everyone involved in the project can share and understand why the project exists.

Everything else you are told about the project can be compared to this objective statement – if it is not consistent with it, or not relevant to it, it should not be considered as part of the project. It is therefore critically important to get this right.

Some simple examples of valid objectives might be:

◆ The objective of the project is successfully to design, develop and launch the new product for the SME market consistent with the business strategy and focus.

◆ The objective of the project is to tailor and implement the new financial accounting system within the finance department and the corporate office.

◆ The objective of the project is to design and complete the re-fit of the Northumberland offices so they can meet the growth requirements of the 2006 strategy.

These are simple statements, which are clearly understood, but which also provide a basic scope for the project and from which anyone can easily determine whether activities they are performing fit within the project.

A warning flag: if your objective can only be defined as a series of statements and can only be linked in one sentence by using 'and' several times you should question whether this is logically a single project or a set of unrelated tasks.

Scoping question 2 – What are the deliverables?

Every project produces some output, known as the deliverables. The production of these deliverables is the *raison d'être* of a project, and until they are produced the project will not be over. It seems obvious therefore to say that the starting point for planning out a project must be to get a definition of what the deliverables are. Obvious, but often not done clearly enough, or assumed rather than captured from conversations with the customer. I have seen numerous projects where, when the project manager has been asked what the deliverables are, he has been unable to reply with full confidence or clarity, or when the project manager has been surprised at a late stage by something the customer is expecting to receive that the project manager has not considered.

The first thing to understand with any customer, on any project, is what the expected output will be. What does the customer expect you to deliver?

This is not about performing a detailed requirements capture – or even necessarily a complete deliverables list, but getting an understanding of the customer's expectations of what the project needs to produce. Without this understanding it is not possible to even get as far as planning a project with any degree of certainty. The most important, and simplest, scoping question the project manager must ask therefore is 'what is the expected output from the project?'

The deliverables may include tangible objects such as a new building, intangible outputs like the development of some intellectual property or software, or some result such as a business change. Whatever it is and however it is defined the project manager must hold this definition close to his heart for the life of a project. Only when this is understood is it worth asking the remaining scoping questions.

Subsidiary question 2a – Are there deliverables required by the project which it is explicitly not responsible for?

For the objective of a project to be met will require the development of a range of deliverables, but there may already be other projects running producing some of these. There is no point in doing something twice, and in fact trying to do so can cause problems (think, for example, of the situation where two projects are both trying to deliver the company's new financial system).

> You must identify what you are *not* responsible for delivering

In this situation you must identify what you are *not* responsible for delivering and, instead of developing a detailed plan with component activities, simply show an external dependency. This removes the delivery task, but gives the project manager the very different task of managing an external dependency.

Subsidiary question 2b – Are you working to deliver a finite set of deliverables or provide some business capability?

This is a somewhat subtle point, but it is fundamentally important. I have seen many projects being a success in the project manager's view but a failure in the customer's eyes because the project manager has delivered what he was asked to deliver, but the customer cannot use it fully. A simple example of this is the classic case of an IT system. As the project manager for a project are you delivering a piece of software – or are you delivering the business capability to use it? The first means your team would predominantly comprise software developers, the second that you would have to consider all sorts of other issues: staff training and possibly staff recruitment, business process change, staff access to the software and much more. An IT system is just a piece of software, a business capability is the full set of skills and ability needed to utilise the software and deliver the associated benefits.

When you have agreed your list of deliverables with the customer look at them and think of any reasons why this alone may not enable the customer to fully utilise it. What does that set of deliverables do for the customer? What additional capabilities does it give him? Is that capability achieved completely with just these deliverables? Ask your customer if he needs the other things too. Check whether your customer can really achieve what he wants with those deliverables alone. If not, go back, re-scope and re-plan the project and include the missing items. It may take longer and cost more, but the project will fail without doing this.

For many business projects it is worth considering the process, systems and organisational impact of any project. If you are delivering a new IT system – do you need associated process and organisational changes as well? If you are delivering a process improvement – are there implications for the organisation design and the supporting IT systems? If you are delivering an organisational change, such as downsizing, are there implications for business processes or IT systems?

Subsidiary question 2c – Are you working to deliver a set of independent deliverables or an integrated end-to-end solution?

Most projects have a number of discrete deliverables. These may have a sensible and complete existence as discrete entities at the end of the project. On the other hand with many projects, especially the technology projects, these deliverables need to be integrated together. The integration of separate items, such as separate IT systems, or other pieces of technology is not a trivial task. And yet I have seen dozens of projects that deliver these discrete items very effectively only to get to the point at which someone points out that they now need to be integrated together and there is no systems integration team, and no time or tasks planned for integration. Sometimes the need for integration can be quite obvious – as when delivering several pieces of software, on other occasions it can be more subtle. (Think of setting up a computer system, and then linking it over a data network to another system. People will generally test the systems, and someone will generally test the data link, but who is responsible for testing both together?) It is far better to work this out at the start of the project.

Subsidiary question 2d – How will the quality of deliverables be determined?

Depending on the nature of your project, and the type of deliverables produced you may have specific chunks of work to include within your plan which encompass quality checking and acceptance of the deliverables. In most cases if you are familiar with the business context of your project you will already know this and may feel you do not need to ask this question. No competent IT project manager would design a plan without a full testing regime included. No experienced new product project manager would develop a work structure without thinking about customer trialling. However, it is worth asking your customer if there are particular testing, trialling, assessment and auditing needs or if there are specific defined standards for deliverable compliance (which may include legal and regulatory standards, etc.).

Scoping question 3 – Are you working to implement a specific solution, or to solve a problem?

In other words are you working in the solutions set or the problem set? This may sound a little esoteric – so let me put it another way. Is the project you are running set up to solve a specific problem to which the solution is not yet known, or are you working to implement a solution that has already been defined? This is best shown with an example. Let's consider the case of a company that is running a project to achieve some growth in sales. A possible way to deliver the growth in sales is to deliver a new product that can be sold to a new market segment the company does not currently address. Your project could be either defined as having to deliver the new product, which achieves the benefit of the sales growth, or it could be defined as achieving the sales growth. Isn't this the same thing?

Well, no, not really. In the first case you will be successful if you implement the new product, whether or not it actually achieves the sales growth. That is the solution you were asked to deliver. In the second case, where you own the problem of sales growth, you may well decide to do something altogether different which delivers better sales growth – and if you do decide to deliver the new product and it does not achieve the required sales growth you have not achieved success. If your project is framed around solving a problem the first step will most likely be some analysis and selection of possible solutions prior to their implementation. If your project is framed around delivering an already selected solution then there will be no such step.

It is driving for an understanding as subtle as this, at the very early stages of project formation that will change an ordinary delivery of requirements into a value adding project management job. It may also completely change the direction and outcome of the project.

A specific example I was involved in was a project in which we were asked to increase the geographic area a television station could be picked up in. We worked hard, but could not come up with an economic way of expanding the station's coverage. Actually we had missed the point, because the problem the customer had was not really how to expand their coverage – but how to convince their board that they were doing a good job. The board was convinced the management were failing because they thought that the coverage could be expanded. The solution the management asked us to come up with was expanded coverage – even though they themselves doubted it could be done. The alternative would have been to have asked us to help them convince the board that it could not be done. When we really understood their problem we developed a very structured and rigorous analysis of why coverage could not be expanded and presented it to the board. The board accepted our analysis, and from that time fully supported the management. The unfortunate thing was that developing this analysis, while complex in itself, was a fairly small piece of consultancy work. The original project to expand the network had been far more expensive!

Subsidiary question 3a – Are you responsible for the delivery of deliverables or for achieving the business benefits?

This is an important, but specific, variant on question 3. Let me phrase it another way, if you deliver the agreed deliverables and these do not achieve the benefits expected who is accountable? Are you? If you are, then focus on the benefits, not simply the originally scoped deliverables – they may well not deliver the benefits required (or may over-deliver implying the project could have been done more quickly or cheaply). You will need to track benefit achievement through the life of the project, not simply assume they will be met by handing over the deliverables at the end of the project. Your work will not be over until the benefits have been achieved.

To give you an example, a colleague of mine was involved in a project to cut the cost of a company's order processing. The chosen solution was a new order processing system. He was employed to implement it, which he did successfully. The problem was the sponsor did not achieve the benefits that had originally been expected (i.e. the cost was not sufficiently lowered), and he felt it was the project manager's responsibility. My colleague had unfortunately never fully clarified his responsibility and felt it was simply to implement the computer system. There was much argument and difficulty as a result.

If you are new to project management my advice is to take responsibility for the deliverables, not the benefits – that is the project sponsor's role. If you are a skilled project manager, you really want to earn your keep, and you have the option, then take accountability for the benefits too. People value someone much more highly who says things like 'I will achieve the cost savings', or 'I will see the profitability of the company delivered' rather than 'I will deliver the IT system' or 'I will launch the new product'. However, if the sponsor wishes you to take responsibility for benefits you may in turn require more decision making and scoping powers than a project manager typically has. The key point is to be absolutely clear about what you are responsible for.

(If you do take responsibility for the benefits you may then want to ask the question whether you are still really a project manager or a more general business manager, but that is a detail!)

Scoping question 4 – How is the customer going to measure success at the end of the project?

At the end of every project the customer will assess whether success has been achieved. This may be formally done through some structured process, or it may be an informal assessment done on 'gut feel'. Although you may be more comfortable with the gut-feel approach as it can seem to give you some leeway, my advice is to always get success criteria formally documented at the start. As a project manager you need to know how the customer will assess the success (and this may be much broader than simply listing the deliverables). If you do not have this guideline to measure against on a daily basis you cannot be sure that you are moving to deliver everything that is required. In addition, the customer's views of what is a success will often change as the project progresses – without formally documented success criteria you do not have any baseline to control these changes against.

Scoping question 5 – What, from the customer's viewpoint, can flex?

Every project manager knows that at some point on almost all projects things do not go according to plan. In fact, if they always go to plan it is in most cases either something so simple that a project manager was not required, or you have so over-engineered the plan as to cover for all eventualities and therefore absorbed much more resource than absolutely necessary. I believe that if things never went wrong you would never need a project manager!

So when things go wrong what can we do? It is at this point that project managers should start thinking and talking about time–cost–quality trade-offs. The argument being that you cannot keep fixed on all three of these. If you absolutely must stick to the cost and quality of the deliverables, you may need to flex the time it takes. If you absolutely must stick to the time and cost, you may need to flex the quality. Project managers regularly mention this time–cost–quality model.

I completely agree with this fundamental project manager model – although I think it is a four- rather than three-dimensional trade-off – time, cost, quality and scope, or functional richness. I separate quality (how well does the end deliverable match the needs) from functionality (how many of the original requirements have been met) as they can be flexed separately. As an example I can change the functionality of an IT system (i.e. make it do more or less) without impacting the quality – alternatively I can alter the quality (i.e. make it more or less reliable) without impacting the functionality. The importance of these four factors is that they can all be flexed and often there is a trade-off between changing one dimension and the others.

> **If things never went wrong you would never need a project manager!**

So far most experienced project managers will be thinking 'so what, this is old news'. Perhaps true, but what project managers who understand this well often forget to do is:

◆ Ensure the customer understands this at the start of the project. Tell the customer that at some point he or she is likely to be returning to make decisions based on trading off the length of time a project takes, its cost, its scope and the level of quality. This is an easy, if somewhat abstract, conversation to have at the start of the project. It can be very tricky if left until late on when these trade-offs are required. It is worth formally presenting the implications to the project sponsor in one of your earliest meetings with him or her.

◆ On top of this project managers regularly assume they understand what the trade-off balance is. Project managers are notorious for making trade-off decisions without clearly understanding the customer's own priorities. I worked in one company in which the project teams strived hard to make sure the projects did not come in over budget again and again. The company was generally short of cash so they concluded this was the right thing to do. They regularly hit the cost targets for the projects and hence thought they were doing a great job and yet the particular department they were working for was not that restricted on budget, it had more money to spend than was currently allocated to projects, but what it could not afford was any time delays. Ironically, in the effort to minimise spend on resources and hence save money, the projects regularly overran on time. In another organisation I saw a team valiantly working all hours to bring a project in on time and budget, and to achieve this the quality was jeopardised. As the final result was a consumer product for sale in a competitive market bringing it in late would have resulted in a financial loss for the company. However, lowering the quality was a total disaster as the product simply did not sell.

Let me challenge you – if you are working on a project right now can you say with absolute confidence whether delivery time, total cost, quality of deliverables, or the scope of the deliverables is more important to your customer? Can you say with confidence by what amount you can flex these factors? If the answer is 'no', or a statement like 'we cannot move any of them', then you need to go back, check and deepen your understanding.

Do not be surprised if your customers find a conversation about trade-offs difficult. They may initially at least give contradictory answers, or state that they need everything. This is not helpful, but from a customer perspective it is actually quite a sensible state of mind. The customer may reasonably think – if you have already agreed to deliver a project to time, cost, quality and full scope – why you are now asking to change it. To counter this you need to ensure the customer understands you will try to deliver everything on time and cost, and to the full quality and functionality, and this is not an excuse or get out for you, it is a way of ensuring delivery *if* problems or changes arise. To refine clarity ask questions like 'if x occurred would you rather y happened or z'. Where y and z are shifts respectively in time, cost, quality or functionality.

Start by asking generically, for example, 'would you rather the time increased or the price?', then move to specifics, 'would you rather the time increased by 1 week, or the price by £10k'. In this way you can start by getting a general prioritisation you can use on regular decisions (for example, if I have an issue to resolve is it better if the resolution impacts time or cost?). By driving to specific values you can start to understand absolute tolerances – time cannot shift by more than a few days, quality needs to stay high, functionality can be de-scoped a lot, and cost cannot increase by more than 20%. These tolerances will vary from project to project, but give you the basis for great management control once you understand them.

In doing this find out if there are any absolute constraints on any of the four dimensions of project management:

◆ Is there a time when, if the project goes beyond it, it becomes pointless? (Is there a critical event that must be hit, or does the business case start to break down after a point in time?)

◆ Is there a cost which the project cannot go beyond? (Is there an absolute budget, which irrespective of business case is all that is available? Is there a cost which once hit means the business case starts to break down?)

◆ Is there a minimum scope below which the project will not deliver anything of value?

◆ Is there a minimum quality standard which in practice or for external reasons cannot be undercut?

Once you understand what the customer considers to be his or her possible points and levels of flexibility – do test them for *reasonableness*. Customers may make bold statements without thinking through the full implications. Your job is not to ignore their needs – but it is to ensure they understand the implications of what they are asking. I was responsible for running a programme once where the sponsor was very clear that the thing that mattered more than anything else was the delivery date. He reasonably told us we could increase the cost if necessary, and we could reduce the scope to a limited degree. From a project management perspective he seemed an ideal customer – he knew what he wanted and understood he may have to make trade-offs to get it. He was also not concerned about quality, or at least he did not really understand the issue when asked. To hit the time we had to make compromises on quality, because we could not do the full testing we ideally wanted. We kept asking for delays to build in quality by better testing.

His driver was only time. When we completed the project it was a major success for his company and the share price duly went up and up. It was only after a few months when his end customers kept complaining about the fault rates in the product they had bought, and started to turn away from the company, that the true cost of hitting the date at the expense of lower quality was revealed and that he fully understood the requirement he had imposed upon us. This was a painful lesson for me – if we had done a test for reasonableness at the start we could have foreseen the outcome.

Subsidiary question 5a – Do you want predictability or speed?

There is a specific trade-off question that is worth asking if your customer rates speed of delivery as of paramount importance. Speed can be critically important and late delivery can often adversely impact a business case far more than people realise. However, sometimes when people ask for speed what they really want is to be able to predict delivery times. This is particularly common where your project is a part of a large set of activities that must all be brought together at one point in time. Predictability is quite different from speed – when stated bluntly it is obvious as the words have different meanings. It is, however, quite common subconsciously to confuse the two, or to have a mental model of the word in which they are closely related. In reality they are quite different things, and are often contradictory.

Scoping question 6 – Are there any other constraints on the project?

When a project is initiated there are often some constraints on how it can progress. Examples include: solutions that are unacceptable in the particular environment; people who must not be used or involved; maximum budgets that are available; or maximum time that can be taken to deliver are some of the most common. Before you develop your plan you must know these constraints.

Subsidiary question 6a – Are there any currently known issues, risks or opportunities?

Assessing issues, risks and opportunities for improvements is a core part of the project work. However, it does no harm to ask the question at this stage to identify anything the customer is aware of that may take you some time to find out.

Subsidiary question 6b – Are there any external considerations?

Many organisations are subject to a raft of external considerations that must be understood and considered by the project manager. Typical examples of these are legal issues, regulatory concerns, specific social guidelines because of the nature of the organisation, and health and safety rules. In some cases these can fundamentally alter the approach that must be taken to a project with significant implications for the resources used and the timescales taken.

Scoping question 7 – How does your customer want to work with you?

Successfully working with people is not just a matter of doing what people want, it is also a function of working in a way that people like, or at least are comfortable with. So, for example, does your customer like daily verbal updates, weekly reports by e-mail, or monthly presentations? Different people like different approaches and you should not assume you know best. Meeting your customer's preferred working style may be a small detail, but at the other extreme may have to create a significant overhead and, as it is a critical success factor, it is well worth determining it now. In addition, if his or her demands are unreasonable now is the time to start managing their expectations. A short discussion on how they like to be briefed on issues, risks, progress, spend, and how they like to be involved in development and decision making, etc. at this stage will enhance your relationship and avoid misunderstanding as well as aid plan development.

Subsidiary Question 7a – How will decisions be made on the project?

During the life of a project you will need to make a continuous sequence of decisions. A project will never simply follow a series of pre-arranged steps. Resources need to be shifted around, options to solve problems chosen, different changes must be accepted or rejected. You can save a significant amount of pain and wasted time by broadly agreeing now with your sponsor what type and level of decisions you can make within the project, which ones you need to go to the sponsor to agree, and finally which decisions need to be made by other customer groups or stakeholders.

An example of this is: can you as the project manager raise and authorise unplanned purchase requisitions – and to what value? Essentially the question is what is within your decision making authority, and who should you involve for other decisions.

Subsidiary question 7b – Can your sponsor allocate all the resources the project requires or do other stakeholders need to be involved?

The task of resource allocation and resource management is described in Chapter 5. Needless to say it is important to understand who you must work with to get resources allocated to the project. Ideally your sponsor should be able to allocate all the resources you require. In practice this is rarely true, and although legitimacy for the project comes from the sponsor's involvement you will frequently have to deal with a range of resource-owning managers. This not only adds to the complexity at the start of the project, but also through its life as these people may remove resources at any stage unless the relationship with them is well managed.

Subsidiary question 7c – How high is the project in your customer's overall priorities?

You do not actually need to know the answer to this question to scope out a project – but you do really need to know it to plan out the project once you have the scope. All projects require resources whether it is money, specialist equipment or people. Your access to these will be a function of what resources the customer has and what else they are being used for. The determining factor will be how high the project sits in a customer's list of priorities. If the priority is set as high as possible then you can assume the customer will give you access to the resources he has available. If it is low you need to plan accordingly and timescales or scope need to be adjusted to reflect this. What really matters is not absolute priority to the customer, but priority relative to other things your customer is doing. For example, even if you are the second most important activity a customer wants completed out of hundreds, it does not help if the highest priority project uses the resources you require.

> What really matters is not absolute priority to the customer, but priority relative to other things your customer is doing

The prioritisation may also impact the type of resources you require. For example, a low priority project will typically not have access to key staff members who will be allocated to higher priority work. Therefore lower priority projects may rely on contract staff or consultants. As such resources are usually more expensive this ironically increases the budget required for lower priority projects.

I discuss prioritisation in detail in Chapter 10. All I will say here is that at first your customer may be reluctant or find it hard to give you a prioritisation. Although everyone has an implicit list of priorities, few people have an explicit documented list. If you think of your own life it is quite hard to prioritise all the activities you do relative to one another. It is hard because it requires making decisions about options – and this is difficult, but your customer must do this. (Customers also sometimes employ assertive project managers specifically to get projects delivered in the face of a low prioritisation.)

You do not need an absolute priority ranking but you do need to get a view on whether you will be within your rights to get people allocated from other work – or if there is work at a higher priority you should not impact if it can be avoided. I am a firm believer that you need to understand this point. Your job as a project manager is to get the work done, but it is not to go against your customer's wishes. I have frequently seen project managers working on low priority projects forcing through success on a project by their personal drive and, especially, nagging people to do the work required. The project succeeds, but if the cost is that work with a higher priority in the customer's mind gets delayed then you have not actually helped your customer.

Subsidiary question 7d – Who can legitimately put requirements upon the project?

A view of the range of people whose input must be actively sort to define detailed requirements once the project is running. The reason this is important depends on the size of the list of names given, and the nature of the people on the list, as a project may be considerably more or less complex to run. Additionally, many people may have an opinion about a project and want to influence its direction, you need to know whether you should listen to them or not. A project with a single person acting as the source of requirements may be unusual but it is simple then to collect the requirements. Larger lists offer problems not only of the logistics in collecting requirements, but also mean you may have to get involved in resolving conflicts between different stakeholders' views of requirements.

If the list of names becomes very extensive challenge and discuss the implications of this in terms of time and resource usage with the sponsor. Also, be clear what sorts of requirements different people can contribute towards. Some may only have a remit to comment and add to requirements in one specific part of the project.

> *Scoping question 8 – Are there any implicit requirements, assumptions or needs that the customer has that are not defined in the scope or requirements documents?*

This is effectively a re-stressing of the point made in Chapter 2 about not making assumptions, and regularly checking understanding. Needless to say, keep checking with the customer throughout the development of both the detailed requirements specification and the project's scope definition that they cover everything the customer has on his or her mind.

4

Some key traits

THIS CHAPTER DEFINES the key personality traits required by project managers.

Let me start by giving you a scenario. I need a project manager to manage a piece of work for me, and I have a number of choices so I am going through a selection process. If you have ever had to employ project managers I am sure you will be familiar with the procedure. I have someone in front of me with a good CV. So far this person sounds good, they know how to communicate and they seem to understand all the things a project manager should know. What else am I going to look for? Beyond basic fitness for the role I am going to try to find out three things about this person:

◆ Do they have a sense of ownership for what they do – and are they involved in it?

◆ Do they have good judgement?

◆ Can they be creative?

Beyond communication skills these are the other things that really differentiate the excellent from the average project manager.

The sense of ownership and involvement

Key lesson

To be the most successful project manager you must feel and externally display a sense of complete ownership for the project and its outcome.

To me a sense of ownership is that pattern of thinking that drives people to care passionately about how well and how hard they work. It is an emotional state that derives pleasure from success, and displeasure from failure. It is the mentality that makes someone act as if they are fully accountable for something, even if they are not. It is the force that makes people get involved in an activity and avoid being remote from it.

If you are a project manager you cannot control everything within the project, but you still need to feel accountability for it all. We can have a long debate about the difference between accountability and responsibility, but in terms of the sense of ownership required these two need to 'blur'. You are the one and only person who has the overall responsibility, and in addition you need to feel as if you have full accountability. Don't evade it – take ownership even when a project is a mess. The true sign of someone worth having around is the person who puts up their hand and takes ownership for things when they are going wrong. Act like this and people will thank you, reward you, and seek you out to work with them again!

> When a project manager has delivered without this sense of ownership it is usually because the project has not been that difficult

A project can be delivered by a project manager who does not have a real sense of ownership for its content or outcome. I have been involved with lots of projects that have achieved their goals when they were managed by someone without a full sense of ownership. But when things go wrong, get tricky, or are otherwise demanding, the sense of ownership drives success. When it is midnight and a little more is needed to complete the work, passion will drive you. When a project manager has delivered without this sense of ownership it is usually because the project has not been that difficult or complex.

How can I tell when a project manager has this sense of ownership? You can only tell when the going gets tough. The project is going to be late – maybe for justifiable reasons – perhaps an issue has arisen which changes things. Do you feel 'oh well I have managed the process and this is the result. I have done my job and can do no more', or do you ask yourself, 'ok, this has occurred – what can I do to bring it on track and keep it on track?' If the former applies to you, you are going through the motions, if the latter, then you have that sense of ownership for the project.

If I am recruiting a project manager what do I look for? Essentially, I will question and probe them to tell me about situations when things have gone wrong and ask them to describe what they did and how it felt. I will ask them about situations in which they have failed to deliver – what did they do and how did it feel. What I am looking for is a picture of someone who is tenacious in overcoming obstacles, who derives pleasure from overcoming them, and who feels he or she has failed if they cannot.

How can you know if you have this sense of ownership? My trite answer to that question is like the old answer to the 'how will I know if I am in love' question – the wise simply respond you just do. You know when you are committed to something. If you are unsure, ask yourself this question: how will you feel if the project does not achieve its end goals for reasons outside your control? If you are simply going to shrug your shoulders and think, 'well, it was not my fault', then you do not have the sense of ownership; if, on the other hand, you are going to feel disappointed and unsatisfied then you probably have it.

Great project managers feel passionate about meeting project success goals, they do not just treat project management as an algorithm that either comes up with the right answer or does not. Great project managers will go that extra mile to find solutions and ways around when things go wrong, they do not accept answers from their team about how long things take, or how much they cost, without rigorous and structured challenge. Great project managers escalate issues to get things done – not to dodge responsibility. When you have escalated to the most senior person available, you still know you are the one who has to bring the project in and you treat the escalation as simply another task you must manage – not a handing over of responsibility.

Great project managers do not only use their sense of ownership to drive themselves to deliver. They project this passion onto the teams they are managing, and onto the customers they are delivering for.

A good analogy is with sports. Everyone can participate in some sports. Most people can win in some situations or against some opponents. But being really successful is not about winning when you can choose your competition, or winning only now and again. It is about consistently winning. This cannot be achieved without the passion to win. All sport's psychologists will tell you that while ability and fitness are necessary to excel at sport, your mental state and attitude is also critically important to success. Similarly, project managers need project management competence and abilities, but they also need passion and drive.

Such a sense of ownership is not about project managers achieving impossible things, it is about project managers having an emotional state of attachment and engagement with the work so that their personal feeling of success or failure is aligned with project success or failure. I am not saying that without this you cannot ever competently manage projects – you can. You can be competent, but you will never excel. You may keep busy, but people will not go that extra mile to seek you out to manage their projects.

Ownership is not a remote sense – ownership needs to be experienced and displayed through total involvement in a project. As a project manager you are not an absentee landlord who occasionally returns to make sure that your tenants are behaving well. You must be an integral, active member of the team sitting at the centre of the action. Ask yourself a question: what is your mental image of yourself as you deliver your project? Do you see yourself as a knowledgeable observer of the project, trying to put some shape and structure onto a series of events you have only partial control over, half-impotently trying to change things, your main weapon being your ability to track what is going on and bring more senior management in when you need to escalate? Do you see yourself as a powerful but impassionate deity sitting above the project whose role it is to oversee, report, and occasionally give directions and move people and tasks around in a giant game of chess? Or do you see yourself as a core component of the project, responsible for its delivery, fighting alongside everyone else to get it done and fundamentally involved in the day-to-day workings of the project? If your image is anything like the first two, you are doing the wrong job, it needs to be close to the last one.

If you want to be great you need to feel total ownership for the project, and remain intimately involved in it throughout its life. And a final factor that makes commitment important, work is personally more enjoyable if you are committed.

Good judgement – project management style

Key lesson

Each and every project is different and a project manager needs to adapt to each one. Although tools and processes will help, the basis for this adaptation must be the project manager's judgement.

Project managers have a whole family of processes and tools, they may also have tick lists and systems to support them. However, project management is not an exact science that can be applied like a mathematical equation to provide a precise answer. Every project is different and the approach to managing the project must be adapted. Project managers require judgement. (In the rest of the book I will continually refer to the need for good judgement.)

Judgement, by its very definition is more an art than a science. Occasionally people seem to be born with good judgement, but usually it comes with the scars of practice. It is learnt by experience more than taught in the classroom, or learnt by reading a book like this. It is not a theoretical subject, and I cannot give you good judgement – you have it, you develop it, or you don't and never will.

However, I can at least be of some help. Good judgement is critical to the project manager, and if I cannot bestow good judgement, I can at least point out some areas in which your judgement needs to be applied.

> I cannot give you good judgement – you have it, you develop it, or you don't and never will

The following list covers a sample of fifteen key areas where a project manager regularly needs to apply judgement. It is not an exhaustive list. These points are not like Euclidian geometry with absolute answers in any situation, but require you to make a decision based on balancing different issues. Being able to find this balance is what makes really successful project managers. I have chosen these specific examples as they represent everyday decisions project managers must make and give a feel for the spread of judgements required.

The fifteen areas for judgement I have selected are:

1 What is in scope?

2 What should be in the plan?

3 Which elements of project management process to apply and which to ignore.

4 When to escalate.

5 When to get into the detail and when to skim.

6 When to do and when to delegate.

7 Who can you trust in your project team?

8 What is an acceptable level of risk?

9 What is an acceptable level of parallel activity?

10 What is an acceptable level of change?

11 When should you enforce the change management process?

12 When is it reasonable to progress based on an assumption?

13 How many levels of project management organisation do you need?

14 When to consider broader stakeholder groups.

15 When is the project complete?

Judgement 1 – What is in scope?

In Chapters 2 and 3 I outlined the importance of understanding a project's scope and defined a series of questions you can use to ensure you know it well enough. I also described an inability to understand or communicate the scope as the closest a project manager can come to a cardinal sin. It is one of the most important things a project manager discusses with his customer, and by using the questions I outlined you should get a good definition of scope. However, the reality is that unless you are working for a very structured customer (or perhaps an ex-project manager), the final definition of scope is subject, to some degree, to the project manager's judgement.

An assertive project manager can usually influence a customer in the definition of scope and support defining it more or less broadly. A less assertive project manager may simply be at his customer's mercy. Project managers usually understand the issues to do with scope better than their customers, so can, to a limited degree, if unscrupulous, manipulate it to suit themselves. In each case there is a danger. Over-rigorous definition of the scope to a very constrained set of deliverables may help to ensure delivery, but it can risk effective project failure – if not everything that is actually needed is included you may, on paper, have achieved the result required but, taking a more customer-centric view, you have failed. It also risks producing unsatisfied customers. No matter how well it is documented and signed off by the customer, if the end result is less than their expectations then they will be unhappy. The counter-balance to this is that an over-broad definition of scope can lead to a situation in which a project never finishes. The skill, therefore, is to help your customer define a scope for the project that is achievable with the available resources and time, and which also meets their real needs.

Common actions that can result in an over-broad definition of scope come about from what is normally known as scope creep, and the customer's desire to use a project to deliver a host of unrelated needs. Scope creep is the tendency for apparently successful projects to be subject to a constant series of additions to scope (often without change control). Customers may also add unrelated requirements to a project's scope, simply because a project team exists and they may feel it can be used to achieve all sorts of extras they may need. Scope creep is dangerous – it can lead to a point at which the project becomes too big to complete. Unrelated requirements added at a customer's whim, have the same, if not greater, dangers upon a project team.

The judgement you must make as a project manager is to balance the following questions:

◆ Is the scope defined broadly enough to add value for the customer?

◆ Is it defined narrowly enough to be achievable with the resources and skills available and in the time required?

◆ Is it defined in a meaningful way that is consistent with the project's objectives and can be easily communicated?

Judgement 2 – What should be in the plan?

Once a project's scope is defined the next thing a project manager must do is to build the project plan. I discuss planning in Chapter 5, but it is worth taking an early look at the subject.

Project planning in itself is not a conceptually difficult activity, but it is very powerful. The project plan will form the basis for deciding the resources required, the length of time the project will take, and will also throw up other issues and risks the project manager must resolve.

The judgement in project planning is essentially to do with the level of detail the plan includes, and how many activities that are not within the project's scope, to include in the plan (external dependencies). A common mistake for new project managers is to make a massively complicated plan, showing every activity down to a very low level of granularity. At the other extreme some project managers simply spend a few minutes putting together a very high level summary.

Before deciding the correct approach it is worth making sure you understand what the plan is actually for, and how you will use it in practice. One way to look at the purpose of a plan is that it should help you achieve the following four management tasks:

1   It is there to enable you to understand how long the project will take and what resources are required through the various stages of the project to deliver it. In doing this it needs to have the capability of enabling your 'what if' analysis. (For example, if you add one more person to a team for a few weeks what will be the impact on the plan, or what will be the impact on the plan if you remove some people for a period of time.)

2   It will enable you to allocate work to the various people or teams involved in the project and to ensure the tasks that they perform all come together to achieve the end result required.

3   It is there to help you measure progress. Without a plan it is not possible to decide in any one period of time whether you have done enough to get to the end point, or if you should have done more.

4   It is a communications tool to explain to people in the project, customers and other stakeholders, what they want to know and what you need them to know.

The next thing to understand is how the plan will be used in practice. It is a tool and not an end in itself – it needs only to be good enough to achieve the four purposes outlined above, nothing else. It will be subject to change and needs to be a living document throughout the life of the project. No matter how well you plan, on a project with any degree of complexity, tasks will have to be added, timings will change – and the plan will help you manage this. Make it too complex and the task of updating it will become unmanageable.

Too high a level of planning and you will not be able to achieve the results defined above. For example, if a major programme is defined in single tasks, each a month long, you cannot work out the resources required. Too low a level of planning and the plan becomes an end in itself and as the project manager you will spend too much time creating and updating it. Also, it then becomes easy to get bogged down in low level detail and stop seeing the wood for the trees.

If your plan is sufficient to achieve the four purposes described above it is sufficiently detailed. Include any more detail and you are just making work for yourself. The primary aim is to show the work that falls within the scope of your project, external dependencies should be shown, but only at a very high level. Do not try and plan out all the external dependencies in detail in your plan. (Though see Chapter 10 for issues in managing external dependencies.)

Judgement 3 – Which elements of project management process to apply and which to ignore

If you try to apply every project manager discipline in every situation you will spend your whole life applying process and nothing will actually be delivered. There are some things (like planning and managing issues) which probably need to be done on every project, but there are others which can be excluded. I regularly see project managers producing all sorts of documents and following processes which are not relevant to the project they are managing simply because they are mandatory in the organisation they work in. There does need to be a minimum mandatory set of common activities for project managers, but this should be a small set with the implementation of other processes being dependent on the judgement of the project manager. For example, if levels of risk are low, and the impact of late delivery is minor, don't bother with contingency plans.

You should remember that the project management process is there to help you, not to hinder you. So use it carefully when it helps, but on the occasions it gets in the way or does not add value then ignore it. There is an overhead in using good process, but this overhead will be repaid in greater efficiency, effectiveness, or lower risk in the longer run. However, where it is not achieving these returns consider working without it. As a project manager your management approach should have priority over the process. If you are a junior or inexperienced project manager – use the process. One of the key things to learn as you become more experienced is to learn when to break away from it. As project manager it is *your* tool – not your straightjacket.

Judgement 4 – When to escalate

The judgement required here is not only to keep to the 'no surprises' rule (see Chapter 2, communication lesson 16 on expectation management), but also to avoid overloading the sponsor and adding no value. Put simply if you escalate everything then you are adding very little value. Your job is to resolve issues and manage risks, not simply to act as a channel to more senior managers. When you hit a roadblock your job is to remove it. On the other hand, you need to give sponsors and customers adequate warning of issues and risks that you will not be able to resolve. If you escalate too late you increase the risk of failure. Being able to judge between when it is inappropriate to escalate and when it is essential is a key capability.

> **When you hit a roadblock your job is to remove it**

It is also important to remember that when you escalate you do not cease to be accountable for resolution of the underlying issue. You are still the project manager, and you are still responsible for delivery – it is just that one of the tasks is being done by someone more senior.

Judgement 5 – When to get into the detail and when to skim

To some extent this depends on the size of the project. But assuming I am talking about big projects or programmes this becomes a critical decision. Skim too high and you are likely to miss important details, go to low and you will stop doing the project manager job and become overloaded. The secret is to identify the members of the team who are fully reliable and those who are not – go into more detail with those who are not rather than in the area you happen to be most comfortable or knowledgeable with. The second thing is to make sure you have a robust progress tracking mechanism – this will soon show up where you need to focus your attention.

Judgement 6 – When to do and when to delegate

This is a general management challenge that all new managers struggle with but must learn. Asking and trusting other people to perform key tasks rather than doing all of them yourself comes naturally to people who are experienced in their jobs and is often difficult the first time you manage people. All managers must delegate; if you cannot then you should not be a manager. It is easy if the task to be delegated is not your area of competence, then it is obvious that you must rely on your experts. However, you must also use delegation regularly even for tasks you feel you can do well. If you are managing the project properly you will not have time to do anything else. But remember, a good rule from the military is don't ask your team to do anything you would not be willing to do yourself.

Judgement 7 – Who can you trust in your project team?

The project manager will have to look across a wide range of areas, managing progress and helping to remove any roadblocks. The main control mechanism the project manager has in this situation will be progress assessments against the plan. Where issues or problems occur the project manager will need to get into more detail. In big programmes it is frequently true that the project manager cannot cover all the areas in sufficient detail to be absolutely sure of progress and resolution of issues all the time. A good way to cover this is to be able to determine which members of your team you can trust to be good at following the agreed project plan and who will escalate to you when they need help. Then you can focus more of your time on those members of the team who need more detailed tracking.

There are two dimensions here that the project manager needs to be aware of. Trust on a personality basis means that when someone says they will do something you believe them. There is also trust based on whether someone has the skills and competencies to do the work required, so that when they say they will do something you know they are capable of doing it thoroughly.

Judgement 8 – What is an acceptable level of risk?

There are two separate risks you have to be aware of when managing a project. Risk to the project (i.e. what can derail it and how likely is this?), and personal risk (i.e. what is the risk to yourself in terms of things like reputation should this go wrong?). I cannot talk about personal risk, as by its very definition it is an individual issue. It is something you should be conscious of and have a good self-awareness of. The degree of project risk that is acceptable varies from project to project, and organisation to organisation. Assuming you have a robust risk management process and do actually understand the degree of risk you are undertaking, the things to think about when assessing whether the level of risk is acceptable are:

◆ Do you fully understand the risk or is it just the tip of an iceberg?

◆ Are the risks independent issues or are they interrelated and cumulative?

◆ Have you got a way around this risk – can it be reduced, can you mitigate it happening, or do you have a contingency plan should it happen? (Is the plan viable and are there resources to implement it?)

◆ How risk-averse or risk-favouring is the organisation you are working in?

◆ How critical is it that the project is delivered – if the risk derails the project will that have a significant impact on your customer or will they cope easily?

◆ How good is your project team? A strong team is usually better able to handle and resolve risks.

Judgement 9 – What is an acceptable level of parallel activity?

To many people the ideal way of doing anything is to perform one task at a time – in other words to do things sequentially. Some activities have to be done sequentially – as a trivial example you cannot physically test a new car until it has been built. However, if you conduct all activities on a project sequentially then it can become impossibly long. Hence, most projects have a degree of parallel activity – in fact, you could argue this is why you need a project manager to manage across the various parallel work streams (in the case of a project), or parallel projects (in the case of a programme). The issue usually only becomes a problem when in the desire to speed up activity, or the desire to catch up following a delay, tasks that were originally planned as sequential become parallel. This can increase risk and you should feel instinctively uncomfortable when too many tasks are brought together in this way. The questions you need to ask yourself are:

◆ Do you have sufficient resources to do the work in parallel? It may speed up progress but it will also eat resources up more quickly.

◆ Are any of the tasks now in parallel logically only possible sequentially? However much you may want to complete some tasks in parallel, perhaps they should or may only be done sequentially.

◆ What is the impact on testing and training? I pick this out specifically as testing and training is normally the last task on a project. It is often therefore testing and training that get this treatment. Acceptable testing short cuts involve developing test and training plans before deliverables are ready for test, testing individual components before all components are ready. Where it becomes higher risk is when integration tests, user acceptance tests and operational readiness tests are performed in parallel. Cut testing at your peril.

◆ Can you, as the project manager, actually manage this, can your team do it? A project with half a dozen parallel tasks is much easier to manage than one with twenty. Managing twenty tasks in parallel increases the management overhead and also the skill required. Effectively making task pathways more parallel removes the margin for error and makes delivery to date critical. In most projects if a deliverable date shifts by a small percentage it can be recovered – when all activities are performed in parallel this may not be possible. Parallel working increases the need for a skilled and experienced team.

One final point about too many parallel activities – it is not only the planned tasks that you have to avoid becoming too parallel. If too many issues and risks are arising which need resolution you can get to the point where work on these also becomes too much to manage, a simple roadblock becomes gridlock. Although it is not a good point to reach, the pragmatic project manager does have to accept that at some time not all issues can be resolved at the same time and, potentially, additional time has to be added to the project plan to resolve some issues sequentially.

Judgement 10 – What is an acceptable level of change?

The project manager's dream project is often one on which nothing changes. When nothing changes it is easier by far to deliver reliably. In fact, some project managers use the change control process more as a mechanism to stop change rather than to control it. And yet change will occur – it is a reality. In some situations it may be a positive benefit (many professional companies selling project-based products and services to a customer often make most of their money on changes as opposed to delivering the base requirement). However, as a project manager you do have to be able to manage the degree of change to some extent. Constant change makes a project almost impossible to complete. If the degree of change is too great you must talk with your sponsor to reduce it (which may be achieved, for example, by slowing the project down until requirements are better understood, or by agreeing that you will deliver against the existing requirements and deal with the changes as a separate, subsequent project.)

The judgement you need to make is at what point is the level of change too great to successfully deliver. In many ways assessing whether the degree of change is too great is like deciding whether the level of risk is too great – different projects can absorb different amounts and there is no absolute rule. The key things to do are:

◆ Make sure the project has a robust change control process in place. People often focus on the forms to log and raise a change – this is important, but there is more to a change control process than this. Critically, there must be a clear process for accepting change, which needs clarity over who has the final say in accepting changes. It is also important to make sure that the project team do not agree to changes without using the change control process.

◆ Develop an ability to explain the impact of change unemotionally. Do not get caught in the trap of disliking changes because you personally find them irritating. This will show in your communications with the customer. It is your customer's project and if they want to make the change they can, but they need to understand the impact fully. When customers really understand the impact of a change on timescales or costs of projects they will often not go forward with it. Unless you take time to explain this, then from a customer's perspective making changes seems essentially to be 'free', and they will tend to ask for changes willy-nilly.

◆ Determine how important the change is. Is it nice-to-have or is it really essential? It is worth challenging hard, it is interesting to see how many so-called 'critical' changes, when really analysed, are not desperately important when people fully understand their impacts – especially if they are asked for more money or delays to the project to implement them.

◆ Determine what the impact of the change on the project is. How does this impact on the customer's time–cost–quality–scope trade-off? If a customer really has a time priority for delivery then change generally needs to be minimised. On the other hand, if the scope and quality of the end result are of paramount importance then the amount of change that can be incorporated is greater.

◆ Assess how the project team are handling it. Too much change can eventually be demotivating for a project team, especially if hard work is wasted as a result.

Judgement 11 – When should you enforce the change management process?

The judgement here is to ensure the change management process achieves what it is set out to achieve: to manage the process of changes occurring to the project, to manage the risk associated with change, and to ensure that the change is fully assessed and its impact understood before it is implemented. So, in general terms, the change management process should be activated whenever it is applicable. On the other hand, project managers and project management

> **Project management approaches are often fairly accused of too much bureaucracy**

approaches are often fairly accused of too much bureaucracy and with the best will in the world change management processes will always have some degree of administrative overhead.

Two factors for a project manager to consider when thinking about changes are:

◆ The impact of a change upon a project depends not only on the change, but also when it is asked for – it may be quite easy to make what are quite fundamental changes to a project early in its lifecycle without affecting the overall cost or schedule. On the other hand at the end of a project even minor changes may require significantly more work. (A simple example: if you have a project to build a car from a kit, and you decide at the beginning you want to change it from a two-litre to three-litre engine it may be easy, but at the end of the build when the car is complete, changing the engine size will be complicated and will delay completion of the project.)

◆ Many people may want or request changes, but some (such as the sponsor), have a more legitimate right to expect their changes to be implemented than other stakeholders.

When it comes to changes there are small things that are asked for early on in the project's lifecycle that can be done with a very minor impact on the project and which do not need to go through the full change management process. If a change is not going to alter the time, cost, resources or plan for a project it is reasonable for the project manager to accept it without fuller assessment, though even here it should be an occasional and exceptional change rather than become a behavioural pattern.

This is a useful judgement to be able to make. However, if you are in doubt do stick to enforcing the change management process on all changes. I would also never tell the project team that it is permissible to avoid the change management process lest uncontrolled change becomes the norm.

Judgement 12 – When is it reasonable to progress based on an assumption?

People make assumptions all the time, and projects are not immune. Sometimes it is done as an explicit action, on other occasions it is implicit in activities and thought processes. In projects people make assumptions when they do not have full information. For example, in a project to deliver an IT system you may need to know the number of users to scale the hardware required for the system to run on. It may be that you can make an assumption that the same number of people will use this system as another similar one. This is not a proven fact, but it may seem a reasonable decision to make to allow you to progress with hardware planning. A further example may involve the delivery of a new product and you do not know how many will be sold. You may assume a sales rate based on your experience of other product sales, and from this plan your manufacturing volumes.

The power of assumptions to a project manager is that making an educated assumption allows rapid progress to be made when there is not time, it is not possible, or it is not pertinent to actually prove something. The danger with assumptions is that, of course, they may be wrong, and this may have a detrimental impact on the project. Making assumptions is a perfectly valid thing to do – never making assumptions will usually lead to a very slow development activity, and there are many things you can assume without too much risk to a project. If you try and make everything certain you may never progress, but making too many assumptions, or taking on too much risk by making critical assumptions around key components of the project needs to be avoided.

The judgement required of a project manager is to find a balance between the answers to the following three questions:

1 What is the impact of not making an assumption? (Will your work be delayed, cost added, etc?)

2 What is the risk of making an assumption? (How likely is it that it will be wrong, and what will the impact be if it is?)

3 How easy/difficult would it be to confirm the assumption you want to make?

Underlying this is a need to understand when assumptions are being made, and to then make them explicit; and to have an assumption management process to manage them through. (In Chapter 10 I lay out the essence of an assumption management process, which I regard as a core project management skill.)

Judgement 13 – How many levels of project management organisation do you need?

In various projects I regularly see many layers of work-stream, work-package, project and programme managers. It is important to remember the end goal is to deliver, not to manage delivery. Once the project is complete all that matters is that the deliverables exist, not that there was a magnificent management structure. Only the very largest of projects should need several layers of management. The issue is as much one of presentation (too many layers look inefficient, like empire building, and like laziness on behalf of the person at the top – all of these factors look bad to customers, sponsors and project team members). One simple way of looking at it is how many people do you have *managing work* as opposed to *doing work*? If your number of managers is not a small percentage (less than 25%, perhaps as low as 10%) of the doers then you have too many layers of management. I have seen projects where 40–50% of the team seem to be managing rather than delivering – this is too high. Countering this – if you have significantly less than a 10% management overhead you probably have too few managers.

Judgement 14 – When to consider broader stakeholder groups

If I define a stakeholder as anyone who has impact upon the project or who is impacted by the project, when you take this to extreme you could virtually include anyone. On the other hand, if you ignore stakeholders beyond the obvious customer and project team you may miss a group which can disrupt progress, or an impact on the success of the project. To some extent use your intuition, but it is worth doing some formal stakeholder analysis to identify those people or groups with potential major impact. This can be considered as a risk management activity, the aim being to reduce or remove the risk of external impact on the project. The types of people to consider are:

◆ Those who can have major influence on the continuing allocation of resources.

◆ Those who can influence the acceptance of the project or its deliverables.

◆ Those who may otherwise cause significant risk to the project.

In Chapter 10 I look at stakeholders again and discuss processes around this a little more.

Judgement 15 – When is the project complete?

It is theoretically very easy to understand when a project is complete. It is complete when it has met the agreed requirements. For some projects this is black and white, but for many others the situation is less clear. The reality is that a project is complete when both the customer and the project team agree it is complete – and there are many situations in which reaching this agreement can be contentious.

The lack of clarity normally involves handover periods and bedding-down situations. For example, a new piece of computer software will normally have bugs in it – does the project end when the formal development is complete, or once all the bugs have been found and corrected (noting it may take many months or even years for some obscure bugs to become apparent)? Alternatively a project team may be required to support new users through a training and familiarisation period. Once the users get used to having support all the time they may be unwilling to let go. After what length of time are users capable of supporting themselves? A different example occurs when a new building is finished. It may have faults or snags. Normally a snagging list is agreed and the items on it must be fixed before a customer accepts the building work is complete. But when is something legitimately a snag and when is it a change of requirements?

Achieving completion may also be contentious when, at the last minute, the customer suddenly understands that they cannot use the deliverables for some reason, or realises there is a gap in them. I have been in several project handover meetings when someone representing the user community or customer says 'but we need this as well, otherwise we can't use it' or 'otherwise we won't achieve the benefits'. There may be a gap in requirements and scope – though you may have delivered absolutely everything you were asked to. There is still a problem that you cannot just walk away from.

You should not leave your customer in the lurch with poorly functioning or sub-standard deliverables, or deliverables they cannot use. Even if the gap is the customer's fault it is not productive to state, even in the most politically correct language, 'that was not in scope, so it's completely your problem'. On the other hand, if a project team is never able to disband it is at the very least an ineffective use of project resources. It may directly cost money resulting in arguments about who should pay, and there is an opportunity cost arising from the alternative work the team members could productively be doing if they were not still tied up on the project.

In terms of finishing support for projects once they have gone live, the secret is to:

◆ Ensure you manage a robust requirements capture process in the first place. This reduces the likelihood of customers turning round at the end and saying there are other things they need.

◆ Agree both a timescale and clear criteria for support to end once the deliverables have been handed over.

◆ Plan to release staff incrementally through the support period.

◆ Build upon good expectation management about the quality and impact of deliverables.

With regard to the timescale and criteria for support to end, agree this early on, not at the end of the project. Then you can build the support time into your plans and budgets – and add some contingency around it. For example, in a project to launch a new product the project team may support live operations until end users are sufficiently familiar with any new supporting processes and to cover if there are any problems with the product once it is in end customers' hands. A guideline may be agreed such that support will be provided for one month post-launch and until no major issues have occurred for two weeks. Although these criteria may not coincide (so, for example, you may have run out of planned time, but still have had more than one major issue in the last two weeks), they at least provide a basis to manage expectations around and provide a framework of understanding which you can use to extricate yourself from a project you consider complete. In my experience post-launch support is never completed more quickly than anticipated, and the less pre-planned the longer it takes. For complex deliverables post-launch support may need to last several months.

Setting such exit criteria should not be arbitrary, but normally cannot be done totally scientifically either. Deciding what is a major issue that stops launch versus a minor issue which can be lived with requires constructive dialogue with the customer. You need to balance your desire to close a project when there are more effective and efficient (or interesting!) uses of your time, with your customer's ongoing need for help.

You do not have to maintain all the staff on the project team through a post-launch support period. It is generally most efficient to let the team diminish gradually until you have only a skeleton crew in the final stages of support. Ideally you need to get agreement that any key team members you have released can be released back to you if major issues arise.

The other basis for successful completion is managing the customer's expectations about the quality of deliverables and the likely impact on their organisation. If the project's timelines and budgets have forced you to make compromises tell your customer. A customer who understands a deliverable will not be 100% perfect, and will cause some pain as well as benefits to his organisation, is more likely to be supportive of letting the project team go than one to whom this comes as a complete surprise.

The alternative scenario, when, at the last minute, the customer realises that the deliverables are not complete or are unusable even though the project has delivered its full scope, is more complex to resolve. There is no single approach to fixing this problem and its solution ideally rests on a strong relationship with your customer. Whenever a conversation starts debating whether a deliverable set is complete or not there is always the danger of confrontation between project and customer – but if you get to a point of confrontation then disaster is looming. When you have a perceived gap between deliverables and customer needs make sure you and your customer are communicating – both listening and talking. If you are just arguing you will get nowhere. Try to keep the debate open and resolution focused rather than pointing fingers. If you must do it, the finger pointing can be done once the problem is solved.

If the customer really has forgotten something it is not unreasonable for you to point out, in sensitive language, that this really is their fault. But you should not simply wash your hands of it. Agree an extension to the project and do the work – if you are an external company then, yes, you should be paid for this, but you should also do it. You don't want your customers saying that what you delivered does not work whatever the cause.

The greyest situation of all occurs when project requirements have been forgotten by the customer – but when you were hired as an expert in this specific type of project. The customer may legitimately think that although they signed off the requirements you should have advised them on the gap. I can remember several meetings with consultancies when they have claimed they did not do something because they were not asked to, only to have the response that they were employed as experts and advisers and should have noticed the gap. *This is a reasonable view for the customer to hold if you have sold yourself as an expert.* Cracking this problem will vary from situation to situation. My advice again is to focus on resolution and not on pointing fingers. Be willing to compromise on responsibility (and hence cost). Try to make reaching resolution a negotiation and not a dispute.

Finally, do not confuse the act of completing a project with meeting a date on a plan. Ideally the two coincide, but regularly they will not. Often organisations focus on time at the expense of all other issues – and it can be in a project team's own interest to complete on the due date. There can be an explicit, or more often unconscious, conspiracy to finish on time at all costs between project teams and certain stakeholders. You should avoid the temptation to put your or the project team's needs in front of your customer's when it comes to delivering on time. While late delivery is bad – it may often be a lesser evil than simply stopping when the scheduled time is up. Your thinking may be 'if I don't complete on time, I have missed the deadline for the project – surely this is failure?' Missing deadlines and project schedules on a regular basis is symptomatic of poor project management. But you must not let your need to be perceived as a

> Missing deadlines and project schedules on a regular basis is symptomatic of poor project management

heroic project manager who always delivers on time get in the way of supplying a high quality deliverable. Do not make the mistake of confusing the importance of hitting time and the fact that very occasionally it is *the* critical factor, with the knowledge that in most situations a specific date to finish the project is an artificial constraint. Unless there is some critical event – such as completing building works for the start of the Olympic Games – which is not going to move, time is important but only one factor among several that are important. Cost is important, scope is important, quality is important, business benefits are important. Yes, if you do not deliver in time you have not achieved full success, but if the cost of hitting the timeline is a sub-standard deliverable, or worse still something that actually disrupts the organisation it is being implemented in, then you need to make a balanced decision about what is best for your customer. This may mean drifting beyond the end date – and if your personal reputation for delivering on time takes a little knock, so be it.

Let me give an example where speed of delivery was put ahead of 'real' completion of a project. I worked for an organisation which was implementing a major software package that could significantly enhance operations. As with such packages the work to implement it was highly complex and required much data collection, data cleansing, process design and process change, as well as organisational change. The package was implemented, and the result was operational chaos. Parts of the system did not fully function as expected, the data in it was not fully accurate, and the impact on existing operations was greater than expected. This was explained as normal teething problems, but those involved in operations knew it went far deeper than that. The organisation survived and eventually thrived, but not without great pain. At the end of the project the project manager proudly announced that the software had been implemented in nine months less than in any other organisation. This no doubt improved the project manager's reputation – but left many of us thinking it would have been better to have taken nine months more to get it working properly. A poorly launched set of deliverables can end up costing far more than the business benefits it was meant to deliver.

Project management judgements – summary

This list of areas where judgement is required could be continued almost indefinitely, as there are many judgements a project manager has to make day in, day out. Some of these will be specific to the project he or she is running. All I have done here is to give you some key points to think about.

I'm afraid that beyond this I cannot tell you how to develop a sense of judgement. I would love to be able to – it would enable a lot of new project managers to short-circuit painful experiences. But I would be lying if I did not say that experience and scars have tremendous value. It is not that a brilliant inexperienced project manager cannot deliver a complex project, it is just that you will find it harder and often your fingers will get a little burnt on the way.

To begin with as a project manager you may struggle finding the balance point, especially as it varies from situation to situation. However, if you find, over time, that you cannot develop this judgement it is really worth asking yourself whether project management is the right career for you. But assuming you get better over time, when things do go wrong, learn from them and be positive about it. Very few, if any, people are born with perfect judgement and therefore accept occasional mistakes as a learning opportunity. Good project management process requires you to review projects when they are complete and at periodic intervals during projects. When things have gone wrong ask yourself, 'if I had made a different judgement in that situation would it have gone better?' If the answer is 'yes', learn for next time.

When things have gone wrong I find it helps to reflect on Nietzsche's famous phrase – 'what does not kill me makes me stronger'!

A touch of creativity

Key lesson

Never be creative with your customer's requirements, but always look for creative ways to deliver those requirements.

Project managers are responsible for managing the delivery of particular sets of things – be they documents, processes, computer systems, buildings, new products or otherwise. They deliver them against a requirements specification, and generally according to a defined project management process. Typically the solution itself is not defined by the project manager, but by some specialist person or team, such as a group of design engineers, who the project manager manages. They are doing this work normally for someone else, a customer, who needs the end result. In this situation, surely the last thing needed is creativity, and surely what is really required is an ability to manage a process robustly and effectively?

There is some truth in this statement, and, in fact, there are many parts of a project that you do not want a project manager to be acting creatively in. A creative attitude towards your customer's requirements is generally unacceptable. Project managers who change the project requirements to ease the work or reduce risk – and I have seen it done – hazard almost certain failure to meet the customer's needs. Such changes must be driven by the customer.

So where is the place for creativity? The place for creativity comes when it is necessary to solve problems and remove roadblocks from a project. Things happen on projects that are unplanned and that get in the way of progress. Such roadblocks need to be removed or worked around for success to be possible. To do this creativity helps. For example:

◆ **Customer challenge** – the project manager is there to deliver the customer's need and not to define it. This does not mean you should feel you are not in a position to challenge the customer's requirements if you see they will result in problems. The mindset to avoid is one in which you, as a project manager, are thinking, 'you do not really want that'. However, based on your experience and what you can see when you plan the project it is very productive to help the customer understand if any specific requirements add significantly to risk, cost or timescales and help the customer to understand that they could get a shorter, simpler or easier project if they removed them. Alternatively you may see that additional requirements may easily be met by the project – again it is worth raising these with the customer. The mindset to adopt is of a professional adviser – the customer in the end must decide, but sometimes a little creative advice can be helpful. If the help is not wanted then stop giving it, but if you do this with sensitivity, you will find that in many situations this helps to build trust and a productive relationship.

◆ **General planning and approach** – your plan defines, to a great extent, the approach you will be taking to delivering a project. There is always more than one way to do anything. For example, there are multiple ways of defining a work breakdown structure for a project, and then to plan out the sequencing of work following this. This becomes especially useful when resources are scarce, or time to complete is short. When you have completed your plans really challenge yourself – was there a better way to organise the work? Remember you can change the plan anyway you like as long as it meets the needs of the scope.

◆ **Project organisation and structure** – how will you arrange the team on the project? Again there are normally multiple ways of doing this, which will have different strengths and weaknesses. If you are finding team interaction and team management problematic try looking at the way you have organised them and come up with some alternatives.

◆ **Issue resolution** – finding the way around a problem or roadblock for a project is a great use of creativity. It is amazing how often seemingly intractable problems can be resolved with creative insight.

◆ **Risk reduction** – how often as a project manager have you seen a risk as a *fait accompli*? The risk is a fact and you feel there is nothing you can do other than accept it. Rarely, in fact, is there *nothing* you can do about it, you are probably simply not being creative enough.

◆ **Contingency planning** – developing good contingency plans and alternative options that do reduce risk and do not excessively increase the cost overhead for a project requires broad thinking and an ability to develop new ideas and options.

◆ **General challenge and insight** – challenging specialists without being a specialist and without taking everything they say at face value can be helped by looking at the problem they are trying to solve from different angles. The stereotypical specialist is notoriously conservative in his thinking in his own field and challenge in new and novel ways can often result in better solutions. As the project manager you are not responsible for specialists' work, but it is part of your job to probe and challenge and ensure the solution they are proposing is fit for the purpose. Project managers need to become adept at recognising creativity, or a lack of creative thinking in the project team.

In addition to this list I would argue that people management can be improved by creative thinking about the way you engage, motivate and drive the project team. This is not a request for constantly off-the-wall behaviour or bizarrely novel ways of interaction for the sake of it – more a desire to see project managers use their judgement about *when* an alternative approach is required – and to creatively seek it out and apply it.

Creativity has its roots in many places. In practice, the main sources of creativity are:

◆ **Yourself and the project team** – the most obvious and easily available source of creativity is yourself and other members of the project team. Do not fall into the trap of thinking you are not creative. Everyone has creative potential in the right situation. This may mean simply mulling things over overnight, or cutting yourself off from the project for a day or so – to give some breathing space for creative thinking as there is nothing like work overload to destroy creativity. Encourage a project culture where people need to deliver their tasks according to plan, though this does not mean that they should avoid thinking. As long as progress is being made to plan regular discussions. Bouncing ideas around should be praised. Encourage unusual suggestions even if you do not implement them. One of the keys to creativity is to develop an environment in which people are excited by the concept of coming up with new ideas.

A significant factor to consider with yourself and the team is the phenomena of 'group think' – which simply put means you as a team start thinking in the same way and it is effectively a creative straight-jacket. Oddly this is a particular risk for close and high performing teams who can convince themselves that there are no other solutions than those they currently see (equally, they can convince themselves that what is actually a major risk is minor).

Real creativity sometimes entails a willingness to take a degree of risk. Obviously this needs to be managed and understood, but creative risk appropriate to the outcome is acceptable.

- **Other people** – people outside of the project environment can often be a great source of creative insight if you are not finding solutions within the project or project team. You should remain open to other people's ideas. In a project situation getting external advice can help. Ideally, choose someone you trust, and clearly and concisely structure the problem you have without giving too much contextual information (as this can inadvertently constrain thinking). Then go to this independent third party and see what their view is. Often a fresh pair of eyes really can add creative insight. If you can find someone who will listen, without breaking client confidentiality, then take advantage. I know many project managers who will talk through such issues with their husbands and wives – finding they can give naïve responses which are surprisingly helpful.

- **Formal processes** – there are a number of formal approaches to creative thinking that are useful. These can be as simple as the well-known brain storming technique, or can be more complex and involved. If you regularly find yourself needing to search for creative solutions then it is well worth seeking out for some formal training in these methods for future projects.

5

Getting your project started

THIS CHAPTER LOOKS AT THE WORK required to take a project manager from the situation in which he has a definition of what he is meant to be delivering (the scope), to the position in which he knows how he will do this and has the resources ready to start delivering. Like getting a large boulder to start rolling – these steps of planning activity, resourcing the work and mobilising staff are often the hardest part of a project. Having the idea to get it rolling was not difficult, keeping it rolling is not so tough, but overcoming the inertia to get it started can be very difficult.

A lot of good planning and resourcing has less to do with the art of the being a project manager, and has more to do with a real understanding of project management mechanics and tools. These are not the primary focus of this book – and therefore I make no claim that this is a particularly exhaustive or complete study of these topics. What this section will do is overview the basic principles and hence provides some context for the rest of the book. For the person who is not an expert in mechanics this will add value. The real benefit of this chapter is to give you a framework to help you think and test whether the way you are approaching planning and resourcing is sound. In addition, it looks at the reality of doing this in a live environment and the difference between the theoretical situations in which you may learn project management, and the real life experience of setting up a project.

In terms of what you have learnt so far in this book – implementing the learning in this chapter in practice will depend on the clarity and completeness of the scope you have defined, your continuing ability to communicate, critically your good judgement, and to some extent your creativity. The other point to hold in mind is that every project is unique – use your plans and resources from prior projects to help your thinking – but they must be adapted to the specific situation you are now managing.

> ## Key lesson
>
> The way you plan and resource your project will set the framework and constraints within which you will operate through the project. Take the time and effort to do it properly.

Planning

The first skill that people coming into project management need to learn, and the activity that non-project managers most closely associate with project management, is planning. Planning is fundamental – without a plan thinking or saying that you are on time, late or early, on budget, over or under budget is meaningless. To scale its criticality I know of some very successful project managers who can spend up to 30% of their time scoping and planning a project.

Simply entering data into a project planning tool will never deliver a good plan

I think it is important from the outset that you differentiate between planning and planning tools such as the almost eponymous Microsoft Project. It is like the difference between writing and a word processor. The software is extremely useful – and you would be foolish not to make use of its powerful facilities – but simply entering data into a project planning tool will never deliver a good plan. Good planning requires you to use your brain.

Before you start planning you must ask yourself what you are planning for. If you cannot answer this question it is likely that the plan you develop will not be particularly useful. There are typically three possible answers to this question:

1   You are developing a plan because you need to form a view of what tasks there are in a project and from this how long it will take and from this be able to derive what resources will be required. This is the plan and the core project manager's work.

2   You are developing a plan to explain to senior managers and other stakeholders how a project will be delivered. This may be to get

approval and support for your plan, or simply explain status and issues to people who need to know. This is the plan as an external communications vehicle.

3 Finally, you may develop a plan to enable people involved in the project to be allocated to work and for them to understand how their work fits within the project. It is worth really understanding that a project plan is as much about ensuring that people are allocated to the right tasks as it is about looking at timings. This is the plan as a work management and internal communications vehicle.

Now the reality is that at some stage in most projects you need a plan to be able to do all three of these things. These three tasks should be interrelated and the plan that is used in each case should be derived from the same base information. But do not assume it is the same plan in every case. As a project manager you must be able to alter the level and scope of detail and the style of presentation in each of these situations – and potentially in different variations of these situations. A senior management presentation will typically want to see a high level milestone chart; an individual working on the project will want to see the activity breakdown relevant to them, and you as the project manager will need various views depending on the task you are undertaking. Every time you present a plan, therefore, you must be clear about:

◆ The level of detail required in this situation.

◆ The presentation format. (For example, a work breakdown structure, Gantt chart and network diagram communicate different things to different audiences. Network diagrams are a very powerful project management tool – but are, say, of limited value as a senior management communication vehicle.)

◆ The degree of 'specificity'. For example, is it generic about resources and resource type, or is it specific and names a particular individual?

The process of planning is in theory not desperately complex, though in practice it can be both intellectually and physically(!) demanding. Good planning starts with a full understanding of scope – although thinking about planning while developing the scope can help with checking that you have enough information to plan – in essence, 'planning in anger' cannot start until the scope is clear and understood. The basic process is:

◆ Build a work breakdown structure – there are many formal definitions of this term. In this context I mean simply to break the overall project into its component tasks, and then iteratively decompose these tasks into lower levels of detail until the plan is detailed enough to manage.

◆ Add the lengths of time each task will take – this is where estimating skills come into play.

◆ Build in the dependencies between the tasks – and suddenly with any planning software you will have some form of schedule appearing.

◆ Determine the resource types and quantities you need to meet this plan.

◆ Add in your resource availability – in some cases this will lengthen tasks, in some cases it may shorten them. Once you have done this you have a complete first cut plan.

In implementing this process there is a complex set of more detailed and difficult considerations to layer on top. How much you need to go into these will really depend on the scale, scope and complexity of the project you are managing. In my perspective the most important considerations are listed below. Each one of these is the subject of many textbooks, and for some project managers it is essential to build up in-depth capabilities in these. In my general experience, on the average project, understanding the top level basics and applying common sense to the situation you are in is quite sufficient.

◆ **Who helps you develop the plan?** In a project of any complexity you will not have the knowledge or skills to develop all the plans. You may not have the specialist skills to understand the work breakdown for some tasks, and you will not be able to estimate the task durations. You will need to call on others' expertise to input into the process. However, whoever is involved it is still your plan – you must integrate the components and you are fully accountable for the end result.

◆ **Milestones**. A plan is a list of tasks and you can, as project manager, track and report on every single one. More constructively it is helpful to break the project into a series of stages – the completion of each stage being marked by a milestone. These stages may overlap or may be purely sequential. The aim of a milestone is to have points on the plan that enable a *visible*, *measurable* and *communicable* show of progress. For example, in developing a new product saying to someone that you have determined the colour is typically not useful in providing a flag pole for how much progress has been made, on the other hand, having a milestone to say all the requirements have been captured is. For milestones to be really worthwhile they should not simply be the measure of the completion of a set of tasks, but they should result in the development of a tangible and useful deliverable. Views on milestones have changed over the years; my belief is that good milestones should be relatively frequent on a project. For example, on a very large project, lasting more than a year, I try to have a milestone every month or so. Without this it is difficult to keep up the pressure to drive progress on a project. It is human nature to strive to meet targets and milestones, as externally visible targets, help the project manager in driving progress.

◆ **How many plans?** One of the mistakes new project managers often make when they start their first very large project is to try and put everything in one master plan. A better way is to have various components of the project broken down into their own plans. A summary of these is shown in the master plan only. Otherwise the master plan ends up having thousands of lines, which may look very impressive when put up on a wall, but in practice almost no-one can actually manage against this type of plan. This is easy with modern planning software which allows the rolling up of individual plans into an overall higher level project or programme plan.

◆ **The level of detail in your plan**. I discussed this in Chapter 3 in the section on judgement. It is a very common issue for inexperienced project managers. The level of detail should enable you as the project manager to allocate work, and then measure progress against the tasks. This does not mean you need a minute-by-minute, hour-by-hour or even day-by-day plan (though there are exceptions). Typically, tasks down to about a man/week decomposition is sufficient. If you have an experienced and trustworthy delivery team then it can be longer than this, although much longer than this and control of individuals can be lost. If you need to, or decide to go to a lower level of detail do not be surprised if plan management and maintenance starts to become unwieldy. It is also easy with very detailed plans to loose sight of the overall objective and timelines.

◆ **Differences in levels of detail in different stages of the plan**. Having decided what level of detail your plan requires the next consideration is can you or should you plan the whole project at the same level of detail.

For simple or short projects the answers is almost always 'yes'. For complex programmes lasting many months the answer is often 'no' – you may not yet know enough about later stages to plan them in detail and doing so can be a waste of effort. In this situation you need a high level plan for guidance for later stages, but really breaking it down into very detailed tasks and times is likely to be fruitless.

◆ **Task size**. Task size needs to be set not simply to reflect the length of time a task takes, but also to give you a management framework. To manage you need small, discrete pieces of work, that you can measure progress against on a regular (weekly is a good guideline) basis. If you find each of your tasks is several months long decompose it to smaller activities you can track the completion of.

◆ **The types of dependencies**. The way dependencies are built into a plan, and hence activities are scheduled has a fundamental impact on project length. The first type of dependency everyone knows is the one where one task cannot start until another has finished. Such 'start to finish' dependencies are the most common, are the easiest to manage and communicate, and will result in a clear sequential plan – which often is very long. You can make tasks dependent in many other ways, the most useful of which are:

– Finish to finish – one task cannot finish before another one does.

– Start to start – one task cannot start until another one does.

– Offset – a task starts a defined number of days after another.

Working through the dependencies in a plan and ensuring they are correct is one of the more intellectually demanding tasks for a project manager. If you are unsure stick with start to finish.

◆ **How much parallel activity will you allow?** Once you pull your plan together you may end up with it all sequential, which generally results in unacceptable lengths of time to complete. Alternatively, an aggressively managed plan can result in it all being parallel. There is nothing wrong with this, except highly parallel plans are inherently more risky and require more focused and able project management.

Whatever way you use to develop your plan do it with the expectation that it will need to change. No one can absolutely accurately forecast or foresee all eventualities (and I for one am inherently suspicious of projects that actually run exactly according to a plan). The success of a good project manager is not *never* changing a plan – it is meeting end goals in the face of a changing plan. For this reason it is worth finding the balance: you need to take enough time to make your plan robust and representative of what is required, but do not spend for ever on it, it will never be perfect.

> You must always remember that the plan is a tool not an end in itself

I have presented planning here as fairly manually mechanistic, and there are lots of wonderful tools you can apply to make planning easier and more robust. Not using planning software nowadays is foolhardy at least. Remember, though, that however well they present your thoughts and facilitate planning activities they do not create the plan – you do.

Like most other project management tasks, judgement is critical (see Chapter 4).

In addition, you must always remember that the plan is a tool not an end in itself – this is sometimes forgotten by the more over-zealous lovers of control and beautiful documentation. It needs to serve a purpose and as long as it does this it is good enough.

Key lesson

Be prepared to change your plan – the measure of success is not an unchanging plan, but meeting the end goals within the reality of continuous change.

Resourcing

Simple logic determines that having completed your plan you should go on to look at the resources to deliver it. In practice, the activity of resourcing must be integrated tightly with planning, and a good project manager iterates rapidly between planning and resourcing. If the theory behind good planning can become complex and academic, that underlying resource management can be truly intellectually demanding.

In this book I am not going to go to those extremes. Again this is because I am more focused on the art of project management than the mechanics, but also because only in the most demanding situations is it really necessary to understand the fine points of resource allocation, resource levelling and other resource scheduling activities.

As with planning, the starting point for resourcing must be to ask why you are resourcing. The obvious answer is to determine what resources you need for your project and how you can get them allocated. It should not be considered as simply an exercise in accumulating talent and skills, it is a process to help you achieve your project goals. It will also help to build the bridge between your project and the organisation you are working in, and this should be an important consideration in both the people you ask for, and the way you organise your team.

The problem with resourcing is that it is the point at which your project stops operating in a vacuum. Until you need to start getting resources a project manager can happily develop scope documents and plans by yourself with a little input from stakeholders and supporting experts. Now your project clashes with the basic reality of everyday business life. The resources you need could well be allocated to another task, and there are always more tasks than there are resources to do them. Whatever resource planning you do within the confines of your own project it must fit within the broader resource planning and allocation of the organisation you are working in.

Assuming you can determine resource needs from your plan, resourcing is not then simply a matter of getting the resources for the tasks you require. There are three additional questions you need to be able to answer for yourself at least, as a project manager:

1 Where are you going to get resources from? Do they have to come from the organisation you are delivering for, or can you make use of additional external resources such as contractors and consultants? Does your sponsor have the authority to allocate the resources you need?

2 How are the people allocated to the project going to interact with the organisation in which they work? So, for example, are they going to be allocated to a project 100% of their time, located in a special project space and managed purely by the project manager for the life of the project – or are they going to remain in their line functions, with the project manager managing them in a matrix function in coordination with their line managers?

3 How are you going to organise the project team members within the project?

The basic points to resource allocation are:

◆ To determine from the plan what skills you require, and how many people with those skills you need for how long. How long in this context does not mean the elapsed time people can be involved in the project for – it means the actual number of hours they are available to work on this project (not on holiday, sick or working on other things).

◆ To work with resource owners (generally line managers), to get the necessary people allocated to the project.

◆ Aggregate resource usage across the plan to understand your points of overload and underload. Focus on the resources that are continuously overloaded as this is the key risk area. These are used to replan and reschedule. (You can use the facilities of any software planning tool to do this. Take care though with the resource levelling function. It may help to think about rescheduling, but if you are constantly overloaded it cannot really help as it cannot create resource. Also you should try to understand what it is doing. The various planning tools use different algorithms and approaches for this and will not all come up with the same answer. You should assume that however good the tool, it will need manual intervention.)

◆ Do not fall into the trap of thinking that the resolution to every problem is to add more resource. Adding resource does reduce the workload for others on the project and may make tasks possible that otherwise are not, but each additional resource increases management complexity and the project manager's coordination and communications overload. Hence with every project there comes a point at which adding more resources reduces rather than increases efficiency and effectiveness.

◆ To reiterate the plan taking account of the actual resources available, which may be different from those you originally requested. You may reiterate between planning and resourcing several times. (In fact, to some extent this is a continuous interplay for the life of the project.) It is the combination of resourcing and planning that provides you with the actual framework in which you will deliver and manage delivery. I often see plans without consideration of resources – these can provide help and guidance but offer no degree of accuracy or certainty.

Once you have some idea of the people you need you will need to define how they will be organised for the project. There is no right or wrong answer, but the factors you need to consider are:

◆ Size of project – the larger the project the more you will need a formal and structured organisation with very clear roles and management levels.

◆ Stage of a project – the organisation may adapt as the project progresses. A project in a feasibility stage, during implementation, or during post-implementation support may have very different needs.

◆ Complexity of the work – is everyone doing very similar tasks or is there a large variation?

◆ Type of staffing – are they dedicated or part time? Are they junior technicians or senior specialists like lawyers? Each need to be managed in different ways.

◆ Relationship to end users – are you working with end users during the project, or are you separate from them and will handover once complete?

Like planning, resourcing is an estimate, do not go into infinite detail (like the hour-by-hour resource scheduling I once saw). Reality will always bring in many factors to move your plans and resources around. Your resource plan provides the baseline to manage against.

When you allocate resources to tasks it must be done in such a way that accountability for delivery of each component of the plan is clear and lies with either a single individual, or, on bigger projects, a single team. This is more to do with management of delivery than resourcing, but it impacts the resources and the task breakdown. You do not want to be in the situation of having to resolve the question 'if an individual item needs to be allocated to several people – who is accountable when it is late?' To avoid this problem, ensure you allocate tasks to single points of accountability and if you cannot, decompose the task further until you can.

When planning around the people on your project do not assume full-time availability. If you are running a big, well-funded project that is accepted widely by the business as being critical then you may have a complete full-time project team. In practice much of a project manager's time is normally spent coaxing and cajoling work out of part-time resources who have twenty other tasks to do. This is not especially efficient, but it is what happens. When combining your plan and resources you must understand not only who is available to you, but for what proportion of time. For part-time resources it is then essential to confirm that the assumed availability actually matches their real availability (businesses constantly overload key resources).

The final point to make about resourcing is that we generally focus on people. Actually we need a whole load of other resources which need to be managed and allocated in the same way. This can be money (a budget – see below) and specialist equipment required. A typical resource problem on a new project is access to desks, PCs, and even building passes if you are using contractors or consultants.

Budgeting

I could use the word budgeting with regard to any resource, but in this context I mean planning the amount of money you need for your project. Budgeting and tracking of spending are often the weakest part of project management and some organisations ignore it almost altogether. One reason for this is that it is often easier to get away with overspending, as it can be hidden in many ways, but it is hard to get away with being late. To be a fully qualified project manager you must understand how to budget and manage cost and manage trade-offs between cost, time, quality and functionality.

There are many costs that must be budgeted for, but the main components are:

◆ Items the project must buy as components of deliverables (for example, raw materials used, or computer software that is purchased).

◆ Items the project must pay for as they are required to do the work in the project (for example, do you need to rent office space, or pay for PCs for the life of the project, etc?).

◆ External resource costs – contractors and consultants. (Maybe a day rate or a fixed cost. Do not forget expenses, which for top-end consultants may add 20% to the cost.)

◆ Internal resource costs – staff from your own organisation. (Assuming they are 'free' is poor management and often results in inefficient resource allocation.) Even if you do not actually cost for them you should at the very least track time they spend on the project.

At the simplest level your budget is a total cost from all of these items. There are, however, a number of other factors to consider. The key ones are:

◆ The finance system and approach of the organisation you are working in. For example, is there a cross-charge for the use of internal resources, or are these effectively 'free' to the project? Are some activities capitalised and some not – and do you need to be able to track this? What are the reporting and tracking requirements?

◆ What is the attitude in the organisation to overspend? Is it better to forecast an accurate budget and hence risk overspend, or is it better to forecast a full budget and hence risk having money left over at the end?

◆ How is budget allocated, and how is spend approved? Do not fall into the trap of assuming just because you have a budget you can spend it. Authorisation may still be required for actual spend even if you have a fully approved budget.

◆ How you will track spend against budget, and, for example, do you need to link into the company's finance systems or not?

◆ What cost was assumed within the business case for the project? Most organisations require business cases for any significant project, i.e. assessing the cost against the benefit. The business case cost is often a broad estimate, and reality in detailed planning may come up with a different answer. Often the business case cost will act as a maximum budget you must operate within.

> **Often the business case cost will act as a maximum budget you must operate within**

I have left this section until after planning and resourcing as it is dependent on them. However, once you layer your budget and your financial constraints on top of your resourcing and plan you will almost certainly need to reiterate your thinking on the resourcing and plan.

Thinking about contingency and risk

Key lesson

Having contingency built into a plan is essential and is not a sign of poor project management. The critical factor is how much contingency, and how you allocate and manage this. This should be related to the degree of risk of your specific project.

To this point I have discussed the various aspects of planning as though we can plan and estimate accurately. This is never perfectly true and before you finalise everything you must consider the degree of risk on your project. The ability to understand and manage risk is an absolutely fundamental project management skill, and it starts now, at the planning stage.

The response to risk at the planning stage is contingency. Contingency is used in two related ways in this book:

◆ Contingency – as a buffer in your plans to enable you to respond to change and risk occurring. This should exist in every project plan.

◆ Contingency plans (see Chapter 10) – which are specific alternative activities carried out, usually in parallel, to your base plan. They are only implemented when the degree of risk and business importance of a project is sufficiently high to warrant development of an alternative solution (or partial solution), should the main plan fail to deliver. This is not discussed further in this section.

Having contingency built into a plan is essential – it is absolutely not a sign of poor planning or weak project management. What is important is the degree of contingency you build in, and how you allocate it. I am always inherently suspicious of project managers who always claim to bring projects in on time and budget and never show any risks. If it was so easy we really would not need project managers in the first place!

It is worth starting by thinking about the key reasons for uncertainty in our plans. They are:

◆ You simply cannot predict everything, risk at one level or another is inherent in everything we do.

◆ Things change. We can argue that change should be managed through a change control process – true, but the change may be due to something like a poorly or misunderstood scope or requirements. From a customer perspective nothing has changed. Alternatively, a team member being ill is not really a change in the change management sense, but it is a change in terms of the validity of your plan.

◆ Your estimates may be wrong. An estimate is simply that – an estimate. Estimation is a notoriously inexact science.

◆ Your sponsor or customer may expect you to be able to absorb a minor degree of change without recourse to formal change control and impact on the project.

◆ There is risk inherent specific to the project you are planning. This comes from four sources – technical risk (can it be done, has it been done before), management risk (how complex is this to manage), requirements risk (is what is wanted really understood), and environmental risk (something changes outside of the project that has an impact upon the project).

The first step in building some contingency into the plan is to consider how you estimate task length. The way you estimate task lengths depends on the type of task you are planning. To be able to estimate with any degree of accuracy you need to have experience and expertise in the specific task you are estimating the length of. What typically happens is that people overestimate how long tasks take. *In extremis* they plan a task to give themselves virtually 100% certainty of completing it, even though this means that tasks are all longer than they will actually take on average, and the overall plan duration is then also far too long. I think people do this through a combination of wanting an easy life, and also not wanting to be seen to fail. A better way is to get people to estimate the tasks down to the length they think it will take on average – and not allow them to build in any contingency time. You, as the project manager, then need to build in blocks of contingency time which you can allocate when the inevitable happens and some tasks take longer than planned. The advantage with this is that you will almost always find many tasks are delivered on time, and overall project length is shortened. (The disadvantage is that it may make contingency explicit to other managers with a poorer understanding of the reality of risk and uncertainty who ask for it to be removed.) There are a number of cultural issues to resolve in centrally holding contingency – essentially you need to build a project culture in which people do not think they are being punished when they overrun and need to dig into the contingency pot, but balancing this they need to treat it seriously and try their utmost not to.

Put into a simple summary:

◆ Avoid building contingency into every activity.

◆ Hold your contingency pot centrally.

◆ Manage people to hit the plan – but release contingency when required.

◆ Manage and monitor your contingency pot. If it is disappearing faster than progress on the project you have a problem looming.

Contingency is not just about time – it should also be considered with regard to the resource budget you have available. Finally, remember it is there to give you a tool to manage risk, not an excuse for poor performance or poor management!

Mobilising

You have a plan, you have a team of people to deliver the plan, and you have an approved budget to spend. There is no great difficulty in mobilising a project team when you are in this position, but mobilisation must take place. It needs to be a specific activity, which it is the core responsibility of the project manager to undertake. Mobilisation can be equated to the situation where a brigade of soldiers is ready for a battle, they have their weapons ready, and they understand what they must do. But they still need someone to actually give the order to commence work.

The basic task of mobilisation is a communication task. You can use all the skills defined within Chapter 2. The style and approach you take to mobilising staff can have a significant impact on your relationship with them, and hence how successful you will be in managing them during the project's life. The objectives of mobilisation are:

◆ To energise and align the project team. If it is a large project team this may take some considerable effort (see Chapter 8).

◆ To ensure the broader stakeholder community is supportive of the project and ready for it (or you have activities planned to overcome resistance where necessary).

◆ To ensure project team members understand the objectives of their involvement, the specific work tasks that have been allocated to them, and how they fit within the overall plan.

Once this is done project delivery can commence.

There is a final point to make clear to everyone during mobilisation. The plan provides the framework we will work to and be measured against, but they are each individually responsible for their tasks. Having a defined plan does not remove the individual need to think. The plan is an aid for them and you, but it is not an abrogation of responsibility.

Projects in the real world – common practical issues to overcome

Key lesson

Project management theory often defines the ideal environment to set up and run a project in. In practice, not all ideal environmental conditions will be achieved and as a project manager you must learn to deliver in sub-optimal situations managing a variety of constraints and compromises.

I have, like many writers on project management, avoided the constraints that occur in practice on projects. However much you plan and develop the right structures to manage, when you are working on a project you will be subject to a host of real world issues. The list of these is endless, but in this section I have picked a few common issues to be resolved at project start up and discuss what you can do about them.

> You are allocated people, but they don't actually have any time to give to the project

Eleven real world issues that I commonly experience are:

1 Unclear requirements and objectives. It's quite difficult to deliver if the requirements and objectives of the project are unclear. Even if you go through the scoping process described in Chapter 3, if the customer fundamentally does not know the answers then you cannot just make them up.

2 The wrong team. You may be allocated insufficient people, or a team with sub-optimal skills or competencies.

3 You are allocated people, but they don't actually have any time to give to the project. This is surprisingly common. A manager allocates people to too many tasks at once. An alternative to this is that you are allocated lots of people, but only on a part-time basis which makes your logistics complicated and extends the project timelines.

4 Location and set up of team. You are allocated a team, but they are physically located all over the place and getting them working

together will add significant overhead to the project you have not planned for.

5 Not allowed contingency time. The project has risk and you have planned it efficiently, but to cover the risk you have built yourself a pot of contingency time or budget. Your customer sees this and asks you to remove it.

6 There are too many stakeholders or requirements owners. The effort to collect all their views and input, assess and collate it and resolve any conflicts will be too large to hit the timelines.

7 Your sponsor does not actually have sufficient positional power to support the project. He wants it and has employed you to do it, but he cannot actually allocate the necessary people or budget to deliver it.

8 The project is more complex than you have ever managed before and you are concerned it is beyond your abilities.

9 The budget, timeline or the resources are fixed before you plan, but they do not match your need when planning has been done. This is the classic project management dilemma, and the most common examples are having to keep to a budget that was set during an earlier budgeting cycle – or the advent of a 'critical event' – an event that must be met and cannot be moved in time.

10 There is no known solution for the problem the project is trying to resolve.

11 You do not have enough information to plan with any degree of accuracy.

These are all constraints on the project you are trying to run. Hopefully they became clear when you were defining the scope of the project. Sometimes they become clear later on in the project's lifecycle, and may, for example, become exposed through your assumption management process (see Chapter 10). There are many others that can exist but, generally, faced with a constraint of this type, what can you do about it?

◆ See the constraint as a constructive challenge – quite often you will find that a challenge does generate creative thinking about alternative ways of resolving problems.

◆ Plan your project without the constraint at first. If you start with the constraints there is a risk you will become more focused on these and not on meeting the requirements of the project. (If the constraint means you do not have all the information make explicit assumptions and plan using them.)

◆ Assess what the impact of the constraint is. Do not immediately panic and get yourself into a negative mindset about it. If this constraint is real what does it actually mean for your project? Statements like 'it's not possible' are not constructive, they need to be quantified. Specifically, what is not possible?

◆ Then review your approach to your project – are there things you can alter that would make this possible? What would the impact be upon the scope, quality, cost or time of the project? For example, if it is time that is capped much shorter than your plan shows can you increase resource and cost to deliver on time or can you reduce scope or quality to deliver on time? If you have a specific resource bottleneck, such as limited access to desk space or a specific system, can you work shifts instead of trying to use the limited resource in parallel?

◆ Look at the project lifecycle you are implementing and see if additional stages need to be added. For example, if there is no known solution to the problem the project is trying to resolve perhaps you need some form of solution selection phase before you start your project. Alternatively, if you do not have enough information to plan with any degree of accuracy put a formal feasibility stage in the project to provide this information.

◆ Are there mitigating actions you can take? For example, if your sponsor says you cannot have an explicit contingency pot of money or time, can you call it something else, or build it into the plan another way? Another example, you have lots of people on the project but only part-time. It can be mitigated by at least arranging for them to have the same times available each week to work on the project.

◆ Talk to your customer and explore options. Start by making sure he understood your baseline plan and why it gives the answer it does. Then determine if this is an absolute constraint that cannot be changed, or whether it is something he has decided upon for some other reason. Sometimes managers put such constraints in place simply because it makes their life easier, or because they believe that setting a challenge is a good management approach. Make sure they understand and accept the implications of the constraint.

◆ In doing this, present them with options, not a *fait accompli*. For example, if your customer wants everything done in less time than you have planned give them the option of giving you the extra time or an alternative such as extra budget or reduced scope to hit the timelines. Best of all is a range of options.

◆ Make an explicit decision on how you will manage this constraint – do not just fudge it.

◆ Having decided which path you are taking, re-plan the project accordingly and communicate the changes. Do not ignore the constraint and assume it will have no impact.

◆ Realise there is always a choice. Even the most critical of critical events are only worth achieving at a certain cost!

Finally, remember project management is all about balanced judgement and creativity. There are often alternative ways to do things which can meet objectives within defined constraints – look for them. But you must have room for manoeuvre, and you are not a miracle worker. No matter how senior and powerful or opinionated a boss you are working for, he or she will not make the impossible possible (see Chapter 11).

6

Personal styles

Key lesson

There is no right interpersonal style for a project manager – successful project managers have a variety of styles. But there are certain approaches to avoid, and some key attributes of style to develop.

THIS CHAPTER LOOKS AT PERSONAL STYLES. Firstly, those which I would counsel any project manager to avoid, and, secondly, those attributes of personal styles to be encouraged in project managers. If you do find you are drawn towards the first set of traits it can limit your success and so you need to learn to moderate them. You may not naturally have all of the second set, but they can be learnt to some extent, or you can bring people into your team who have these skills.

Styles to avoid

Key lesson

Certain interpersonal styles will limit your success as a project manager.

There are many styles of project management, and there is no one type of interpersonal skill and style that ensures success. I have seen many thoughtful and introspective project managers, some who are extroverts and compulsive and continuous communicators, some who deliver by understanding the technology and using logical analysis to drive people to the right conclusion, and others who build a team and a consensus towards delivery without getting into the details. There are endless approaches and options. There is no single right personality style to be a good project manager, but what I do believe passionately is that there are some methods of interaction to avoid. Core among these are four styles you may recognise. These are stereotypes – but stereotypes based in reality, and you may be familiar with them already.

Stereotype 1 – Bully boys

You will probably be familiar with this type of person. The bully boy is known by everyone (perhaps I should say bully person, but my experience is that they are more often men). These are the people who manage by fear and when things go wrong start shouting. The general approach is to make sure that everyone knows they are the boss. They talk a lot about respect, which they confuse with power. They misunderstand leadership and instead like to 'put people in their place'. They thrive on people giving in to them, and they tend to be obsessed with titles and position in organisational hierarchies. This person is the grown-up version of the playground bully. They bully through a lack of understanding that delivery not only does not require bullying but may also be impaired by it.

Use this style sparingly and at your peril! It is not so much that bullying never gets results. I would be lying if I said it never worked or that it is not occasionally useful to be able to direct staff robustly – sometimes this is essential. It is recognising the difference between the occasional demanding request, and the grinding bullying of people into submission and delivery. In reality apart from being an obnoxious style, bullying is a very poor way to deliver anything reliably and consistently. It has several core weaknesses:

◆ It does not develop trust (which is a two-way thing). If people think you do not trust them, they in turn will not trust you. Successful project teams which do not have any trust are hard to find. In my experience the most productive team is the one that works harmoniously and not the one that works in an atmosphere of fear.

◆ It creates problems from the very outset of the project. If people think they will be put under unreasonable pressure in an unpleasant manner when they are late they will tend to over-estimate the lengths of tasks to ensure they can be completed within the schedule.

◆ People who fear you will avoid or delay telling you the truth, especially if it is bad news. People will seek to cover up or put things in a defensive way. Really good project management requires the project manager to know the risks early, and know when things are going wrong immediately. I have seen situations, on several occasions, in which the project manager was the last to know the project was going wrong because people were too frightened to tell him. I even remember one specific programme with a budget of several hundred million pounds, that almost everyone on the team knew was a disaster except for the programme manager. Needless to say it was a failure, and he was fired.

◆ Sometimes team members you have to manage or get deliverables from or tasks done by are actually more senior than the project manager. Acting the bully boy in these situations generally does not get good results.

◆ Team members working for a bully may work hard from fear, but are unlikely to be enthusiastic or passionate. Passionate, enthusiastic people will produce more and what they produce is more creative. People who are bullied rarely deliver high quality results. They produce just enough to stop the bullying – and will often go behind your back whenever they can to undermine you.

◆ Finally, people, and often the best people, will avoid you, and try hard not to be on your projects in future. Consistent delivery depends on other people too. The project manager is a participant, not the whole team.

If you are of this type, next time you feel yourself going red, and being tempted to bang the table and shout at everyone take a deep breathe and calm down. Try to manage in a more humane way – the toughest, most effective and efficient managers rarely let themselves get to this state. Really ruthless people never do.

> Passionate, enthusiastic people will produce more and what they produce is more creative

Well-respected people get things done well because people want to deliver for them rather than because they are frightened of them.

Stereotype 2 – Process nuts, compulsive planners and detail obsessives

Another style of poor project management that is not uncommon to see is the person who is more obsessed about some detail or other of the project than its overall progress.

It is important to note that I am not criticising people who like detail more than high level views. There is nothing wrong with being interested in the details, and being focused on too high a level can be dangerously risky. However, the project manager is there to manage the overall project and except on the smallest project usually does not have time to be aware of every detail of everything.

There are three typical forms this takes.

Firstly, there are those who obsess about the process of project management more than the project itself. They focus on making sure they have carried out every possible project management activity and ticked every box on all their tick lists. Satisfaction only comes when they know they have done all the process tasks, and when the project goes wrong they tend to see this as inevitable rather than as a result of too much management process and too little managing. The correct use of process is to apply balanced decision making. Too little process can result in chaos – too much can be sterile. Good process is powerful, but it can never cope with every situation, and the skill is to use it rigorously when appropriate, but to rapidly be able to assess when it is necessary to go outside of the process boundaries. The bureaucratic process obsessive will often think 'I will not do that, it is not part of my job' – some things are not the project manager's job, but if progress is to be achieved you are the person who needs to sort it out, and process constraints must not stop this.

Secondly, there are those who continuously focus on the plan, updating it at every opportunity trying vainly to keep it perfectly correct. On a daily basis there is a vast collection of status data, tasks are realigned and the critical path reassessed. I have known project managers spending literally hours every day keeping the plan up to date. The point they miss is that plan is merely a tool; it is not a result in itself. Planning is essential, plans are powerful – but they are a means and not an end in themselves.

Finally, and somewhat differently, there are those who become obsessed by the very low level details of the content of the project. Often these people have a technology focus. They try to understand and have an opinion on every aspect of the project, and may even become stressed when they do not understand all the details. At best this type of project manager gets overloaded, at worst the project fails because the broader picture is being ignored.

There are two basic reasons for people focusing on these types of details. Firstly, they may be more interested in them than the delivery of the project. If this is true and you do actually want to work on projects you may be better off working in a project office than as a project manager. Project offices offer more scope for very detailed management of plans and focus on project management processes. The second reason is that they have not built up the skills and knowledge to do otherwise – inexperience tends to result in poor judgement on what is important as a manager. When people do not know what to do they typically cling to a lifebuoy, and in this case the lifebuoy is feeling good because you are busy with the details. If this is true and you are unsure what else is important for you then seek out some help from a more experienced project manager.

Success for a project manager is only measured in terms of delivery of a project. Once it is complete the beauty of your plans, the completeness of your paperwork, and how detailed your understanding of every aspect of the work are irrelevant. Think in terms of other professions. A decorator wants good paint brushes and will clean them well after work, but knows that all that matters to his customers is the quality of his painting. An accountant will worry about his compliance with agreed accounting approaches and processes, but what counts at the end of the day is the accuracy and completeness of the accounts he puts together. An engineer will try to use the agreed algorithms and theories in designing a new machine, but again, in the end all that matters is that the machine works to the performance parameters it was designed to. So it should be with a project manager – use the tools and understand the details, but only so far as is necessary to achieve the desired results.

Stereotype 3 – The Teflon man

There are some people who can seem to get away with everything, when things go wrong they come up smelling of roses – it was always somebody else's idea. These 'Teflon men' (and women) never let anything stick to them. You will have come across them in any large organisation. They carry the scent of politics, but never show it directly. Somehow they are never incorrect, never in the wrong place at the wrong time, and always have a valid reason for error or failure.

This style of being able to dodge all bullets and claims to fault can be successful in the short term. The problem is that project manager is essentially a profession about taking responsibility. In every situation sometimes something will go wrong, and if you are taking responsibility you must shoulder some of the blame. If things never stick it means you are not fully taking responsibility. You are ducking the necessary sense of ownership.

The problem with this style is much more subtle than the problems with the previous two styles as some people have built apparently successful careers around it, and have even reached senior levels in management hierarchies. The main issue is as much to do with the project team as anything else. People resent others who work like this and can wriggle out of every situation, and therefore the project team is less likely to be aligned with the goals of project manager like this. If nothing sticks, it may well be sticking to someone else who will have honest grounds for resenting you strongly. When your boss takes some painful flak to support you it generates goodwill and trust, when it constantly slides off your boss onto those around him or her it generates bad feeling. The same is true for project managers. I think we all know the answer to the question: would you rather have a team working for you which resents you, or one which respects and admires you?

You may not fail with this style, you may feel you actually do quite well with it – but you will not excel, nor will you do as well as you can. Do not think 'oh well, it works for me', think 'how much further would I have got if I did not work like this?'. You may be getting away with it, but do not think it is invisible to your managers or your team.

Stereotype 4 – The panicking manager

Some people stay calm in all situations, they remain as cool as a cucumber whatever life throws at them. Many of us aspire to be like this, but these people are few and far between and can occasionally seem inhuman. Occasional doubt and feelings of lack of control are normal, however, do not confuse this with the tendency to panic. There are some managers whose first reaction when the pressure steps up or something goes wrong is to panic.

In the old BBC TV series *Dad's Army*, there was a character, Corporal Jones, who whenever something was starting to go wrong, which was often in this comedy, would start to rush around and shout 'don't panic, don't panic'. And, of course, he was rushing around aimlessly and panicking. This is precisely the problem with panicking. Someone panicking tends to spend more time managing their panic and trying to get their brain to work again than actually doing constructive work.

When you do feel the pressure, avoid panic. It is never constructive. If you do find the tendrils of fear grabbing you and pulling you towards panic resist. It is quite normal to be concerned, even to feel a little stress, but once panic sets in you cease to be productive. Worse still, panic tends to have a knock-on effect, and once one person panics it has a domino effect. The worst person to panic on a project is the project manager – this sends a clear message to the team, and they will be thinking 'if he is panicking it must be really bad'. Over time, if you panic regularly people will loose trust and faith in you.

When things are tough it is the time for good leadership, and good leaders may be afraid and may even have doubts, but they do not display this to their teams.

Styles to encourage

Key lesson

Choose the personal style that best develops your personal brand. Build the attributes of good style to help you succeed.

This section defines the building blocks of personal style that project managers should consider.

There is simply no one best style for project managers. Different styles suit different people, different organisations, different industries, different project teams and different types of project. At heart I would always advise a project manager to try to be true to yourself, and to avoid going with a style that is completely unnatural to you – adopting a completely unnatural style is often transparent and can lead to problems because of this. However, that is not to say the project manager should not, over time, learn to have different styles for different occasions, or should not try to learn new styles. The style you adopt, display to people, and use is to a large extent a personal choice, and be conscious it is a choice, and it has an impact on performance.

Elsewhere in this book I talk about how you have a personal brand as a project manager. We all are attracted to branded products – a brand is something that gives people a feeling of confidence. We select things with brands because the brand is a promise of a certain minimum level of quality and to a specific experience. A brand is initially about presentation, but as any good marketing manager will tell you unless the reality matches the hype a brand will not survive. If you are influenced to buy a certain type of car because of its brand, and it does not live up to your expectations then the brand will be devalued in your eyes. A brand can be both powerful and fragile, every time you buy a brand of food or drink the experience can encourage you to buy anything with that brand again, or it can make you avoid it for ever. This principle can also be applied to people. We build up a brand over time, usually accidentally, but by choosing the optimal style to adopt you can manage and improve on your personal brand. If you want to be a successful project manager, who is asked to run the most interesting projects you must think what your personal reputation and brand

> You must think what your personal reputation and brand is – and how you build and maintain it

is – and how you build and maintain it. Although a large proportion of people's judgement of us is related to our success in delivering projects, much of this is also due to the personal style we assume. I am sure you know people who are excellent at their jobs but do not excel in their careers because of their personal style.

When thinking about your personal brand you must therefore think through which attributes of personal style have the largest impact on people's perception of you. There are eleven factors I find are usually most important. They are really a combination of personality traits and competencies:

1 Empathy with your customer.

2 Management and leadership skills.

3 Ability to handle stress.

4 Respect for people.

5 Dynamism and positivism.

6 Networking skills.

7 Political sensitivity.

8 Having sufficient presence.

9 A sense of humour.

10 Being sensitive to your environment.

11 Adapting your style to the situation.

The following section is therefore less about whole styles and more about attributes of style. If you do not have these attributes try to develop them, or think about how you can bring others into the project team who have them.

Attribute 1 – Having empathy with your customer

A project manager is not the customer and needs, at times, to be able to distance himself from the customer. Constant affinity with the customer may start you thinking exactly like the customer and through this can limit creativity and broadness of vision. And yet at the same time as a project manager you need to be able to think things through from the customer's viewpoint when it is relevant. For decades now the fundamental mantra of business has been 'the customer is king', this is also true from a project perspective. Treating the customer as king requires an ability to see things from her viewpoint, and communicate in a way that is helpful to her. This is what I mean by empathy with the customer.

The times when it is really important to be able to adopt the customer's viewpoint are:

◆ When you are collecting the initial requirements and developing an understanding of what the customer wants.

◆ When decisions or changes need to be made to a project – if you were the customer is this trivial or is it a core issue that needs serious debate and consideration?

◆ When communications are being made or planned – what does the customer understand, what is important to them, and how do they like it being communicated?

Every time you are in one of these situations try to put yourself in your customer's position. Ask yourself:

◆ Why are they acting this way?

◆ What do they need?

◆ What help can I be to them?

◆ How is it best to approach them and provide this help?

◆ What are their sensitivities and how can I avoid these or approach them carefully?

◆ If I cannot help them – is there anything else I can advise them to do?

People who work to understand their customers best and respond in the most productive way are the most appreciated. This is not saying you should do whatever your customer wants – if you think it is wrong you need to say so, if you cannot do it you must tell them. But this should be done in the most constructive manner.

Attribute 2 – Displaying both management and leadership skills

There are huge amounts of paper dedicated to defining and explaining good management and good leadership. I will not in the few words here try to encapsulate it, but I will point out that while there is some relationship they are different activities. Project management is by its very definition a management task and it goes without saying that project managers need good management skills. Project managers, at times, also need to be leaders.

Without writing down all the things in a project management approach the management task of a project manager relates to assessing the work that needs to be done, assessing the people available to do the work, and then providing the project team with clear roles and defined goals. The sum of the goals delivered by the specified roles will deliver the end project. The ongoing management task is then to monitor progress and remove issues as they arise. Although the approach is specific to project management, the basic task is the same as any manager has to do: prioritise and chop up the work that needs to be done, allocate it to the team you are managing, and manage them to completion.

Although much is spoken and written about leadership, and we all intuitively have a view about it, leadership is a more nebulous concept. At one extreme, leadership is about providing the motivating speeches and a good example to the team, and these are important but not the core task on a day-to-day basis. To me, leadership is about the framework which is developed for people to operate within – how do you present and communicate the objectives of the project? what is the culture of the project team? how much space do you give people to do their tasks in? how do you get and maintain approval and support from the project team? what examples do you praise and what behaviour do you clamp down on? The need for leadership on projects, especially those which require large teams of people is evident.

The management role is solely the project manager's, whereas the leadership responsibility belongs to a wider group of people including primarily the project sponsor. However, leadership is needed on a project and the project manager cannot assume this will be provided by the sponsor or anyone else. The project manager's leadership role is really to assess what leadership is required, determine what is being provided and fill the gap with what is needed. There is no one leadership role for a project manager to take – it will vary from situation to situation, depending both on the leadership required by the project team and the leadership that is being delivered from other sources. A hands-on and inspirational project sponsor may provide all the necessary leadership, but a backroom decision maker who is invisible to the project team may provide none. A key task for the project manager is therefore to make an assessment of the leadership requirement and work out what she can do to fulfil this.

A core skill for project managers is to drive things to happen when you do not always have legitimate line authority over all the people on the project. We can all talk and dream about fully dedicated teams, but a lot of project management is about getting slices of people's time. Time that is a scarce resource for them. So why should they give it to you? Well, partially this may be because you are perceived to have authority to do so, but partially it must be that your management skills combined with the leadership you project encourages them to do so.

Project managers who understand and can implement their management role, and can determine in any one situation the leadership required will thrive. Being successful will require you not just to manage well, and when required to lead well, but also to be seen to be a good manager and leader.

Attribute 3 – The ability to handle stress

Projects can be tough environments to work in. The work can be intense, the work can be difficult, and the available time, budget and other resources can be limited. Project managers need to be personally committed to the end point or goal. The end result of this is that project managers are liable to great stress.

An example of a typical stress driver for a project manager is the rate of change. You need the ability to handle the fact that everything will change – timescales, requirements, resources, budgets. They flex, and yet you are expected to have the ability to manage through and deliver to expectations! Depending on your personality type, this can be stressful. Plan proactively, but be willing to react when you need to. People instinctively do not like change and a frequent response to such constant change is a feeling of stress.

There are many mechanisms to handle stress, including being naturally laid back, doing a hard workout, having a drink or talking things through with people. Whichever it is, if you are liable to stress you need to find a mechanism to handle it or else a career as a project manager may end up being more trouble than it is worth to you. I have counselled several people liable to stress to reconsider their choice of being a project manager.

The other point about stress is not only to manage it in yourself, but also to avoid displaying it overtly to your team. People are less likely to trust someone who is regularly showing stress, and when things are hard people will often look to the project manager. They will sometimes be looking for help, but on other occasions they may be looking simply for confidence. A stressed out manager does not exude confidence.

Finally, do not get stressed because things are going wrong from time-to-time. It is worth remembering that normally the world will not end if your project is late or over-budget. This is not to shrug off your sense of commitment to the end point, but to put it in context. Also, remember if it all went smoothly there would be no need for a project manager. Recovering from difficult situations is the sign of great project management and something people value highly. It is true that if all goes perfectly well you may end up being invisible – and it is right to conclude that is a sign of success not failure – but in reality people best remember those who have recovered projects from difficult situations.

> I have counselled several people liable to stress to reconsider their choice of being a project manager

Attribute 4 – Respect for people

Project management is largely about managing people. It is a job that is all about interacting with people on a daily basis. You need to respect the people working on the team for two reasons. The first is simply that people are more likely to respect you if you respect them. The second that people work better when they feel they are respected and valued. You are dependent on your project team doing a good job and anything you can do to improve on this will increase your chance of success.

If you do not respect your project team because you legitimately think they are not up to the job, try to change the team. You may shake your head when this is suggested as it will be very hard, but unless you do, you will jeopardise the project and it is your job to enable its delivery. If you cannot change the team, try at least to hide your contempt.

Having respect for people does not mean being weak or wet. When you respect someone you tell them the good news as well as the bad; you give them constructive criticism as well as the praise they deserve; you ask them to do the tasks that need doing, not just the things they want to do.

Attribute 5 – Dynamism and positivism

There are two attributes that every manager seeks from every member of their team – a positive attitude to their work, and a dynamic style of performing work. This can be flipped on its head – good project managers should lead by example and display a positive outlook and attack work in a dynamic style.

The ability to come across as energetic will inspire energy in other people. Non-dynamic teams are less fun and people are less motivated. A dynamic project manager will help. Well managed and funnelled energy will deliver many times the result of an unenergetic project team.

A positive project manager develops a feeling of confidence in the team – and confidence helps people overcome everyday obstacles with ease. This is not a cry to underestimate or ignore problems, but to face them with the attitude that they can be overcome. I do not know how the human mind works, but when it comes to solving problems, people who face them in a positive frame of mind regularly solve the problem more quickly and more constructively.

I have often been in the situation of having to choose between well-qualified, cynical experts and a young and dynamic person with bags of energy. You need a good balance on your project team, and there are times when I have to choose the expert, but these are, in practice, in the minority and when I can I will always choose energy and enthusiasm over experience.

Attribute 6 – Networking skills

Project managers need to get people onto their project teams, they need to be able to get help and other input during the project's life, and they need to engender an environment that is supportive to the outcome of the project. A great help in these situations are your personal networking skills.

One way to look at a network is to see it as a framework of personal relationships that you can call on when you need help or advice. You should build a network and use it for finding people and resources that you need, and for informal communications which underpin our daily lives (both to transmit and receive information). Such a network is about having ongoing dialogues around the business so you know what is going on, you know who can help you, and you understand which people are good to have on projects. It is about having subtle negotiation skills that convince people to free resources to you, encourage team members to come onto the project, and induce people to support your work. A good network provides information and promotes action.

Some people are natural networkers. We can all think of someone we know who knows everyone in the office, hears all the gossip and news first, and can always lay their hands on whatever they need. But networking skills are not only possible to the gregariously extrovert. A personal network can deliberately be built by identifying those people who it is useful to know and by engineering situations in which to talk to them. It is quite acceptable to be completely open about what you are doing – most senior managers understand the need for personal networks and will respond well if you simply ask for a short slot in their diary (try 30 minutes, or even less), simply to introduce yourself. Having done this it is much, much easier to ask them for advice or support at a later date.

Ironically one of the best groups I find for this is smokers. There are very few reasons to be jealous of smokers – but one is their informal networks. In modern environments smokers have to go to a specific place to smoke and the people who go there often share information well. I would not suggest you take up smoking to get your project delivered, but do learn the example of regular informal communications and a personal network.

Attribute 7 – Political sensitivity

Project managers should avoid playing politics, but you do need to be aware of it. Projects often fall foul to political games going on in many organisations. You should try to avoid getting involved in them, but you do also need to develop the ability to feel when strings are being pulled behind the scenes and when you need to approach your sponsor for help.

Usually people play these games because they have some vested interest which is endangered or negatively impacted by the outcome of a project. Some good stakeholder assessment will often provide a good basis for understanding the political landscape (see Chapter 10).

Not everyone likes being in a political environment. If you really cannot stand the pressures of personal manoeuvring and vested interests then there are certain projects you should avoid. Projects related to topics such as business change, organisational transformation and post-merger integration work tend to be highly politicised. If you do not like politics avoid these types of projects. Also, in some organisations there is a very political culture (for example, I find government bodies and academic institutions places where political games are played regularly), and projects in these are more likely to have a political undercurrent than in other organisations.

However hard you try, unless you stay on small or very focused projects it is unlikely you can avoid politics altogether. Be sensitive to it, and seek help when it is interfering with your project.

Attribute 8 – Having sufficient presence

Not all project managers have natural presence, and it is not a critical problem – it can be balanced with the strengths of your key sponsor. I know some introverted and very successful project managers.

However, there will be times when you need to be able to hold an audience and generate respect. This is especially true for large programmes, and for situations when things are not going well – then a project team will look to the project manager for guidance and confidence. There will also be opportunities to interact with senior managers and executives who respond well to presence. It is worth trying to develop; seek out feedback on whether you do have presence or not and what you need to do to encourage it.

Attribute 9 – A sense of humour

The ability to generate and enjoy humour is an extremely positive trait with a project manager. People enjoy working with someone who can raise a laugh. Project management can be stressful – and the ability to laugh about it will help you manage your stress.

If you are not a natural wit do not worry. A good substitute is simply to smile a lot. People like people who smile. It sounds trite, but do not underestimate the value it generates. A well placed smile can completely change the dynamics of a conversation and can lift an individual from a negative to positive frame of mind.

Attribute 10 – Being sensitive to your environment

As stated many times in this section, project management is primarily about people management, and people and groups of people vary tremendously in how they behave and how they expect others to behave. A style of interaction that is perfect in one environment is completely unsuitable in another. As a project manager you must learn to be sensitive to your environment.

There are many triggers to different environments and different behaviours. There are four factors I always try to consider:

1 The country I am working in.

2 The type of organisation the project is for.

3 The type of function the project is working with.

4 Anything specific to the organisation I am operating in.

At the highest level on this list is the culture of the country you are operating in. An example of cultural differences is that a casual use of first name terms is the norm in the UK, almost obligatory in the USA, but completely out of place in Germany. Next is the culture of the organisation you are working in. In most media companies if you are dealing with creative departments wearing a suit will place you at odds with most people, but wearing jeans and t-shirt in a financial services company is also likely to be poorly regarded. Thirdly, I consider the function I am working in. Engineering departments have a very different ethos and language from marketing departments. Engineers tend to be focused and pedantic about detail; marketers are often very hard to pin down to specific requirements and will often talk in terms of ideas and concepts. Finance and legal departments often work alongside each other and are seen as 'corporate' functions policing people as much as helping, but their styles and approaches to work vary tremendously. Finance departments often start work early in the morning; I find legal departments usually do not, but they think nothing of still being in the office at 10pm. Finally, there is the organisation itself – some companies strive to develop a specific culture or attitude, whether this be open and honest, or driven and focused. Some companies have a caring culture where you help people succeed, others have a ruthless focus on delivery and any hesitation is seen as failure.

If you are not sensitive to the culture of the organisation you are working in you will find that, over time, you do not develop support, people will try to avoid working with you, and confidence and trust in your abilities will not develop easily.

Once you have got used to a specific organisational culture you will find yourself naturally following its patterns of behaviour. This is good, but when the project is over do not take those behaviours to another organisation unless they are directly appropriate.

Attribute 11 – Adapting your style to the situation

The final thing to say about personal style is that not only is there no single correct style for all project managers, but any one style is not right for all situations. To take an extreme example, laughing and telling jokes is expected at a wedding, but is out of place at a funeral. Most of us will automatically adapt our style when we move into a different situation, and we would not even need to think about the appropriate behaviour to adopt in my example of a wedding and a funeral. Projects are no different; on a day-to-day basis they will put us into many different situations, and just because a certain way of interacting works for you some or even most of the time, do not maintain it in every situation. Adapt your style as appropriate.

> Any one style is not right for all situations

However, do not automatically adjust your style without thinking about it, but *consciously* manage the style you adopt as this will avoid you inadvertently taking on a poor style. For example, if you feel yourself becoming defensive it is not always good to actually adopt a defensive style of interaction. Think about what will be most productive in any one situation. Failure to adapt your style can leave you looking wooden and unimaginative, and people will start to develop potentially false assumptions about what you are feeling and thinking.

7

Managing your project

Key lesson

To manage projects a project manager must understand what she should be managing, have a mechanism to provide information to understand when management action is required, and finally implement action when the information tells her it is necessary.

THIS CHAPTER LOOKS AT THE CORE DAILY WORK required of a project manager on a live project – actually managing the project. It may be surprising to some readers therefore that this is one of the shortest chapters in the book.

To be an effective project manager I cannot deny that it is important to have a good grasp of project management processes, methodologies and tools. As I stated in Chapter 5 these mechanics are not the primary focus of this book and therefore I make no claim that this is a particularly exhaustive or complete study of these topics. What this section will do is overview the basic principles and hence provide some context for the rest of the book. For the person who is not an expert in mechanics this will add some value. The benefit of this chapter is to give you a framework to help you test whether the way you are approaching managing projects is sound. More fundamentally this section is short because if you have set up your project correctly as described in Chapters 3 and 5, if you use the communications tools described in Chapter 2, and if you have the attributes of personality described in Chapters 4 and 6 – the truth is that day-to-day management of projects is not the hugely difficult and demanding task that it is often presented as. (This is reflected by the fact that it has taken me until Chapter 7 to even start discussing this topic.) On the other hand, if you have not worked hard to scope your project well or put the correct plan and resources in place and if you do not attempt to use good communications skills, then managing your project may soon become a complete nightmare.

To be able to control a project you need to be able to keep in mind what you should and can manage, understand what is going to trigger you to take management action and, following on from this, actually how you manage.

Key lesson

The degree of difficulty in managing project is closely related to how well you have set the foundations (in terms of expectations, scope, plan and resources) in place.

What should you manage?

When you start out on your career as a project manager it is often easy to get bewildered by the number of things you have to do on a day-to-day basis. The plan is complicated. There are lots of people doing activities more or less under control, and more or less relevant to your project. There are various external stakeholders trying to influence the project. And finally there are huge numbers of things that are completely outside of your control that you feel you must worry about. So what should you be managing?

> There are only five things that you are really responsible for managing

In your role as a project manager there are only five things that you are really responsible for managing. These are difficult enough at times, but keep focused on these and your life will be much easier. Anything else you are involving yourself in should be because it has an impact on these five. They are:

1 **The time the project is taking to deliver** – this is typically measured as progress against your plan.

2 **The resources you are using to deliver** – again this is typically measured as resource expenditure (man/hours, money, etc.), against

your original plans. This is generally harder than measuring progress and relies on a number of estimates. In addition, you must work to ensure you continue to have access to the resources you need – this cannot be taken for granted. Often people focus totally on time and ignore or under-emphasise resource usage – this can be because it is quite hard to monitor, and also because a less than fully scrupulous project manager can more easily get away with using more resource than with failing to deliver on time. Inefficient delivery is as much failure as late delivery.

3 **The quality of the work done** – where the quality of a task is determined by assessing whether it is good enough to allow following tasks to be done adequately, and therefore allow the overall project's goals to be met. Additionally, you should look at quality in terms of the project process you are applying. This can be the hardest part of managing a project – though it is one often thought about least.

4 **The scope** – are you continuing to meet the scope of the project, and is this scope still relevant?

5 **Your customer** – are still meeting their expectations?

How do you know to take management action?

A very large part of project management theory, processes and tools are given over to providing the project manager with mechanisms to deliver information to know when management action is required. These are described in more detail in Chapters 2 and 10, but in summary the key tools a project manager has are:

◆ Formal progress reporting and progress monitoring:

– Progress reports and other formal inputs from the project team. (One good tool that is frequently not used to its full advantage is timesheets for team members.) Do not forget that progress needs to measure what has been produced relative to time spent – not simply how much time has been spent.

– Ongoing planning and monitoring – and there are a variety of tools available to help this including mapping progress against plan and using tools like earned value analysis. Remember that such monitoring is not simply a measure of how much time has been used, tasks done, and resource used. It is a measure of how much has been used relative to where you expected to be.

- Budget and spend tracking – both from the project itself and from any financial systems supporting you.

- Project team meetings – the team's own assessment of progress.

◆ Use and assessment of outputs from project management tools, e.g.:

- Risk management.

- Issue management.

- Assumption management.

- Change control.

◆ Quality control and quality audits of deliverables – both formal and informal. (This is normally not regarded as a project management tool as it is specific to the content of the project – my view is that as a project manager you need to know how quality of deliverables is going to be assessed. Otherwise how can you know if the project is delivering what it is meant to be? For some types of deliverable such as software there are well described processes and approaches for testing them. For many other deliverables there is no defined standard methodology.)

◆ Informal day-to-day conversations and communications. No matter how good formal information flows are do not forget how powerful it can be to keep your ear to the ground.

◆ Direct feedback from the customer.

All of these tools provide different sets of information to a project manager, and as a project manager you must be aware of the range of tools in your armoury and use them appropriately. With all of these tools the depth and quality with which you use them should be a function of the situation you are in – they are simply tools and not the end result. When you need to hammer a nail into a piece of wood you will use a cheap hammer, when you need to break up several tons of concrete you at least need a pneumatic drill and possibly something bigger. So it is with project management tools. Their effectiveness should only be measured in one way – do they have the optimal balance of being as simple as possible, yet giving you the best information with which to make management decisions in the context in which you are working? When you are setting up your project you must determine which tools you will need to what degree.

The decision to take action then comes down to your ability to structure the output from these tools to give you worthwhile information, your analysis of the information and judgement of what action is required. Look for two things, firstly specific individual problems or issues and secondly trends. For example, a one-day slip from one team member in one team in a large programme is probably not relevant to the project manager – a one-week or one-month slip is. On the other hand, a continuous trend of one-day slippages does need to be managed.

How should you manage?

If you know what to manage, the next question you need to determine is how should you manage? This is somewhat more difficult, but again if you have the fundamentals in place it is where all your hard work comes together – and this is where the successful project manager makes life look easy and the less able project manager struggles. To use an old cliché – this is where the rubber hits the road.

Again, this is not intellectually complex if we think in terms of the actions a project manager can actually take. No matter how senior, how experienced, and how clever a project manager you are – there are a very limited set of actions you can take in response to a need to manage something. The management levers you have are:

◆ **Change the way the team are working** – this may be as simple as encouraging them to work a little harder, asking them to work more time on your project, reprioritising or refocusing effort, or looking at the way they are actually working.

◆ **Change resources on a project** – if a project is running late, or occasionally it is ahead of schedule you can attempt to change the resource level – or release resources from the project. The basic parameters are either to get more resource, or different resources. A more subtle, but equally important thing to do when you need resources is to have the priority of the project changed to make accessing resources easier.

◆ **Change the scope of a project** – a project that is suffering can be made more likely to deliver by reducing the scope and focusing on a smaller set of critical deliverables or requirements. (Alternatively, a successful project may have more deliverables or requirements added.)

◆ **Add tasks to the project** – not quite as broad as fundamentally changing scope, but, for example, in response to issues or risks you may add resolving tasks to the workload of project members.

◆ **Change the plan or approach** – a plan is only a plan, it becomes a statement of fact only on the day a project completes. If it is wrong it can be changed. This may be fundamental re-writing, or it may be to try and move some dependencies around to see if things can be improved. Projects often get fixated on one approach. There are normally many ways to solve a problem. If an approach is not working then it is worth taking a creative look to see if there is an alternative approach.

◆ **Change the quality** – changing the quality of deliverables of projects can make a huge difference to the time a project takes and the resources it absorbs. This should not be undertaken lightly – and should be explicit. I have seen numerous examples on technical projects where engineers have striven for a level of quality that far exceeds what is necessary on the project and hence have used more time and budget to deliver. More often people cut corners to get their deliverables complete. In the intense focus on time and money that many projects operate under changes to quality happen without really being noticed until a sub-optimal end result is achieved.

◆ **Make decisions and escalate** – one thing a project manager must do on a regular basis, either by herself or in conjunction with different customer and stakeholder groups is to make decisions on actions (see end of this chapter). All the changes noted above need some form of decision making and, if significant enough, with external agreement, but there will be other decisions required on a day-to-day basis by the project team.

◆ **Terminate the project** – a valid option that is always available is actually to stop a project. Of course, this should not be done without serious consideration, but in my experience it should be done more often than it is. Any project which will under-achieve its original business case should be considered for termination – if the under-achievement is material to the decision to start the project in the first place. Of course, if you get to this place it is best to get there sooner rather than later, and don't fall into the sunk cost trap. What you have spent you have spent, what you need to focus on is how much time and effort it will require to complete the project from where you are now.

The important point about these levers is that this is really where individual judgement comes in. Most project management tools and texts are about getting you to a position in which you can make a decision on one of these activities – they will not actually help you that much in making the decision.

Taking action is the heart of managing a project. If you do not or cannot do this then you should not be a project manager. If what you love is understanding and analysing projects then consider a role in a project office – if you want to be a project manager it is about driving delivery through action. It is not just that you do this, but how well you do it.

When issues or problems occur that need management action, the action must be driven by getting a better result, not simply about understanding why it occurred. In fact, understanding how an issue or problem has arisen is less urgent than understanding how you are going to resolve it. A lot of time can be wasted determining who did what and who is to blame. This is generally unproductive and even if necessary can be done later when the more

> Taking action is the heart of managing a project

urgent task of solving the problem is over. When the problem is understood and some action is being taken to resolve it, it is sensible for you to give this some more focused management attention – but do not confuse that with smothering everyone with a need for constant and continuous updates. Updates are required – sometimes daily, sometimes even more frequently, but if people spend the whole time updating you they will not actually be resolving the issue. This is the time for good leadership and balancing your need for information for control and managing customers, and giving people the space to deliver.

Once you have determined and agreed upon a course of action it needs to be communicated. You must therefore have a structure of meetings and communication channels in place to ensure this is done – and the team should be prepared for it. The team should understand that the plan they are working to is a framework, and not necessarily the final answer. They must expect regular updates to agree what actually needs to be done given the current status of the project.

> ## Key lesson
>
> The success of a project manager depends on an understanding of what can be managed and sources of information to trigger management action. The measure of success is only dependent on the taking of the action and its result.

Change control and management

> ## Key lesson
>
> Change control provides a mechanism for a project manager to respond to changes in a project's scope and requirements in a controlled fashion. It is essential to successful project management to have a robust change control process supported by ongoing expectation setting.

So far, both in terms of setting up the project (as overviewed in Chapter 5), and subsequently managing the project (as defined in this chapter) I have described the baseline for the work as the scope (described in Chapter 2). In practice, neither the scope of a project, nor the detailed requirements stay static and the whole of the management process that is based on it being consistent is therefore in jeopardy. The response to this is not to reject change, but to control and manage changes. This is where change control and change management come into place.

The primary source of change should be the customers of the project – they want additional requirements included, they desire to expand the scope. Alternatively, but much less common, the customer can want to decrease the scope or requirements – this is a change and they may expect the project to be done more quickly or more cheaply as a result. There will be some changes that are driven by the project team rather than the customer (for example, if it is found that a chosen approach does not work and the plan needs to be modified). Finally, changes may be driven by the environment a project operates in. This may be something as fundamental as a legal or regulatory change that must be conformed to, through to more simply a change in an external dependency.

There are some changes which are not optional – something happens that must be responded to. But in most cases it is worth remembering that accepting or rejecting a change is an optional choice. A key part of change management is therefore about delivering the information to make the best choice.

While you may have built some 'fat' or contingency into a project plan to respond to minor changes, and as discussed in Chapter 4 you may occasionally accept small changes without explicitly using a change control process, change control is not an option for the project manager. It is central to project success. Poor change management is a very common reason for project failure.

The basic process for any change control system is fairly straightforward:

◆ Capture and log any changes that are proposed – what is it, why is it wanted.

◆ Understand and assess the change. Specifically determine the impact of the change upon the project. There are two views of the impact of a change:

- *A project management view*: will it increase or decrease time, will it increase or decrease resources, will it change the cost, and will it impact the quality of the project?

- *A customer view*: if this change is implemented will it still result in a project delivering what the customer wants and will it still result in the necessary benefits or business case being delivered? The impact of change upon benefits realisation is often ignored and yet it is critical as without it you may alter something that means the project does not deliver what it was set up to deliver in the first place.

◆ Determine viable options for responding to the change. For example, if it is an increase in scope you may be able to respond by lengthening the project, or keep the time the same and increase resources.

◆ Discuss with the sponsor and agree whether to accept the change, and if so which approach to take towards it.

◆ Adapt your plans accordingly.

A key factor in successful change control is supporting it with good expectation management. Set the customer's expectations early on that if changes occur they will have an impact on the project – and when changes do occur communicate and reinforce the impact to make sure it is understood and accepted. An essential part of this expectation management should revolve around educating the customer. If your customer wants a project with an absolutely committed plan, minimal contingency in time, cost or resource it is unlikely that you will be able to change anything significant without altering the cost, time or resource levels. Alternatively, if change is likely your customer should hold a contingency budget to be prepared to handle this.

Decision making

Throughout this chapter I have mentioned the need for the project manager to make decisions. No matter how good and accurate your planning and preparation are, things will occur that require decisions to be made to resolve them. Whenever there is an option you must make a decision. Therefore, while it is rarely explicitly mentioned, analysis and decision making are a core project management skill.

To make a decision you may either guess at the right answer (generally not a good idea), or, more constructively, you can rely on your intuition and experience of similar situations to make a 'gut' decision (which is fine for most decisions we make on a day-to-day basis), or, finally, in the most structured way, you can decide what information you need to make a decision, gather it, identify options, analyse the information relative to the options available and then make the best decision. Good decision making is not 'free' – it requires effort to gather the information you need, and takes time to perform the analysis. A trade-off that all managers must make on an ongoing basis is that between making decisions on a sufficiently speedy basis to maintain progress, and taking the time to gather the information required and to form a valid assessment.

> Good decision making is not 'free'

Projects in this respect are like any other management challenge – all the tools and processes in the world will not provide you with all the information you need to be sure of a perfect decision in all situations. But you must make and implement decisions regularly otherwise the project will stall.

The key points about decision making are that it is a constant trade-off between the following issues:

◆ How critical is the decision and what is the impact if it is wrong?

◆ How critical is the decision and what is the impact if you take too much time to make it? (Many decisions must be made within a certain period of time. The most difficult to make being those that must be made quickly, but which also need lots of information and have a big impact if wrong.)

◆ Understanding who can and who should make the decision. Can you do it? Do you need an expert specialist? Does it need any level of formal authority to make? Is it something for your sponsor to decide?

◆ What is the culture of your organisation? Some company's value considered decision making, others value speed and pace over accuracy.

Don't be afraid of decisions – in most situations it is important to make a decision rather than be absolutely certain it is right. Analysis and decision making paralysis is usually far worse than making a few sub-optimal decisions. The key is to identify the small number of critical decisions and make sure that they are right.

8

The team

Getting the best from the project team

> ### Key lesson
>
> One of the main tasks for a project manager is to manage and motivate the project team to deliver all that is required for the project. Pure project management process and methodologies will not achieve this – a project manager above all else is a people manager.

DURING THE LIFE OF A PROJECT the project manager will personally create a range of tangible deliverables that are critical to delivery. This includes things like plans, issue and risk registers, project charters and the like. The funny point is that at the end of the work when the project is complete these items are largely worthless. They have little or no value outside the life of the project. The real deliverables, the things desired in the first place are produced by everyone else on the project. Whether that is a computer system or a new building – the people the project manager manages on the project produce the deliverables the customer wants.

This is important to remember, because project management is at its heart largely about people management. Even though as a project manager you will usually have no permanent staff of your own, and may even have become a project manager to avoid line management – you will have to accept managing people as being core to your role. Without the project team the project manager's role is worthless. The main task for the project manager is to ensure that the project team is capable of delivering and delivers, and that blockages in their way are removed.

So what are the key things that a project manager can do to get the best from the project team? There are sixteen key people management tasks, split into four groups:

1 Getting the basics right – right people, right skills, right tasks (tasks 1–4).

2 Motivating and building the team (tasks 5–9).

3 Project team management challenges (tasks 10–14).

4 The broader context (tasks 15–16).

Tasks 1–4: Getting the basics right – right people, right skills, right tasks

Management task 1 – Getting the right capabilities and skills

The first thing a project manager must consider when setting up a project team is what capabilities and skills are required to do the project. This should be treated firstly as a paper exercise – not a review of who you have. Once you have an understanding of what is required then review what people are available and assign them to relevant roles on the project.

Often there will be a gap between the capabilities and skills of the team you have, and that which you ideally need. Try to fill it as best you can, but it is naïve to expect a perfect match between the skills you need and the people you get. This gap needs to be managed as a risk like any other risk. (And a key reason for starting your thinking with what you need rather than what you have is to be able to understand this gap explicitly and therefore be able to assess the risk this creates.) Lack of skills to complete the project should appear on your risk register. Do not just ignore this point and accept what resources you are given. Yes, in the real world you do not get a perfect team, but as the project manager it is your responsibility to manage the resultant issues. If the impact of the gap is small you can manage around it – but do not assume that the gap will be constantly small at all stages of the project.

Get a balanced set of capabilities and skills, and do not fall into the trap of choosing people who are all like you. In fact, look for people you can work with, but make sure at least some of them are not like you and so that they may see issues and risks you would not have thought of or come up with creative solutions you may not see. Managing varied people assists in ensuring constructive challenge and helps to avoid the danger of group think. Group think is when a team of people think alike and become blind to issues. This is a risk especially on a small well-motivated and focused project team working in a closed environment.

Find a balance between internal and external resources. You should not fall into the trap of only considering the people you have available within your organisation. There are many good contractors and consultants who can help out. Some unusual skills which your organisation only uses occasionally are often best sourced externally. On the other hand, fully staffing projects with contractors and consultants is both expensive and can lead to solutions that are inappropriate for your specific context. In addition, inhouse staff often resent the situation where a high percentage of external staff are used.

> **Group think is when a team of people think alike and become blind to issues**

Management task 2 – Go for quality rather than quantity.

If you remember no other point from this section, remember this one. When people plan and scope out projects and look at the number of people required there is a tendency to treat people in purely number terms. Do you need 5, 10 or 20 people – as if there is no difference in the quantity and quality of the outputs from some people? When in doubt always go for fewer better people – they will be easier to manage and will produce more. I can quote numerous examples were a smaller group of people have delivered far more than a big team. I have seen situations where a single senior executive goes away on a Friday and comes back on Monday morning with a fully scoped strategy that the strategy project team of ten consultants has struggled over for weeks. I have seen small teams of motivated fitters do more work in one weekend when a building is required than a team of builders twice as big achieved in the week before. I have experienced a group of four superb software developers creating better, more functionally rich and robust software in a matter of a few weeks than a team of 20 or 30 from a major software house would develop in six months. Life is full of examples where a small group of motivated people have delivered far more than a much larger group of less able people.

In terms of people quality always wins over quantity. Get the best people you can afford even if the resulting cost means you end up with fewer.

Do not simply accept the resources you are offered without question. If there are better capable, better qualified, or better motivated people elsewhere in the organisation try to get them rather than the people you have been offered. You may need to act as the salesman to these individuals to get them interested in coming onto the project, and work as a negotiator with their line managers to get them released. This effort will be rewarded as the project progresses.

Management task 3 – Assign clear roles and defined objectives

The starting point for management of anyone in any team is for them to understand why they are part of the project team, and what is required of them. If you have asked for someone to be on the project you should know why you need them – projects are not simply an excuse to collect and stockpile people! It is amazing how often project members find themselves allocated to projects without a clear idea of the requirements being placed upon them. On the other hand, if this is done comprehensively and clearly the chance that the project will be a success is increased greatly.

Everyone on the team should therefore know:

◆ What their role is and what the tasks are that they are expected to perform. This should be defined clearly and succinctly. The best way to do this is not simply to list a set of tasks the individual needs to complete, but to specify the objective or goal you wish them to achieve.

◆ Who on the project is allowed to allocate them work, and who they will be working with or for.

◆ Who they need to interact and work with to complete their tasks.

◆ How much time they are expected to spend on the project (both in terms of duration and percentage of time in this period to be made available to the project).

◆ What the measures of success for their task are.

◆ Why they were chosen. Even if it is true, avoid telling people that they are on the project because they were the only person available as it is not very motivating!

For a large project this is a considerable piece of work, and arguably one of the most important tasks for the project manager. (For projects with several teams this can be done as a cascade with the project manager doing this at team level, and the individual team leaders then breaking this down for the team members.) It does not have to be done in a complex fashion – but unless every team member knows this you risk poor performance and focus on irrelevant activities. Unless you can see a direct linkage between all the activities on your project plan and the work being done by the project team then the project is unlikely to be successful.

Role assignment and allocation of tasks will not happen automatically as the people on the team may never have worked together before. It will certainly need your management.

Try to find a balance between very detailed roles and a degree of flexibility. Given that nothing is fully predictable and it is unlikely that you will foresee every eventuality no plan will cover 100% of all tasks required. New unplanned activities will arise that need to be performed. Roles should therefore be defined so as a project progresses and new activities are discovered you can allocate them to a member of the team without causing disruption. Some of this is about writing role definitions in a way to allow this, but it is also about raising people's expectations up front that their role *may* develop as the project develops.

Once you have assigned roles and responsibilities check there are no gaps, and, almost as important, no overlaps – one task requires one person or one team to be accountable for it – otherwise you will struggle to ensure it is delivered. Blurred responsibilities and accountabilities waste time, increase management overhead, and add significantly to the risk of failure to deliver. Having single points of accountability for tasks is a critical success factor in projects.

Management task 4 – Know when to throw people off the team

What should you do with an under-performing member of the team – especially if it adds some risk to the project? Keeping the right mix of people on the project and removing those who are not pulling their weight is essential. Hopefully it will not be something you will need to do too often – but you need to be prepared to do it.

When you become aware of poor performance take action quickly and start by giving people an explicit chance to perform better. Ensure they are given clear feedback about how they are failing and give them a chance to turn it round. Go through the following checklist:

◆ Does the poorly performing individual understand what is required of him (or her)?

◆ Does he (or she) understand that he (or she) is performing poorly? (Will some constructive feedback resolve the issue?)

◆ Do you understand what is driving the poor performance?

◆ Can any of these reasons be easily resolved?

◆ Is the individual willing and able to overcome the performance issue?

Do not leave such a review until too late. Do not wait until a major problem has arisen – if you do this you are really shirking your responsibility as a project manager. If in doubt my advice is to pull people off the project. Your job is to ensure it is delivered, not to develop staff. This may seem harsh, but it is necessary. They have a line manager to worry about their development and their feelings.

One useful point is that if someone is under-performing and jeopardising a team's output you may be surprised to find that the rest of the team actually support their removal. There is nothing high performing teams dislike more than an individual who is seen to be reducing their ability to deliver.

This is one activity that is normally far easier for a project manager than for a line manager. Assuming the person thrown off the project will not actually loose their job then you do have the benefit that many line managers do not have that you do not have to make them redundant or perform structured performance management activities which normally are time consuming. Advise the sponsor of the risk the person brings and get them off the project as soon as possible.

Poor performance in a project situation should not be measured in an absolute sense – as you would as a line manager, but relative to the requirements of the project. For example, someone may give you a very good but time-boxed 9–5 performance as these are their working hours. Sometimes on projects this is not enough, and a project requires short periods of intense working. In this situation you should consider removing your steady 9–5 performer. The work he is doing is not sufficient for the context of the project you are running – and, equally important, others on the project who are putting in the required time will resent it if you do not remove him.

Tasks 5–9: Motivating and building the team

Management task 5 – The line management challenge – aligning objectives and motivation

The nature of most projects is that the team of people on the project will only be there for a limited period of time, and the project manager is not those people's line manager. The project manager often has limited authority or formal influence over project team members. There is a three-way relationship between the member of the project team, their normal line manager and the project manager. Project management requires the ability to matrix manage, and although it should be minimised in all matrix management there is some degree of greyness, everything will not be black and white.

The first point to any project manager is not to moan about this – this is a project manager's lot. If you want to be a line manager you should have gone into line management. (In fact, a regular positive feature of project management for many project managers is the fact that they do not have line management responsibility.) Most team members have a line manager who can determine things that are important to them and which will influence their performance – such as pay rises, promotions and the like. The line manager may have nothing to do with the project. So if you do not have line management responsibility and the levers that go with this – how do you manage the team?

The first thing you must do is to try to align objectives:

◆ Agree with key individuals on the project what it is that they need to achieve for you to consider them a success. For larger projects actually document this as if you were setting objectives for any other role. This needs to be done in conjunction with, and with the agreement of their line manager. (See management task 3.)

◆ For people who are going to spend any length of time on the project it is worth formally aligning any defined performance measures with project success. As an extreme negative example I have seen project team members who had benefits packages including substantial bonus elements determined by meeting their goals as set by their line managers. These people were on a project for many months and yet their annual performance objectives had nothing to do with the project. Needless to say, much of their concentration was pointed elsewhere. Discuss with their line manager, and if he or she is not responsive, the project sponsor, whether you can have line objectives reflect the work your team member must do on the project.

◆ Try to pick people with a personal interest in the project. These people will often volunteer or request involvement. Excitement, drive and enthusiasm are often worth far more than apparently better skills on paper. Everyone has experienced occasions when the expert has given up, but the motivated and driven non-expert has gone onto deliver. You cannot do without expertise, but do not over-estimate the value of having absolutely the best experts when compared to having the most personally motivated individuals.

◆ Make sure people are aware that this is a visible project that more senior managers are watching. People do not respond well to having someone constantly looking over their shoulder, but people are more likely to be engaged if they know their successes (and failures) will be visible to influential people.

Almost all employees will do their contracted 9–5 hours when asked to. An issue for projects is that almost always at some point this is not enough. Secondly, the content of the work is often stretching or different from what people normally do. This will motivate some employees who like a challenge, but not all. Therefore it is important to be able to motivate people to work outside of their normal expectations of work content, and working hours.

Junior and inexperienced managers often confuse motivation with authority. As a project manager you will often have limited authority. Authority can come from position – and through this the ability to control rewards and punishments (the stick and carrot). In your role as a project manager you will normally have little or no control over these, though you may be able to influence them. Authority can also come from a position of expertise – and you should ideally be respected by the team for your project management expertise but this alone will not generate complete authority as it is only one of many types of expertise needed on a project. But do not despair, as a project manager it is still possible to motivate people once you understand what motivation is about.

The starting point for understanding motivation is the realisation that most people do not like to fail. If you and the team want to succeed the majority of individuals will go along with this. Most people also respond to a challenge, but they must have a fundamental belief that what is required is at least possible. Motivation does not come from your ability to manage the stick and carrot. It comes from people being engaged in the work – this can be that it is satisfying or fun in itself, it is a challenge they want, they like the team they work in, or they are getting learning or development.

Hence, having aligned objectives there is a number of actions you can take to continue to motivate the team to work towards them:

◆ Lead the team by example. You want each of the project team members to see success of the project as their personal goal. As the project manager if you do not act as if your personal goals are aligned with the project goals then it will be difficult to convince a project team to align their goals.

◆ Motivation is about giving people a reason for wanting to be involved in the project and wanting to make the project a success. For some people being motivated is internally driven and is a normal part of their working lives whatever they are asked to do, for others motivation is driven by external factors. The most important of these external factors is usually ensuring alignment of objectives and reward with project success.

◆ Make sure the specific objectives and targets you have set teams and team members are possible – it's ok if they are challenging or stretching but no-one is motivated by the constant thought of missing goals.

◆ Next you should seek to create a motivating environment. The things that make something motivating to any individual vary from person to person, but key factors include:

   – Plenty of regular informal constructive feedback. Positive reinforcement of good behaviour simply by recognition and praise is a major motivating factor for many people.

   – People work best in an environment with a combination of good support and help when they need it, but also challenge. Encourage openness and honesty when there are issues and problems.

   – Work to build a team environment that people want to be involved in and feel a part of.

   – Try to enable individual team members to achieve personal goals through working on the project.

   – Make the environment fun – encourage a positive attitude to work. This can be as trivial as building a team environment in which it is common to smile through to organised social events. No one technique will work for everyone – having a drink or going go-karting will not suit all individuals so you need to be creative in coming up with as inclusive options as you can find.

◆ Avoid doing things that remove people's motivation. The main things that kill motivation are a lack of belonging and lack of alignment with objectives, combined with uncertainty. Many people may say they thrive in changing environments – but typically this is because they are certain they will survive the change, or they have skills that can be readily deployed elsewhere. Clear goals and objectives combined with regular reinforcement and praise reduce uncertainty.

◆ Build a feeling with team members that their impact on the project is valued. Remove poor performers from the team. It is highly demotivating for most people to feel that their good work is being held back by a poor performer – or that their work is carrying a 'freeloader'.

Management task 6 – Building the team

Unless you are very lucky, or working in a situation of a continuous stream of very similar projects it is quite likely that the people in your project team will not have worked together before. You should not automatically assume that people will come together and work well as a team. You may have to work to bring them together.

There is no one right way of building a team and different sets of people will form bonds in different lengths of time. To support this as a project manager:

> **Don't take team building for granted**

◆ Take mobilisation seriously. When the team is first mobilised make sure you communicate the purpose of the project and everyone's roles. Give some time for people simply to get to know one another.

◆ Ensure roles are clear and understood.

◆ Ensure communications channels are open – not just between you and team members but across the team members.

◆ Bring people physically together as much as you can.

◆ Encourage activity between members of the project which you think encourages team building. Stop activity that is detrimental.

◆ Don't take team building for granted. Work at it – and build on tasks 3, 4, 9 and 10.

Management task 7 – Ensure there is personal development for team members

If people are on a project for any length of time it is not unreasonable for them to expect some form of personal development out of it – and it can act as a great motivational driver for team members to feel their skills are being enhanced. One thing for project managers to watch out for is that when people are allocated to projects it is often on the specific advice that they will get some personal development from it. The conundrum facing the project manager is simply that enabling team members the chance to develop normally means giving people the opportunity to learn or do new things. If you are not learning something new you are not really developing – and yet the most effective people would be thought to be those who are doing what they are very experienced with. If you want a brick wall built quickly, you get a great bricklayer – but he generally is not getting any personal development from building this wall.

What should the project manager do?

◆ Accept the need for people's development. It is usually not a core objective for you (normally it is not a project success factor, but can occasionally be), but it may be fundamental to your success. Therefore, try to get a good trade-off between good existing expertise and learning goals.

◆ Face this task early on in the project – ideally when people first get involved. As part of their induction to the project understand their needs and thoughts in this area. If their expectations are out of line or unreasonable then put them straight, it is better to take the disappointment now, when you have a chance of doing something about it, than at midnight (later in the project) when a critical task needs completing before the next day.

◆ Try to sell people on the idea of learning from the things that are naturally part of the project. This is a bit of a selling exercise, but often people are quite happy to learn something new in the project by actually doing things you need done anyway.

◆ Build any reasonable things into the project plan – whether this be training courses or getting people involved in specific things. However, make sure development goals do not divert or alter the project in a way that adds risk.

◆ Make sure, in turn, you do not set any unreasonable expectations that the individual's line manager disagrees with.

Management task 8 – Ensuring people have a home to go back to

Some of the people working on your project will be what I think of as professional project people. These are staff, contractors and consultants who spend their lives going from one project to another. However, many, and often most, of the project team have been pulled out of normal line jobs to be on the project. These line jobs had the security of having no defined end point – whereas a project has a very clear end point.

In the age of regular rounds of reorganisation and redundancies in most industries, do not be surprised that these people are concerned if they are allocated to a project team for any extended period of time. If their normal line role can do without them for several months, or even longer, do they really need them back when the work is over? Whatever the true answer, it is obviously quite reasonable for people to have this concern. Reducing concern in team members is not simply a function of simply 'being a nice person'; the reason this is important for the project manager is that people who are concerned for their future are at best likely to be less effective, may well not be properly motivated, or at worst may actually start looking for another job.

There are ways around this:

◆ The starting point is to prepare for this issue arising before anyone is allocated to a project team.

◆ Get formal and explicit commitment that their job will still be available when the project is finished.

◆ If possible have their role backfilled with another member of staff or contractor when they are on the project. In this way their job still explicitly exists.

◆ For key staff an extreme method is to actually guarantee them some form of bonus or payment at the end of the project in return for taking the risk of coming on it. This is not common practice, but when I have seen it done it is effective.

The final point is that for some people coming onto a project is actually a deliberate way out of their current role. For these people being on the project may be motivational in itself, and they may want to develop some transferable skills.

Management task 9 – Be aware of team dynamics and team politics

Any group of people working together will develop a style of working together. The ability to understand the dynamics of your team is crucial for project managers. The thought that you can allocate people tasks and they will gladly deliver them irrespective of the people they are working with is naïve. There is no one right or wrong team style and there is no right or wrong way of responding to the dynamics of a team. You will have worked, if you are lucky, on great teams with great dynamics, and you will have worked on poor teams with poor dynamics.

◆ Be aware of it and monitor it – don't just ignore it as a fact of life. For long projects on which a team will be together for many months or even years it may be worth doing some form of formal assessment of personality types. This will give you a good insight and may let you see skills or approaches you are missing in the team or over-represented with. This can help you manage rebalancing the team. Such measures, if shared with the team, can enable them each to understand how they may need to tailor their behaviour to other team members. If you do use a formal assessment (whether it is as simple as Belbin, or more complex like Myers–Briggs or OPQ), make sure you understand the results – it is far too easy to draw the wrong conclusions from a poor understanding of the methodology.

◆ Use it – it can be a positive as well as a negative force. Good team dynamics and a lack of politics should be striven for. If you have formally assessed the team members use your understanding to help shape the team and drive individual performance.

◆ Don't assume it is static – it will change over time as the team changes and people get to know each other.

◆ Stop it if it gets in the way – if the team dynamics or politics are reducing performance it is your responsibility as the project manager to sort it out.

◆ Manage it when you need to bring new people on the team – this can be quite disruptive to a well-established team and can be hard for the new joiner.

◆ Encourage openness and honesty – successful teams tend to have few barriers to communications.

◆ You are part of it too, so lead by example – if you don't want politics in the team, do not politic yourself. You want to be trusted by team members, if there are problems or issues you want to know about them as soon as possible and this is more likely if people trust you. If you politic too much you are unlikely to develop trust.

◆ Remember that the team is more important than the individual. It is the team that delivers not any one individual. You will have star performers who need to be looked after, but explicitly treating people to different standards will only create bad feelings and negative mutterings. Similarly, no matter how good someone's skills are do not put up with them if they disrupt the team.

In many projects team members will not have met before – and even if they have met they may well not have worked together in this way before. You must use the mobilisation phase and then ongoing management to help the team form, and manage the way it interacts through the life of the project.

Tasks 10–14: Project team management challenges

Management task 10 – Physical proximity and communications channels

One of the most under-estimated factors is the advantage of close physical proximity for a project team. The basic truth is that people work better when they work together. Issues are resolved more quickly, more creative solutions are designed, and conflict occurs less regularly when people have to sit together. Whenever I am starting up a new project I try to find space for the project team to be colocated. My belief is that bringing a team physically together will have dramatic effects on efficiency and effectiveness. If the project is important enough it is worth putting in the effort and living with the short-term disruption of pulling a team into one location.

In practice, bringing a team to one physical location and sitting them in close proximity is often avoided – as it is put in the too-hard-to-achieve category. It is seen as a lot of effort for marginal benefit, a nice-to-have rather than an essential. Do not give up on this easily – it is worth the effort as when it is done productivity is significantly enhanced.

It is, of course, not always possible to bring a team together. The way your resources have been allocated, the nature of the organisation you are working in, or simply the size and geographic spread of the project may require a very diverse working. If possible insist that all team members do meet physically at least once. More generally in these situations make sure that communications chains are robust, and that people communicate in the most 'intimate' ways possible. By this I mean ideally face-to-face, next via video conference, then by phone and, finally, by e-mail (and e-mail should be seen very much as the poorest way to communicate).

Actively discourage less intimate communications styles. Encourage plenty of continuous informal communications and use tools such as e-mail for what they are good at – and not as the sole communications channel.

Before you bring all your team together be aware that it does have some disadvantages and risks. The primary one of these is that you are more likely to be seen as cut off from the line organisation your project is delivering into. This is a particular problem for the type of projects that need constant interaction with the line organisation, or good buy-in for the results from the project. Potentially this can be overcome by strong and regular communications, but for some projects, for example, business change projects being located away from the main organisation can be a significant enough disadvantage to forgo the delivery efficiencies to be derived from having a single closely located team.

Management task 11 – Managing geographically diverse and isolated staff

If you cannot bring your team together you may have geographically diverse teams, or individually isolated members of staff. This does not need to be a problem, but it is an issue you need to manage – and it will increase your management overhead. It needs careful control.

Useful tips to consider are:

◆ Make the relationships between teams and the way they will interact clear at mobilisation. Try, at this stage at least, to bring people together.

◆ Don't forget isolated staff. They may be happily and productively delivering, or they may simply be ignoring what they are meant to be doing. Unless you are managing them you will not know.

◆ Communicate frequently. Communications must become more

deliberate. The opportunity for informal chats is reduced so you must plan your communications in a more structured way.

◆ Check their understanding and comprehension of the requirements on them – it is easier for them to be in error when you are not sitting next to each other all the time.

◆ Ensure you do not develop any location biases or tensions. These are generally unproductive.

◆ As project manager try to travel to all locations at some time during the project if practical.

Management task 12 – Managing part-time resources

Every project manager wants a fully dedicated team who only have to think about and apply energy to the one project. In practice, on virtually every project I have been involved in some people have other tasks to do outside of the project. These other tasks may include other project work, or may include other day-to-day operational tasks for the business.

Many smaller projects are resourced primarily with part-time staff. The 'virtual' project that has only a project manager who then must beg, steal and borrow resources to get things done is, in textbook project management, a bad thing – but in reality it happens all the time. Hence, in real life much of a project manager's time is spent in coaxing and cajoling part-time resources to focus on the particular project rather than any other task they may be doing. This can be a painful and long-winded process for the project manager, but it can often be the factor that decides whether a project is successful or not. Your ability to do this is an essential skill.

> Communicate frequently. Communications must become more deliberate

Assuming the project workload justifies it, it is worth pushing to try to get as many people as you need full time, but you will have to accept that you will get part-time resources – and you should be capable of managing in this situation.

◆ Make sure that you have enough resource – it is the hours people are available for that counts, not simply the number of people involved in the project.

◆ Get fixed and measurable amounts of time from people – are they available one day a week, two days a week or some other amount?

◆ Monitor them and ensure you get the time you are meant to receive. Staff under pressure on several different projects or activities may simply slip away from your work if it is easy to do and not be noticed.

◆ Try and align availability times. For example, if you have two team members who work only two days a week on the project and need to work together try at least to get them to allocate the same two days a week to the project.

◆ Get yourself dedicated to the project – only for small projects should the project manager not be dedicated.

◆ Build an 'inefficiency' buffer into your planning. Part-time staff can be very productive as they are not soon tired of only focusing on the project, however, generally, a number of part-time resources will be less efficient that fewer full-time staff. Even where it does not alter the number of worked hours needed to complete tasks – it can massively increase elapsed time for a project.

◆ Measure staff on deliverables as well as time. Time allocated should not be an excuse not to deliver.

◆ There will be a small number of absolutely critical people – often in operational roles, and sometimes quite junior in the organisation. They will be very busy and have absolutely tiny periods of time to give you, and you may feel in asking them for time that you are trying to squeeze blood from a stone. Balance your approach here, use your charm and good manners to coax them, and escalate to your sponsor to get their priorities reset to focus on your work. (If you are going to escalate to get someone focused on your work, warn them in advance. This gives them the chance to do it anyway, and also avoids it becoming a confrontation. When you escalate, advise them you are not doing it as a complaint against them, but to help them find the time to work with you. Presenting escalation as an aid and not a threat helps maintain good working relationships.)

See management tasks 13 and 14 as well.

Management task 13 – Managing upwards

Project managers manage a team of people, and these people respond to the project manager's requests, simply because that team has some reason to fulfil the project manager's needs. Often this is because there is a formal level of seniority between the project manager and the team members. However, on almost all projects there are tasks that need to be done by senior managers and disciplines like law with senior professionals who will not automatically 'obey' the project manager.

How should a project manager face this task?

◆ Ensure the individual is pre-warned that the project may require them to do work at some time. This is easier if the senior person has a formal role on the project such as a sponsor – although I have frequently seen projects on which it is a surprise to the sponsor that he ever actually has to do some work. Tell him at the start – there will be issues escalated for resolution at the very least.

◆ Explain the reasons for the work clearly and simply – you must avoid patronising the person, but they should feel that it really does need someone of their seniority doing it and you are not simply being lazy!

◆ Explain your time frames and when you need the task done. Senior people are rarely dedicated to your work (see above), have lots of other important things to do, and regularly do not do all the things they might want to do. Tasks get de-prioritised away – you need to ensure your task does not. Constantly telling senior managers they are late for something may need doing, but it normally irritates them. If they clearly understand the implications of their work being late or sub-standard they will generally deliver.

◆ Be polite, clear and respectful, but be robust in making sure the task is done. Most managers are responsive to this.

Management task 14 – Managing non-dedicated specialists

Project managers will always try to get dedicated resources – sometimes for legitimate reasons and on other occasions because it just makes the management task more straightforward. But, there are some specialists who it can almost never be justified to have full-time support from. A typical example of this is lawyers. I have rarely seen projects with a dedicated lawyer on board. The issue when getting part time support from a specialist is to ensure your tasks get treated appropriately – for people like lawyers your task is often one of many important tasks and giving you absolute priority may not be possible. Also, specialists like this rarely understand the knock-on effect of their work being late – this is not being pig-headed, but lawyers, for example, are often only worried about legal risk and not the fact that there may be a trade-off between removing *all* legal risk and completing work on time. Generalising, most specialists are more focused on quality in their field than hitting your project timelines. Rapid progress which you require may require them to take risks, which they are uncomfortable with. You will all have come across engineers, lawyers and software specialists, for example, taking time to deliver a higher quality output than you require, or than there is time to do. As a result, you will often find lawyers and other highly paid specialist activities on the critical path even if they were not originally expected to be so. This is sometimes unavoidable – but happens regularly because no-one takes the time to really explain the context of their work in the wider project.

All you can do in this situation is to ensure the specialist in question has actually set aside time for your task; fully understands the implication of being late – so she can make a rational trade-off between getting absolute quality in her area versus the rest of the project; has a clear understanding of the quality required and the degree of risk acceptable to the project; and, finally, that they understand you are an important client who needs to be satisfied. Whatever you do, never ask specialists like this for a zero-risk solution – unless you have an infinite amount of time to wait.

Tasks 15–16: The broader context

Management task 15 – Working with the wider organisation

Projects do not exist in isolation – and the primary role of most organisations is not to deliver projects. Any project you are involved with is being done to change something within the organisation it is being run in. And yet it is very common for projects and project teams to forget this – and in doing so forget to manage their relationship and communications with the organisation they are operating in.

> Projects do not exist in isolation – and the primary role of most organisations is not to deliver projects

The need to manage relationships with the wider organisation varies depending on the context and content of the project. For example, on specialised technical projects it may be a small task to think about how the project stays in touch with the wider organisation. On the other hand, on a major change programme it may be one of the dominant sets of activities in your plan. Whichever, you must be conscious that the project only exists for a limited period of time, and usually it only exists for the longer-term benefit of the wider organisational community. The results of the project, if successful, will live for a long period of time.

This community typically needs to understand what will be delivered to them, when and sometimes even why. They must be prepared to accept the deliverables and their expectations must be managed as to the general impact of the project upon them. Assessing the communications requirement to do this, and implementing this as an ongoing series of interactions, whether simple and informal, or a complex set of informal and formal communications needs to be accepted as part of the project manager's role. In special circumstances the project manager will be supported by, or may even be working for a change management or communications specialist who will deliver much of this task. But it is a task like any other that the project manager needs to ensure is performed in a timely and quality fashion.

Management task 16 – Disbanding the project team

Projects come to an end – this is part of their very nature. Therefore, unlike other organisation units there is always a known time on a project when it comes to release people, either onto the next project, or back to the line management function they came from. Don't let this just happen by accident with people drifting off as they feel appropriate. Consider:

◆ Preparing early for this, don't just suddenly arrive there.

◆ Completion of a project should not simply occur when a point in time is reached – closure happens with a conscious decision that the project has been completed and the deliverables are at a standard that allows closure.

◆ Managing the expectations as to when people will be released. Project timelines will often flex a little and original plans to let people go on one date may move as the project shifts. Similarly, manage team members' expectations as to when they will be free to go.

◆ Resisting pressure to let critical resources go too early.

◆ Staggering the release of people – it is unusual to be able to release everyone at once, but also it is unusual to need everyone right to the end of the project.

◆ Explicitly thanking people – especially those who have gone the extra mile. This is not just good manners, you may need the same people later on another project so leaving them with a good feeling is useful.

◆ Feedback on team members' performance to their line managers.

◆ Holding a wrap-up session with the project team to bring together any lessons learnt.

9

The limits of knowledge

SO YOU ARE A PROJECT MANAGER – you know what a project manager does, and you regularly put this successfully into practice. What can limit your success? There are two traps project managers sometimes fall into that can constrain your achievements. The first is to try and apply generic project management skills to the situation in which a specialist is required. The second is to try and do things that are best done by other people. To avoid these traps you need to understand the limits of your knowledge and skills.

This chapter therefore sets out to discuss, explain and then answer two key questions related to the boundaries of project management knowledge:

1   **When do you need a specialist who can manage a project, and when do you need a professional project manager?** In many situations project managers can be caught in debates to do with the fact that on the one hand project management skills are within many people's toolkits of capabilities, so the question arises 'do we really need professional project managers?'; while on the other hand there is a common thought that 'isn't project management a generic skill set that can be applied to any situation?'. This leads to the subsequent thought 'surely someone who can manage one project can manage any other?' You need to understand this argument so you apply your skills on appropriate projects, and also so you can respond to this debate when it occurs.

(Specialist in this context relates to any particular professional or functional discipline, e.g. lawyer, accountant, engineer, HR, IT, etc.)

2   **What is it that project managers really don't do?** In any profession it
is useful to be able to understand what is outside the scope of your role
and what is included. In the case of a project manager this is critical
because the project manager is the person at the end of the day responsible for delivery of a project, so you will often find yourself filling the
gaps in activities or skills not covered by others. There are many tasks to
be completed on a project and there is a tendency for project managers
to do a whole range of tasks which are better off done by others. This
chapter outlines some specific mistakes to avoid.

The generalist vs the specialist

Key lesson

Complex projects are best managed to successful delivery by people skilled
in project management. Project management is largely a generic approach
to managing projects – but being a project manager is not a completely
generic skill that can be applied to any project in any situation. To be
successful, project managers need to understand and be able to use the
language, concepts and ideas which are used within the context of the
project they are managing.

Let me split the world into two categories of people. This is an artificial split,
but it will help with my initial explanation. Let me argue that there are only
two types of people – generic project managers who only know about
managing projects and have no other specialist knowledge and specialists in
various functional areas who know everything about that functional area but
nothing about delivering projects. Which is better, the generalist project
manager, or the specialist non-project manager? The answer to that question
is easy – if the world really did only contain these two extremes it is obvious
that for a project to be completed we need both. One type of person to
manage work, the other to do the key delivery tasks requiring the specialist
skills.

In reality the question that needs to be asked is slightly more complex as
there are two types of people who can reasonably be thought to be

competent to take responsibility for delivering projects – the generic project manager (or perhaps more positively put the specialist in project management) and the specialist or expert in a specific functional discipline, like IT, HR or finance, who can also manage projects. Which is the better in any one situation?

The banal answer is whoever is more likely to achieve success on the specific project in mind. I will go into a little more detail before I leave it at that as it would be fair to say that with this answer I am sitting on the fence. In practice, it depends on the scale, complexity and content area of the project.

As I have stated earlier in the book there are plenty of people who have experience and training in project management, who call themselves 'Project Managers' and who spend their lives delivering projects. There are also other people who have experience and training in project management, who spend their lives delivering projects, and for various organisational or personal reasons have a different job title. This differentiation can be ignored and whatever the job title, both at heart are professional generalist project managers – or specialists in project management rather than the content of the project. On the other hand, there are millions of other types of specialists – whether it be an IT systems analyst, a quantity surveyor or HR professional who may also have project management skills in addition to their core job skills. Which type of project manager is better for which type of project?

There are no absolute rules in these situations as to who is the better choice for a project manager, but my general guidance to people is this:

◆ **Part-time project managers should be used on small projects only**. On small non-complex projects it is perfectly acceptable for the project manager to do other things than project management. In fact, it is very likely that the project manager's role will be contained within one of the other specialist roles on the team. This specialist will have an ability to manage projects while fulfilling his or her own specialist role, and it avoids the costly overhead of a full-time project manager.

◆ **Project management is a specialist skill**. Project management is a specialist skill in its own right. Do not assume that anyone and everyone can do it, or has the time to do it. Apart from the simplest or smallest of projects it is generally worth having a project manager who really knows about managing projects. The overhead of a dedicated project manager will be easily recouped on a larger project. There are lots of factors that can make a project complicated, but my rough rule of thumb would be when there are less than five people to manage on a project then the project manager's role can normally be absorbed within one of the other roles. If there are five or more full-time people on a project it is worth considering a full-time project manager – when there are ten of more it starts to become essential.

◆ **If you have multiple skills in addition to project management choose which 'hat you are wearing' in any one situation**. It is true that many specialists can also manage projects – but if you are working on a large or complex piece of work you need to be clear about your role. If you are the project manager you need to focus on managing the project and not performing your specialist role. If you want to be the specialist then you should be the specialist and leave the project management to someone else. This is simply a function of having enough time to do what on a project of any significant size is a full-time job. (If you are tempted to perform both roles, please also read the next section in this chapter.)

◆ **Project managers do not need to be experts in what they are managing.** Project managers should not seek, unless from personal interest, to be expert specialists in every single discipline required on a project. The project manager who feels he needs to know as much about the content of the project as the specialists working on it is usually not understanding, or doing, the project management tasks required.

◆ **Project managers must have relevant contextual understanding**. The generic project manager will not be successful in delivering every project. It is true that a project manager will do very similar tasks within any project and so it is easy to draw the conclusion that they can manage any project. The issue is really that project managers do not operate in a vacuum; they operate within a specific organisational context and with people who are used to that environment. Such organisations have their own concepts, language and jargon, methods of working, and any specific project can have its own special area of focus within an organisation. Although the project manager does not need to be an expert in any of these, she does need to be able to talk the language of the people she is managing, and without understanding the details understand the concepts and approach of the people being managed. You cannot manage people you cannot talk to and share concepts with. To put it more positively if, in conjunction with relevant specialists, you can plan their tasks, assess risks coming from the performance of those tasks, and you can communicate unambiguously with them, then you probably know enough about their specialist field to manage a project in that area. On the other hand, if you do not understand the basic concepts the specialists deal with and have difficulty talking to them, or understanding what they are doing, then you cannot manage a project in that area.

To help to put this more explicitly I will give simple examples. If someone can manage a software delivery project for a financial system well, then with a little contextual information they can probably manage most other major software delivery projects, but will not be able to manage the construction of a bridge or the delivery of an HR change process without having any concern about their project management abilities and true credentials for the work. On the other hand, if someone is capable of managing a project to deliver a telecoms infrastructure for a bank they should

> Project management is a specialist skill in its own right

be able to do the same for other organisations such as a manufacturing company – as the basic task being managed will require very similar contextual knowledge and almost exactly the same project management skills.

If you are not working as a project manager, but hiring one or bringing in a contractor and cannot find anyone without directly relevant industrial experience, you will have to take someone from a different industry. One of the things to note is how quickly they try to pick up your jargon, your organisational oddities, your ways of working and your approaches. The ones who pick it up quickly and consciously, really are the most likely to be the closest to your needs.

If you are a project manager and are having to consider whether you are competent to manage a project in any specific situation, ask yourself:

◆ Are you comfortable managing this scale of project?

◆ Are you able to operate within the organisation this project is for? Do you broadly understand any specialist language and terminology they use?

◆ Can you plan, direct and control the various components of the project assuming the necessary specialists are available to do the work?

◆ Can you assess the quality of the deliverables, or manage a process that will assess the quality of deliverables?

◆ Can you challenge the specialists competently? (For example, if someone says a task will take 50 days, can you challenge them to do it in 25 and understand the implications and consequences?)

◆ Will the customer accept you and can you project credibility?

If the answer to all six of these is 'yes', then you have enough specialist skills to manage the project. It you answer 'no' to one or more of these, at the very least you will need some support, and you should question your competency to manage the project.

What should project managers not do?

Key lesson

Project managers must respect the need for a range of specialist disciplines on their project, and must fight for all the resources the project needs. Being a project manager on a large project is a full-time job, and even if the project manager has the skills to do other tasks he must focus his time and energy on managing the project and not doing other project tasks.

This section looks at the reasons project managers perform activities on projects which they should not, what these activities to be avoided are, and the impact on projects if they are done by the project manager.

There are a number of tasks that project managers should avoid doing

There are a number of tasks that project managers should avoid doing, but in my experience often end up doing, and in doing them increase the risk of failure for the project. The reasons they do these activities vary, but typically the explanations include:

◆ Project managers take the overall responsibility for delivering a project. They are the only person to do so in any individual situation. Due to resource shortages the skills of project teams are rarely perfectly aligned with the needs of the project. Projects are often short of one skill or another. Frequently, especially on smaller projects, the project manager personally ends up filling the gaps between the skills of the team allocated to the project and those needed. On a small project this can work, but it needs to be managed with care. I have seen many projects fail because the project manager is perfectly competent, but overloaded doing too many things other than project managing.

◆ Project managers often started out in their careers in different roles and so built other specialist skills beyond their project management skills. Think of IT project managers who normally start out in programming or analysis, or technical project managers who often started their careers as engineers. Again, on small projects there is no specific reason why they should not use their original skills, but as stated in the previous section on a big project the role of being the project manager full time. If you are finding that it is not taking up all your time you are probably not managing the project properly. On a big project the project manager's role is to manage, not to work on or deliver the components.

◆ Finally, and often most dangerously, there are a number of specialist disciplines that may not be recognised at all; or may erroneously be seen as synonymous with being a project manager; or are simply not thought of as difficult, complex or time consuming. In the next section I discuss seven 'culprit' skills that regularly follow this pattern. The need for these skills may have been forgotten during the planning stage, and so appropriate resources are not scoped in, or the specialist task may be under-estimated. Again, what happens is that there is a gap between the skills of the project team, and the skills needed to complete the project. If this is happening then my advice to any project manager is to understand your own limitations and avoid over-stepping them by trying to do the tasks yourself. If you have not planned these tasks in – don't bodge it by doing it yourself. Admit the mistake and get the people you need to do them to the quality you need. This may mean you need more time, or more resources for the project which your customer may not like, but better to do this than completely fail on a project. As a project manager you have your own deliverables like plans and progress reports which take time and skill, which you should be respected for. As a project manager you should respect the skills and time needed to do other things.

When project managers do undertake tasks that should not really be done by them there are two specific risks that can occur:

1 The project fails because insufficient time is being spent on managing the project.

2 The project fails because the project manager is doing a task he or she is not expert at and an expert is required. The project manager may do the tasks, but the tasks are not completed to the quality or scope required to deliver the project.

Both of these risks need to be avoided. I next look at what these disciplines to keep away from are. Note that at any time you are responsible for a project and find yourself spending a large percentage of your time doing these you are doing the wrong job.

Specialist skills that should be recognised as not being the project manager's job

Following this introduction is a list of seven 'culprit' skills that often fall to the project manager to do, which I cannot stress highly enough need to be treated as separate activities requiring specialist skills. On small projects all of these can be done by the project manager, on large ones they should not. Business life is littered with projects that have failed, or struggled with great difficulty to deliver because the following skills were forgotten, or thought to be the direct responsibility of the project manager. In some cases the project manager has this background, but as stated before he needs to focus on managing the project not doing these things. What is so difficult about the specific disciplines noted here is that they are all things that project managers do need to understand something about, and in restricted ways may legitimately and regularly get involved in. However, the statement 'legitimately and regularly get involved in' is quite different from taking primary responsibility for.

The seven skills I have selected are simply examples – though common ones. Understanding when you should or should not personally be responsible or involved in a task is a matter of judgement and balanced decision making. The truth is that any situation is rarely completely black and white – so consider the points made here to help make a decision on whether to personally perform a task or not. (See the Summary section on page 185 at the end of this chapter for the decision making criteria.)

Culprit 1 – Business analysis and requirements capture

Many projects, like IT development activities or new product development work, require the definition and documentation of complex requirements. If the requirements are wrong, incomplete, written in an overly ambiguous fashion or otherwise faulty the project may well fail or may end proving to be pointless by delivering the wrong end product or service. In building it is accepted that you need to be a trained architect to draw up an architectural plan for a customer before building work commences. The same thought needs to apply to IT developments and other technical development projects. The skill to understand customer requirements and write them down in a coherent way is that of a business analyst, and not a project manager. Many IT project managers do have analyst skills – but don't fall into the trap of 'because you can do it you should be doing it'. Project managers need to ensure the process for requirements capture is robust, and do need to have a good overall understanding of the requirements – but that does not mean they must collect them.

(See Chapters 2 and 3 for a discussion of definition of scope which is a project manager's responsibility.)

Culprit 2 – Change management

Change management is a much abused term. It has several meanings for different audiences and it is important when using this term to understand which use you are using it in, and to ensure your audience is using the same meaning. The three key uses of this term are:

1 **Project change management** – probably better called change control. This is the managed process of bringing changes to requirements or scope to a project. The objective of this is to ensure that any changes required are accepted by the project team and project sponsor, and the impact is understood before they are accepted. It is a core skill of all competent project managers and is discussed in Chapter 7.

2 **Operational change management** – this is the management of bringing in changes to live systems of some sort. (A live system in this context is any form of technical system or process that is already

operational and is needed for existing work or business services – the project is simply adding to this workload. It is most often used in connection with IT systems or networks, where changes regularly need to be made to a live system.) The objective of this is to reduce the risk to current services from making a change to them. This is often for technical projects the last thing that has to be done – the project's deliverables have to be implemented in the live environment passing through the operational change management process.

3 **People and organisational change management** – this is the management of change and its effects upon people and organisations. Ensuring that the change is successful in the way it is implemented and adopted by the people who will be affected.

So in the context of what is out of scope for a project manager I do not mean change control on requirements or scope of a project, and I am not really worried about operational change management, but the actual management of change to people and organisational units. It is unfortunate that this term has these three quite distinct meanings to three groups of people as this can cause much confusion. The skill of managing the impact of change on people is very valuable and quite specifically different from project change control. Like writing software code or doing an architectural drawing this is a very specific skill set – which many project managers are actually quite bad at. Many projects do require specialist change managers, and experienced change managers usually have at least an appreciation of project management, or may even be expert project managers. Many project managers have little or no workable knowledge of this type of change management, and trying to do without when required will often lead to project failure.

The complexity here is that there is an overlap between change management and project management skills, and they cannot be categorised as completely distinct disciplines. All projects result in a change which impacts someone and therefore are possible candidates for change management. Most changes are implemented through projects. However, a change management skill set is quite different from a project management one.

Culprit 3 – Systems integration and testing

A project frequently has many deliverables each produced by a different person or group of people. The project manager is responsible for ensuring they are all delivered – so presumably he is responsible for ensuring they all work together? Wrong! He is responsible for ensuring the integration and testing tasks are done and that the results are acceptable to the customer. Again we get to the difference between managing a task and doing it. Although many organisations understand it well it is amazing how poorly integration and testing are generally understood as concepts by senior managers and correspondingly they often look to cut them out when a project is running too long or costing too much.

Systems integration is essentially the skill of designing and implementing a solution from an end-to-end perspective rather than from the individual components. Typically on any engineered solution there are specialist engineers who will design and implement each component. There also needs to be someone who looks at all the components and ensures they work together to achieve the overall goals of the solution. A good analogy is with building a dry stone wall. If you are building a dry stone wall it is great to have people collecting each stone – but you need to have someone with a view of how each stone will fit the others around it or else the wall will be unstable and fall down.

Explaining why a project needs a highly paid systems integration specialist when there are already well paid engineers and project managers on a project can often be difficult. But do not avoid having them. Push back hard on any doubting managers – these are critical stages and vital skills in many projects, and you must insist you have the necessary integration and testing skills within your team. Without them the project is at risk, and you personally are at risk, as a failed project will always reflect badly on the project manager.

Culprit 4 – Supplier negotiations

Many people think they know how to negotiate a deal with a supplier – sometimes for as little a rational reason as they get good deals every time they buy a car from a garage. Although it is true that not everyone wants to do it as it can be confrontational and difficult (though if handled well does not need to be), too many people treat negotiating as a straightforward task. Please do not assume you know how to handle suppliers. For many small contracts it is not worth the overhead of professional supplier management types and the project manager does pick up this task. But when it gets tough,

> Many people think they know how to negotiate a deal with a supplier

or the deal is big enough don't avoid using them. A few project managers are trained negotiators, but this is comparatively uncommon.

You definitely need a specialist when the contract is for something unusual or different. The way to negotiate a deal say for cement, will vary hugely from the way a deal needs to be struck and structured for buying TV programmes or IT software. I have worked with very successful negotiators who are specialists in both of these areas – and their approaches, style, and the types of deals they struck were completely different. If you think you know how to handle a supplier and get a good deal then next time go in with a professional negotiator who knows this sector and see the difference.

Culprit 5 – Contract and legal issues

Contract and legal support are most often used in project situations when you are involved with third party suppliers for whom a legal contract needs to be put in place. (On the other hand, you may be a third party delivering for a customer, and then your legal people need to be involved to check your side of the contract.) Sometimes projects have to operate within legal or regulatory frameworks, especially in regulated industries such as utilities, telecommunications or government work. Legal support is normally required to confirm compliance to the necessary rules and regulations. It should not be necessary to describe why you need legal experts to be involved, but it is common on projects I have seen for a senior manager to ask the project team 'have you run this past the lawyers', and to receive an embarrassed shake of the head as a response.

Don't hesitate to involve solicitors or lawyers when appropriate – but do not under-estimate how long their work takes, or how tricky they can be to manage. In fact, the length of time lawyers take to do their work is a good reason to involve them early. It is amazing how often, rightly or wrongly, that the legal team is on the critical path of a project (the reasons for this and how to overcome it are described in Chapter 8).

Culprit 6 – Project office

That the project manager should avoid taking on the project office tasks will surprise many people. After all, should not all project managers be able to manage a project office? Probably, and many project managers have started their careers in or running project offices. The reason project managers should avoid the task is partially down to the much repeated issue here of workload and their need to focus on delivery of the project not doing the administrational support that a project office offers. The other issue is that I often find, rather oddly, that many project managers are not very good at project office stuff, even though most rather arrogantly think they should find it easy. Of course, many projects cannot justify the overhead of a project office and so by default the project manager must do the work. The reality is, however, that on a complex programme a project office provides invaluable support to a project manager and the overall project. Like a project manager, a project office needs to be structured in approach; in addition, the sort of administrative and frequently pedantic focus on detail and adherence to the project management process are skills that not all project managers possess.

In practice there are four types of project offices (or POs for short) that I come across. You could argue whether these all really deserve the title 'project office', but they each regularly get it:

1 **Administrative support** – Sometimes all the PO does is support some administrative functions on projects. Distributing reports, managing documents and arranging meetings. All important tasks, but the project manager is not an administrator. (If you find yourself doing this ask the person employing you to let you go and employ a cheaper administrator instead!) They may also perform the task of managing a document library and, depending on the context, this may simply be a useful bit of administration or it may be a task that is core to the success of the programme.

2 **Policing function** – Checking that project managers and projects adhere to some defined process standards. This can be checking the completion of regular reports, the use of the correct document formats, or confirming that things like issues and risks logs are kept. The policing function may simply be one of process adherence (i.e. checking you follow the steps you are meant to follow), or more substantially checking quality (i.e. checking not only that you follow the steps, but that you perform them well). This is most often done in companies that have teams of project managers on different projects, with the PO supporting the project managers' line manager. It is also often done on government projects where adherence to standards is both mandatory and must be auditable and provable. By its very nature this task cannot be done by the project manager.

3   **Expert support** – Tasks like planning or issue management can be done
    by a central team partially to remove the workload on project managers,
    but also to ensure a high standard is maintained. As an example – all
    competent project managers can plan – but they may not know all the
    planning features of the planning tool they use and expert support can
    help. This type of PO is often staffed by trained project managers who
    like the technical rather than people side of project management. The
    task can be done by a project manager, but the point of having
    centralised support is then removed. Centralisation ensures common
    minimum standards are achieved.

4   **Portfolio or programme control** – The most advanced of POs are
    those that not only administer but manage central plans, risk and issue
    registers and look for and manage common items across projects in
    conjunction with programme managers. They may also consolidate
    project plans and manage inter-project and programme dependencies
    and potentially do cross-project resource management. These POs may
    require the technical skills of a very good project manager, but the
    potentially valuable task they are doing really is supporting projects and
    programmes and not managing them. If this is achieved the project
    office can provide a powerful support to management, but it is in
    practice very difficult to accomplish.

If you have a small amount of administration to do, accept that this goes with
the job. If you are running a large programme or portfolio of projects – set
up a separate PO.

Culprit 7 – Communications

That the project manager should not take full responsibility for all communications may surprise some people, especially as I spent the majority of
Chapter 2 stating how important communication skills are to a project
manager. That is not in doubt. The key person responsible for communicating core information on the project such as progress, key issues and risks,
changes and so on is the project manager. However, some projects have
requirements that go beyond the need to communicate well with project
customers and project team members. Projects that have been set up to drive
things such as large organisational change activities often need much wider
communication – for example, to thousands of staff impacted across a
company. This type of communication is more akin to a marketing, journal-

istic or PR skill set than straightforward communications by a project manager to customers or team members. Under-estimating the complexity and need for really strong communications planning, structuring, development and delivery skills has undermined the outcome of many substantial programmes – especially those that impact large numbers of people.

When there is a significant communications task associated with a project then employ a professional communications manager. Even if they only support you on a part-time basis their input will be valuable.

Summary

Having looked at some areas which are close to the project manager's heart, but critically not his responsibility in all but the simplest project, what actually should he do about these? For every project manager my advice on these topics is:

- Get a basic level of competence in all of these areas – not so you can complete complex tasks in each area but so you can actively and fully interact with professionals in each of these disciplines and so you can manage them. Each of these seven culprit areas is regularly required on many projects. You may be able and have the time to complete the most basic tasks in each area – whether it is simple or small enough is a matter for your own judgement, but if you find any of these areas absorbing significant amounts of your time you are not managing the project.

- Learn when and how to engage people in each of these areas – some of them you will normally only need for parts of a project. In fact, it is very useful to have a personal network of people skilled in these areas, both to call onto your projects but also to go to for advice.

- Learn to use their language and concepts so you can manage and challenge them without doing their job. Not being responsible for a particular specialist's work does not mean you will not be responsible for the quality of the output if it affects the success of the project.

- If you do engage them make sure your project sponsor understands why it is not your task and what the specialist brings. Some of these skill sets are in short supply and can be expensive to use. If your sponsor thinks these are your roles then unless he or she understands the value they bring it can cause tension between you.

Ask yourself four questions if you are unsure whether to pick up a task or not:

1   Do you understand the task well enough to be able to fully scope out what needs to be done?

2   Do you have the knowledge and experience to complete the tasks to the quality required and without exposing the project to unnecessary risk?

3   Is the input of a professional in this area optional? (Some tasks have to be performed by qualified professionals for legal, audit or regulatory reasons.)

> Learn to use their language and concepts so you can manage and challenge them

4   Do you have the time to do this work without jeopardising your project management responsibilities?

Only if you can answer 'yes' to all four of these questions should you do it.

The mechanics of project management

The project manager's toolkit

> ### Key lesson
>
> Project management methodologies contain a rich set of approaches and tools, yet project managers frequently only apply a few of these. Do not forget the other components which on complex and risky projects will be very useful. Successful project managers have a very broad toolkit which they make use of regularly.

WHEN PEOPLE PERFORM ANY ROLE they rely on a combination of the natural skills and common sense they possess, the experience they have built up, the tools that are made available to do the role, the formal processes and procedures which define how the role is to be done, and any training they have had in using these tools and processes. This book has so far focused on improving your natural skills, strengthening your common sense, and describing experienced-based lessons.

I have largely avoided conversation on the typical project management subjects of most project management textbooks – project management organisations and roles, project management disciplines and processes, project management standards and templates, and project management tools because these are not the things that in my experience separate the great from average project manager. But now that we have reached this late chapter it is time for a quick reflection and discussion on these concerns. This chapter is not a master class in these subjects, merely a pointer to them, and an appeal to learn the relevant techniques.

If you know about delivering projects and are honest with yourself you will understand that a lot of being a good project manager is about having and applying common sense, and having an appreciation of normal good management disciplines. In saying this I am not belittling the core specialist skills of project managers – such as an ability to resource work, or to develop a plan and maintain it through the life of a project, or to resolve issues. These are fundamental things every project manager should know that will make life more structured and more reliable than simply applying common sense, and will avoid some of the pitfalls that common sense alone will not navigate around. In reality, the reason I have not focused on these is because of the ongoing success of good project management discipline and training – these things are increasingly a given and therefore do not become the differentiating factor between the average and the excellent project manager. When I started in project management a formally trained project manager was a rarity, increasingly now he or she is the norm. But even with the training and accreditation there are a few core skills that are regularly documented and in which project staff are trained, but which somehow get left behind or forgotten. And we all know project managers who have done every course under the sun, and have every qualification, who are frankly useless, and others who have picked it up as they went along, who are brilliant.

> When I started in project management a formally trained project manager was a rarity, increasingly now he or she is the norm

This chapter briefly overviews the mechanics and toolkit components of project managers. I have excluded the things that are not relevant to this book, or that are simply not differentiating factors in project managers' success. Primarily this encompasses:

◆ Creating standard forms and documents – including documents such as 'project initiation documents', and forms such as those to log issues, risks and changes.

◆ Use of common project management software – such as planning tools like Microsoft Project. Tools are very useful and can make you significantly more productive. They are not covered as the knowledge is really specific to whichever tool you have selected. More importantly, your success is actually dependent not on the tool but on the understanding of projects that you implement with it.

Additionally, I have excluded the things that are covered elsewhere in the book in a significant depth. These are essential parts of the toolkit and include:

- Planning and resourcing – including how to build a plan starting with work breakdown structures. (See Chapter 3 – judgement 2, and Chapter 5.)

- Project change control procedures – how to capture, assess, choose and implement changes with controlled risk. (See Chapter 3 – judgements 10, 11 and 15, and Chapter 7.)

- Decision making. (See Chapter 7.)

- Create weekly and monthly reports to a standard format. (See Chapter 2 – communication lesson 2.)

- Allocation of resources and management using tools such as timesheets and time recording systems. (See Chapters 5 and 8.)

So what is left? There are a number of other things, which should lie within the standard project manager's toolkit, but seem to be used inconsistently. I make no claim that these things are new or novel although my definitions here all contain my perspective on what is practically useful. What I do see is that somehow many project managers fall into one of three traps:

1 They use some of the skills – perhaps the ones they are most familiar with or like most. But they miss others pretty regularly. It is true that many of the skills here are not critical on small projects, but on large or complex programmes they can add significant value.

2 They apply the skills in an extremely complex fashion. The real talent is not to apply these tools in a highly complex fashion. It is easy to blind yourself and your team members with too much science, whereas most of these tools have their roots firmly in straightforward common sense. The great project manager therefore understands what the tool can achieve and then applies it in the simplest fashion relative to the need. This need is usually driven by the complexity and scale of the project.

3 They do not see the full toolkit as a holistic continuum, which must be adapted and used according to the situation rather than purely mechanically applied. Each of their projects has the same set of disciplines applied in exactly the same way.

To overcome these traps project managers must see the disciplines as a toolkit. Each tool should be understood, and before each project and project issue you should assess which tools to use. Comprehending how all the tools come together into the complete framework of project management skills and then applying them appropriately is essential.

The following list is a personal view. It contains thirteen skills in two groups. The first group when combined with the skills described in Chapters 5 and 7 form the core project management mechanics. The second group are supporting skills. Don't worry about the second group until you are proficient in the first.

Skills 1–7 form the core project management mechanics and as are follows:

◆ Management of assumptions.

◆ Sign off.

◆ Management of external dependencies.

◆ The time–cost–quality–scope trade-off.

◆ Basic risk and issue management.

◆ Contingency planning and triggers.

◆ Using escalation effectively.

Skills 8–13 form the supporting mechanics and are as follows:

◆ Benefits realisation.

◆ Stakeholder analysis.

◆ Use of project office.

◆ Administration and meeting management.

◆ Prioritisation.

◆ Use of project lifecycles.

Key lesson

Good project managers accept that each and every project is different, and they therefore adapt their approach accordingly – choosing which parts of the project manager's toolkit to apply in which situations – and applying them in the simplest fashion commensurate with the complexity and scale of the project.

Skills 1–7: The core project management mechanics

Skill 1 – Management of assumptions

Within every activity in everyday life we make a hundreds of assumptions. Some of these are quite reasonable, and the chance of them being false is miniscule. (For example, we assume that when we wake up in the morning there will still be air to breathe, the risk of this not being true is infinitesimal so we do not worry.) Other assumptions don't matter because the impact upon us of them being untrue is limited. (For example, I will assume the chair by my desk will be there tomorrow, I do not worry about it as if it is not I will just pull up another.) But there is a third group of assumptions that need to be looked at because there actually is a risk they may not be true, and if they are not we may be in trouble. (For example, I may assume I do not need to wear a seat belt for I will not crash my car – this needs more consideration as there is a measurable risk of having a car crash and the impact will be large!) Many, and some argue most, risks on projects are due to the assumptions that people make.

Making assumptions is not necessarily a bad thing. There are times when we cannot absolutely know an answer to something, and we cannot progress without making an assumption. In these situations the temptation in projects is often very strong to continue working by making an assumption – as otherwise we may feel we are not making progress. When this occurs it is worth challenging the situation with the question 'do we really need to make an assumption?'.

There are a couple of poor reasons for making an assumption that need to be resisted: firstly, someone may simply be too lazy to put in the effort to find the real answer, and secondly, that by making caveats around assumptions people can avoid making real commitment. So when an assumption is being proposed always check that it is not just laziness or people covering themselves from personal risk. The first is relatively easy to spot, the second is harder to identify. People, especially professional specialists like engineers and lawyers, unfortunately love to give caveats and reasons, often in the form of assumptions as to the fact that although they are giving you their best advice there are several assumptions they have had to make which may mean they are wrong. Feel no qualms about challenging them and asking if the assumptions are reasonable, why do they have to make them, and what they can do to remove them. Specialists generally do not like this, but developing work on possibly shaky foundations needs to be challenged. You are not employing specialists to build a logically great argument from whatever set of assumptions they make – they are being paid to be right.

When making an assumption for valid reasons there is normally an explicit choice between making it so you can continue to progress, or stopping your work to spend time checking the assumption. (In Chapter 4 I look at forming a judgement of when it is valid to make an assumption.) I have been involved in situations in which the assumption was so fundamental that, if wrong, the whole project was pointless. In this position it is worth putting more work into understanding the assumption even if it delays your project. As an example, I once worked on a project to deliver a new product to a customer segment which initial market research had identified. We had to make a number of assumptions about the behaviour of this group, but we did not actually test them as we thought the cost of the necessary detailed market research was too great and would take too long. However, our assumptions turned out not to be true, and unfortunately by this stage we had got quite a long way into developing a product based on them. Once they were shown to be false the product we were developing was largely pointless. A little more investment in market research at the start of the project would have avoided this problem.

So it is essential to minimise the number of assumptions you make. But there may be some left, and indeed, sometimes you should make assumptions but as a major source of risk these need to be managed and the key to managing assumptions is to:

◆ **Document them** – make them commonly visible, make sure everyone agrees with them and make sure everyone is using the same set. Simply doing this has significant power as it is fantastic the amount of clarity it can generate across the team. Regularly, when an assumption is written down, someone in the project team will challenge it, or show an alternative contradictory assumption they are making. If you do nothing else make your assumptions explicit and shared.

◆ **Challenge them** – check they are relevant and reasonable. Do you really need to make an assumption? Is the chosen assumption actually the most reasonable?

◆ **Assess them** – focus on those assumptions that are most likely to be wrong, and those that will have the most significant impact if wrong.

◆ **Give them an owner** – the owner's role is to ensure the assumption is resolved, i.e. it is turned from an assumption to a fact during the project. When it becomes a fact the risk is removed.

◆ **Set target dates to resolve them by** – each assumption must have a clear date in the project that it has to be resolved by. This can be at any point in the project, depending on the nature of the assumption. The aim here is not just to forget them. People have a tendency to list assumptions and then to forget them, using the mentality that if they are listed that in itself solves the problem. By the time the project is finished there should be no assumptions – any that are left should not have any impact on the work and were unnecessary.

◆ **Be prepared** – to manage the consequences if the assumption turns out not to be true. Your big assumptions should appear as core items in your risk management activities.

◆ **Remove critical assumptions** – if the assessment of an assumption shows there is both a major likelihood of it being wrong and there is a major impact on the project if it is wrong try to resolve it. By resolving it I mean turn it from an assumption to a fact. Sometimes with more research and analysis assumptions can be proven one way or another. If the risk to the project is big enough this is worth doing even if it delays the project.

Two examples of poor assumption management I was involved in include, firstly, a project on which we needed three days' input from an academic. The assumption was so trivial as to be missed, yet had a great impact. The academic's work was crucial to the project's success, he agreed to give it, and given it was only three days' work and we were paying well he advised us that with a couple of weeks' notice during normal working time he would be available to support us. We duly went back to him when we knew we would need his input and gave him his two weeks' notice. Unfortunately we had assumed we understood what he meant by 'normal working time'. As an academic this did not include the period from mid-June through to late September (he was working then, but abroad at summer placement in another university). We could therefore not get his input at the right time and the project was delayed as a result.

The second example was a telecommunications project I supported, which was delivering a new product which meant we had to install equipment in our customers' homes. The equipment was not attractive, but we assumed that it would be tucked away in houses and the look was unimportant. For a small fee (about £10 per home, which was not great given the equipment's cost was about £150 per home) the supplier could put a new fascia on the equipment which made it more attractive. We assumed the cost was too great for our customer, and the impact on their end customers was low. In practice, the equipment was generally placed in a visible location in the end customers' homes. It had to be re-engineered at a later date, at a much higher cost as end customers continually complained about how it looked.

In both cases, had we identified the assumptions we were making we could have better managed the situation.

Skill 2 – Sign off

Most good project management methodologies have the concept of getting some form of sign off from sponsors whenever anything major changes. This could be changes to the scope, the time to deliver, or the cost to deliver. Customers never really like doing this, but it is good practice, it is important and problems can occur if it is not done. Almost all project managers understand this. A lot don't bother to do it – when was the last time you actually got your sponsor to formally sign off a change in cost or time for a project?

When discussing such changes with a customer try not to represent it as a *fait accompli* – the customer should not simply be agreeing to an error in planning, he should be making a decision about whether to accept something or not. He therefore needs options. Additionally, check that the change is consistent with the customer's priorities on the time–cost–quality–scope trade-off.

Sign off is not simply about transferring personal risk from you as the project manager to the sponsor – this is not a constructive mindset to have. Sign off is about ensuring that when key decisions are made the signatory is treating them as a serious issue. Without sign off there is a higher risk the signatory will not fully accept what is being signed or will not put in enough effort into understanding what she is signing up to. It is also about providing a formal audit trail of decisions should you need to revisit them at any time.

Skill 3 – Management of external dependencies

Usually, complex projects have dependencies on other activities that are not within the project's scope or responsibility to deliver. This is the well-known concept of an external dependency. The questions that need to be asked in these situations are:

◆ What project or piece of work is delivering the dependency?

◆ Who is accountable for ensuring the work you are dependent upon is being delivered?

It is surprising how often project managers simply write an assumption in their scope document saying they assume that someone else is delivering it, and leave it at that. Even if the customer has accepted this point, a successful project manager does not leave it at that. If the project needs it and it is not delivered the project may fail. Failing to deliver a project because an external dependency has not been delivered may not be the project manager's fault, but it is failure nevertheless.

The balance to find here is that as delivering the dependency is not within the scope of the project it really is not the responsibility of the project manager to deliver. If, as a project manager, you try to deliver every possible dependency you may end up trying to manage too much. All you need to do is:

◆ Try to see if you can remove the dependency – some things that are seen as dependencies when further challenged are not. Find out precisely why the task in the project is dependent on this external activity. (If it is for a trivial reason it is often possible to sort this out within the confines of the project.)

◆ Ensure somebody somewhere is responsible for delivering the dependency. If no-one is, raise this with the sponsor as a significant risk you cannot resolve.

◆ Monitor delivery of the dependency by getting periodic updates on progress so you can assess the degree of risk on the project if it is not delivered on time.

◆ On critical dependencies do not simply accept statements of progress, probe the progress reports as you would any part of your own project to give yourself confidence that they are accurate.

If a dependency is crucial to the project, and you cannot identify anyone with responsibility for ensuring it is delivered, it really is a good idea at least to assess bringing it within the project's scope, even if it increases your workload.

This problem partially disappears if the project is part of a larger programme – then the management of dependencies is usually the responsibility of the programme manager. But even the largest of programmes have boundaries and resulting external dependencies.

Challenge yourself on each project, do you really understand where all your external dependencies are, and who is delivering them?

Skill 4 – The time–cost–quality–scope trade-off

In Chapter 3 we discussed how important it was to understand where the customer stands on these dimensions (time, cost, quality and scope), and what can flex. While virtually all project managers understand and pay attention to this, in practice, project managers are poor at turning it into a structured decision making process and action. Understanding what the time–cost–quality–scope trade-off means in reality, for the project you are currently running, rather than simply as a bit of project management theory, and then using this knowledge to structure and manage your project is critical for success.

Do not fall into the trap of being one of those 'heroic' project managers who delivers on time at all cost, and uses delivery to time as the single measure of success. Project managers, project management literature and business culture have unconsciously conspired to build the image of time as the only factor of importance. It sometimes is the most critical factor, but not always. Don't assume you know how important it is – ask your customer, explain the implications, and proactively use this knowledge in managing the project.

Skill 5 – Basic risk and issue management

Issue and risk management are one of the fundamental disciplines of project management. I have called this section 'basic' simply because they are such vital tools, and also because the depth of expertise required in them in most situations is quite straightforward. You can read huge books dedicated to these subjects – especially risk management, but for most projects complex risk management is not really required.

The first thing to understand about risks and issues is that their management is as much about attitude and proactive management as it is about formal process and tools.

The vital points to understand and apply for both risk and issue management are:

◆ Communicate to the project team that these are important, will be managed, and that there is a defined process.

◆ Define how you do capture them – avoiding bureaucracy. Capturing issues and risks needs to be light-touch, making sure you get the key information in a simple way. I have seen major bureaucracies being developed to capture issues and risks in which the process of capture becomes more important than their assessment. Simple paper or electronic forms capturing the following are sufficient in most cases:

- Description.

- When identified.

- Owner.

- Resultant action.

- Due by.

- Probability (risk only).

- Impact.

◆ What do you then do? Knowing your issues and risks you need to assess them and determine what action to take. Once you know what action to take it should be implemented and managed by the project manager like any other task.

◆ It needs to be an ongoing activity – project managers are often guilty of doing periodic exercises on risk and issue management, then forgetting them in between. These are continuous processes that should be part of your daily routine.

You need to be able to communicate the difference between an issue and a risk. An issue is essential something you need to resolve now to ensure progress can be made – it can usually be phrased as a question which you need to answer. A risk is a prediction of something that may potentially happen that will have an impact on the project. By understanding it in advance you have the opportunity to mitigate or remove its impact should it occur. Remember that understanding issues and risks is about driving management action not simply about collecting information or assessment.

> Good project managers have an affinity with risk

It is worth exploring risk management a little more. Good project managers have an affinity with risk. That is, not that they like it, but they have a sense for it, and they understand that on regular intervals unexpected things will occur. You can argue that project management is risk management – if nothing changed and there was no risk of anything changing once a plan was complete there would be no need to manage the project, it would just happen.

Risk management processes will help you assess and manage risks, but only if you identify them in the first place. You need to develop the ability to predict issues and risks before they arise – and plan what you need to be ready to do should they occur. The sources of risks will vary from project to project, but generically they come from five main sources:

1 Technical – risk that the deliverables being proposed cannot actually be delivered or will not work.

2 Management – risk that there are neither the management skills nor resources to deliver the project.

3 Requirement – risk that the requirements are not fully specified or not understood in the way meant by the customer.

4 Acceptance – risk that the customer will not accept the deliverables once they are complete.

5 Environment – risk that something will change or is not understood in the environment the project operates in and has an impact on the project.

You should have a mental differentiation between personal and project risks. Project risks are those things that may impact your ability to deliver – personal risks are those things that may impact your personal reputation. The reason I highlight this is that in the rush to please and be seen to be effective project managers often hide issues and risks from their customers. You may please your customer in the short run, but if the risk actually develops and the project is delayed you have done no-one any favours, and you have essentially converted what was a project risk into a personal risk. At best you look incompetent, at worst you look like a liar.

Good project managers instinctively know about the need for options when projects go wrong. Unfortunately it is a rare project that actually gets beyond the very basic step of thinking vaguely about options. Risk management should be a continuous living process in a project, not a one-off or even periodic exercise that results in a list of things in a document. The key things to do are:

◆ Where there is significant uncertainty use a phased project lifecycle that enables you to understand and manage risk as your understanding of the project expands (see skill 13, page 213).

◆ Ensure your project has a robust risk management approach, and regularly identify and review the risks that you have. The level of formality here does depend on the context. (For example, a business-critical project using novel technology with a fixed end date may require intense risk management. A project on a familiar subject, following an often repeated path with little impact if the end date is moved only needs a more *ad hoc* and lighter touch approach.) The approach to identifying risks I undertake is to run a brainstorming session at the start of the project. I then periodically regroup throughout the life of the project to reassess this, and to accept risks from team members as they become apparent throughout the project's life. Remember though that the only risks you are interested in are those that can impact the project directly and that you can manage – you are not trying to create a risk management process for the whole organisation you are working in. Be careful therefore quite how much detail you go into in environmental risks – yes, a meteorite may hit the earth and kill everyone, stopping your project, but you cannot change this or do anything about it and adding it to your risk register adds no value.

◆ Assess these risks to see if any of them result in a significant chance of something occurring with a significant impact on the project. If this is true you need to do something about the risk. You can spend a lot of time working out a scale for assessing risks, and then assessing risks against it. Almost universally I find a scale of high, medium or low for probability and impact is sufficient except on the largest of programmes.

◆ Plan what you can do about the risk. This essentially falls into four categories:

 – Maintain a watching brief – i.e. do nothing but monitor the situation and only do something if the risk increases, or the impact increases. This is a valid option if the risk is not currently impacting your work, and is really regularly monitored (and not simply written down and forgotten about).

 – Mitigate against the risk – which essentially means doing things that will reduce the risk occurring. An example of this is in the situation that there is a risk that your project will run out of funds, and so you seek agreement to a contingency budget. The risk of your running out of money has been removed.

– Mitigate against the impact of the risk – which essentially means doing things that will reduce the impact should the risk occur. An example of this in the same situation of risk that funds will run out might be to look at ways a project can be done more cheaply, or even for free using internal resources should your budget run out. In this situation the risk has occurred (you have run out of money), but the impact on the project was reduced.

– Have a contingency plan – i.e. do things now assuming it will occur. This is discussed below. You cannot have a contingency plan for every risk, but if the impact of a risk on a project is great enough, and the project is important enough you should consider having contingency plans. There is a resource-risk trade-off to be made, as even the simplest plan will absorb some additional resource. This is described more in the next sub-section.

Skill 6 – Contingency planning and triggers

Contingency planning is a complex subject, and good contingency plans require insight, creativity as well as structure. A contingency plan can be anything that you can implement to remove the impact of a risk when it occurs. Many project managers struggle when it comes to good contingency planning. The key points to think through with respect to contingency plans are:

◆ **What triggers your contingency plan?** People often assume that what will trigger a contingency plan being activated is a risk occurring. If true, this is ideal as it will avoid using up resources on something that may not be needed. Unfortunately because of the length of time they take to implement, for many contingency plans to be useful they have to be activated before a risk has occurred. The trigger may be something as simple as a date – if delivery x has not occurred by time y we will implement the contingency. Delivery x has not yet actually failed, but for the contingency plan to be effective it needs to be started at the latest by time y. There may alternatively be some other trigger related to the risk becoming more likely or having higher impact. Unless you understand when to implement the contingency plan – it is largely worthless.

◆ **Do you have the resources to implement the contingency plan?**
Here we get to the point that undermines many projects having contingency plans. Implementing contingency plans increases the chance of
success, but it will require resources. The choice a project manager has
in this situation is to take resources from the existing project with
obvious potential impacts, or ask the sponsor for more. Rare is the
sponsor who happily gives up resource to cover for something that may
not happen, remembering that in the event that a risk does not occur
and the contingency is not needed all the work on the contingency is
effectively thrown away. However, if the risk is likely enough, and if the
impact on the project is significant enough then the investment is
worthwhile. It is somewhat analogous to an insurance premium – you
hope you won't need it, if you don't, the money can be said to be
wasted – but when you do need it you will be very glad of it.

◆ **Does it actually reduce risk?** This may seem obvious, but I have
frequently seen contingency plans that are far riskier than the original
project. In the desperation to find a contingency I have seen people
come up with all sorts of creative (but in reality hare-brained) ideas.
The point is that people will often have the best solution in the project
and if a contingency plan has a lower risk solution this should have been
adopted by the project in the first place. If a contingency plan is more
risky than the original plan it may work (as even in a 99% chance of
failure situation you may happen to be in the 1% than succeeds),
however, it is not a good sign. An effective, worthwhile contingency
needs to be significantly less risky than the original plan. A simple
example: if you absolutely have to get somewhere and your car is not
very reliable then you may make a contingency plan based on alternative
transport, but if this is even more unreliable than your car there is no
reduction of risk.

◆ **What can you de-scope if the choice is not delivering?** What often
makes contingency plans less risky is that they rely on delivering only a
subset of the full set of deliverables already planned. This may not
achieve all the success factors of the project and may not be popular
with your customers who will see most components of the project as
'must haves'. However, if people are faced with the choice of de-scoping
or having nothing at all it is remarkable how easy they find it to reduce
the list of 'must haves'.

Skill 7 – Using escalation effectively

Escalation is a core weapon in the project manager's armoury of tools to get things done. It can be used to get involvement of senior people (for example, to get more resources or decisions made), it can also simply be used as a threat to recalcitrant team members. I do not advise too much use of the latter as it is a sign of weak management – but used occasionally and sparingly it can be very powerful. Many project managers are either reluctant to escalate as they see it as failure, or, more commonly, use escalation as a dumping ground for everything they either cannot do or for some reason will not do.

Good escalation is used sparingly, but it is used. Your sponsor or other senior person to escalate to is a part of the project too and will have to do some work from time to time. As discussed in Chapter 4 developing a judgement of appropriate times to escalate is a fundamental understanding a project manager must develop.

When you do decide you need to escalate, put yourself in the shoes of the person who you are escalating to. Gather the information this person will need to help you and do it at the earliest opportunity. For example, if you cannot get a person allocated to your project who you think you need you may escalate to a senior manager to get them released to you. The first thing the senior manager is likely to ask you is what this person is doing now and what the impact would be of stopping that job to work on your project. To save time and appear more professional it is best to be able to answer questions like these straight away.

> **Good escalation is used sparingly, but it is used**

While it is important not to be over-ready to escalate – once it is necessary it needs to be done straight away. The person you are escalating to has the right to expect some time to think things through and receive notice of problems. There is nothing that irritates senior people more than being forced into a corner at the last moment because you have sat on an issue for too long.

When you have escalated, remember you are still the project manager. Just because the item for resolution is with someone more senior does not remove your responsibility to manage the attainment of that resolution like any other task on the project.

Your attitude with regard to escalation should be to see it as a supporting aid to you and the project team and you should limit its use as a threat or weapon. For example, when someone had no time to allocate to your work do not threaten them with escalation as if they will get hit over the head, present it to them as an aid that will enable them legitimately to focus on your work with their manager's support.

Skills 8–13: Supporting mechanics

Skill 8 – Benefits realisation

As projects are undertaken to achieve some benefits, it is therefore not surprising that there is increasing interest in formally tracking the benefits as a measure of success for a project. This is generally a good idea in theory, but in practice is often much harder to do than people realise. There are few formally defined mechanisms for benefits tracking – and given that benefits may be defined in almost infinite ways it is unlikely that a single robust process for tracking benefits will ever exist.

There are four problems with being sure that benefits have been achieved, and formally measuring them in some form of benefits tracking approach:

1 Benefits are often simply difficult to measure. For example, incremental operational efficiency improvements in a complex organisation that are due to a project may be very hard to track. How would you measure the 1.3% efficiency improvement, I saw in one project's business case, in your own work?

2 It is usually difficult to be sure that it was the project that delivered the benefits and not some other change elsewhere. In most organisations there are hundreds or even thousands of small changes being implemented all the time. How can you be sure that the benefits achieved are due to your project and not one of the other changes occurring in parallel?

3 They typically only arise after the project has been completed. If a project will deliver cost savings over three years, then you can only be sure that the benefits have been achieved three years later. By this time the project manager and the project team members are probably dispersed, doing work on something else, somewhere else.

4 Benefits are generally only roughly estimated at the start of a project. Even if a full and detailed business case has been developed it is usually riddled with untested assumptions. These types of estimated benefits are

good for providing guidance, but poor for providing an accurate target – they can equally well under-estimate benefits as well as over-estimate them. (I find that often in the drive to get pet projects approved a sponsor may be over-optimistic when judging benefits, and then commit the project team to delivering them.)

Additionally, measuring benefits can unfortunately drive as much bad behaviour as good if the measures and incentives to hit them are poorly thought through. (For example, if your project is to deliver a headcount reduction in a company, and you are measuring and rewarding people based on achieving this they may only focus on the headcount reduction at the cost of everything else.) The answer here is to apply a balanced set of benefit measures – but again this takes time and effort.

If well thought through and with sufficient effort benefits realisation can be achieved, and can be a very positive force driving success on a project. The activities to perform if you are going to track benefits are:

◆ Define well-estimated benefits at the start of the project. If you are going to track them and measure success against them it is worth really putting in effort to get the benefits reasonable and clear in the first place. Any assumptions made should be tracked through the project assumption management process.

◆ Ensure it is possible to measure these benefits. Projects can be done to achieve unmeasurable benefits, but you cannot track them. A benefit such as a cost saving is conceptually easy to track, something like staff satisfaction is somewhat harder, and benefits like improved company reputation are almost impossible to measure incremental improvements in.

◆ Assign resources and responsibility for measuring the benefits. It is a task that will take some time and will not happen unless someone is assigned to doing it.

◆ Set expectations about how much benefit will be achieved during the lifetime of the project and agree with the project sponsor how benefits will be tracked after the project has been completed.

Behaviour on projects will frequently improve when people know the end results will be robustly and formally measured and tracked. Do it, but do not fall into the trap of under-estimating the difficulty of this task.

Skill 9 – Stakeholder analysis

Formal stakeholder analysis approaches are a useful tool for any manager, but especially for a project manager. The basic principles of assessing people's attitude towards a project (from very negative to very positive), and their power to influence the outcome can give a powerful picture of who you need to work with, and, bluntly, who you can ignore. Successful projects need sponsors and advocates and need to ensure that those who oppose the outcome are either brought on board or that their influence is managed away.

Many project managers have at best a limited theoretical knowledge of stakeholder analysis and at worst no knowledge of it at all. Really strong management of stakeholders is not required on all projects and on some can be pretty much ignored. However, on projects like organisational change or others that impact large numbers of people, or on those that have some faction opposed to them, assessment of the stakeholders and planning of positive actions to change their view or mitigate their actions can be essential.

The basis of stakeholder analysis is so simple as to almost make one wonder why it is so useful. Essentially, it relies on categorising stakeholders according to how much impact they can have on a project, and how favourably they view the project. (Do not fall into the trap of thinking that this conceptually simple task is easy to do – it can take real effort on a major project.) I always stick to a very simple four-way split – people roughly fall into the following four categories:

1 High impact, high support – use these people to get resources and drive support for the project. Your sponsor must be within this group, if not the project will be problematical.

2 High impact, low support – powerful people who oppose the project are the ones you must most actively manage. Think about what you can do to get their support, or, if this is not possible, mitigate against any activity they may do to oppose the project.

3 Low impact, high support – people who support the work, but have little real influence on its outcome. Use these people to help you get work delivered.

4 Low impact, low support – people who oppose the work, but have little real influence on its outcome. Formal processes will indicate how you need to convince these people. My view is you need to monitor them in case their influence increases, but otherwise you can ignore

them. (The main exception here is on organisational change or other programmes where people generally may need to accept the change and deliverables if it is to be a success. Then this group must be managed very carefully.)

Skill 10 – Use of project office

All project managers are aware of project offices, although many will have wildly different experiences of them. When do you need one, and what does it do?

Whatever the theoretical literature and methodologies may state project offices in practice come in one of four types (which are defined in more detail in Chapter 9):

1 Administration pools.

2 Process police.

3 Expert support.

4 Portfolio and programme control (information consolidators).

So the simple answer about what it will do depends on what it has been set up to do. You may set up a project office to carry out some specific tasks for you on your project, alternatively if you are working for a programme manager or a corporate project management function there may be a project office already existing that performs a defined task.

The issues to think through on project offices are:

◆ Do you understand what you may want the project office to do? Be clear about why you need it and what it will do for you and the project. If it is just to do some administrative work for you, get an administrator or PA. You should understand how the work will split between yourself and the project office. A typical example might be:

   – Setting report formats and schedule – project office.

   – Collecting, chasing on reports – project office.

   – Analysis of reports – project manager.

   – Deciding on action – project manager.

   – Managing action – project manager.

   – Report quality assessments (timelines, format, etc.) – project office.

◆ Will this make you more efficient or effective? It may seem very obvious, but unless it actually aids you it is not worth setting up. I have seen many project offices simply blindly enforcing some project bureaucracy, to become more of a hindrance than a help to project managers.

◆ Who has access to the project office resource? Once a project office is set up you will be surprised how many people want it to pick up support work for them. To avoid overload you need to be clear about who can and who cannot use the project office.

◆ Does everyone else understand what it does? Project offices can be seen as an unnecessary overhead unless people understand the value that they bring to the project.

Skill 11 – Administration and management of meetings

Administration generally is a bit of a bug-bear for project managers. Yet irrespective of whether you have a project office or not, being well organised and having good project administration is a significant factor in project success. Project managers without support often complain about the administrative burden and that they are not simply administrators. This is true, a project manager is not an administrator and it is not a good use of an experienced project manager's skills to dedicate them to administration. But you must be prepared to do some administration and do it in a well structured way. The sorts of administrative duties that must be in place are:

◆ Document control and document management:
  – What information is required, in what format, and how often is it updated.
  – Who owns the document and is responsible for change control.
  – Where is it stored, etc.

◆ Schedules and formats for regular reports.

◆ Meeting schedules, set up and arrangement.

◆ Diary management for project team members.

◆ Running standard business operational processes – procurement and purchase requisitions, room bookings, etc.

◆ Others depending on the nature of the project. Typical administrative tasks I come across regularly are access to stationery, building access and passes, arranging desk space and PCs, travel and hotel bookings, collating and analysing timesheets.

Although administration may not seem that glamorous to project managers it needs to be seen as the oil that keeps the machine of a project running. Working on a poorly administered project is painful and inefficient. If the administrative overhead is large then look for support or set up a project office. Developing an understanding of the administrative requirements and therefore the administrative resource and process needs of your project will enhance your delivery.

The management of meetings is an ability most people need – you can argue whether this is a type of administration or a general management skill. As a project manager you will need to set up and run many meetings, and the better you are at it the less time you will waste. Also, you may need to develop and coach meeting management skills within the team. Meetings can be a productive and efficient way to communicate and even to develop deliverables, but if poorly managed and set up they can eat vast quantities of time for no discernible benefit. Projects can develop a culture of continuous meetings which is rarely productive. Some simple points I try to keep to are as follows:

> **Meetings can be productive, but they waste huge amounts of time**

- Start by thinking through why you want this meeting. Is it to communicate, is it to generate agreed actions, is it to develop some deliverables? Meetings can be productive, but they waste huge amounts of time, so, before you have one, check with yourself that it is necessary.

- Always have an agenda – even if it is a short meeting.

- Makes sure the materials and people you need are available.

- Be clear why you have invited people and what you expect of them. Do not invite people just for the sake of it. Brief them prior to coming about what is expected of them and what they are expected to bring.

- Plan for yourself what you want the outcome from the meeting to be, what you expect the outcome to be, and what actions you need to take in the meeting to get your desired outcome.

- Agree who will run the meeting and who takes the minutes – this does not need to be you. In fact, in many meetings it should not be you as you may need to be focusing on being a contributor rather than having time to take the minutes.

◆ Avoid continually changing diary times and locations for meetings – it can significantly disrupt the flow of work.

◆ Encourage plenty of regular informal communications – often this can avoid many meetings.

◆ Follow up on actions.

◆ Take a few moments at the end of every meeting to get feedback on whether it was successful or not. This can seem like overkill but if done quickly will develop your skills and understanding of and rapport with the meeting participants.

◆ For regular, fixed meetings have decision criteria for when they stop happening. The world of business is full of scheduled meetings that should have been stopped long ago. The criteria can be a date, when something is achieved or when conditions change.

◆ Consider meetings as part of your work – if they are not contributing in some way, stop them.

◆ Keep them as short as possible.

Skill 12 – Prioritisation

The ability to prioritise work is a general management skill and as such is not often thought of as specifically part of the project management skill set. Project managers must have a good understanding of the principles and practice of prioritising work, as without it you cannot be sure you are actually working on the most important or urgent piece of work at any one point in time. Project managers need to be aware of prioritisation because:

◆ There are normally fewer resources in a project than are required to do everything possible. Project managers need to prioritise between the various tasks team members may do. If you do not do this team members will regularly do things that are of lesser importance – as their view of priorities may differ from yours. If you are ever on a project with more resource than you need then you may feel lucky, but you are usually not being ambitious enough in what you can complete.

◆ Projects themselves are normally part of a larger prioritisation of activities that goes on within organisations. It is of substantial value to understand this process and where the project you are running sits within the overall prioritisation system. The ability to use and manage an organisation's priority system will ease your access to resources significantly.

Prioritisation is logically very simple. Everyone understands the idea that some tasks need to be done before others – and the idea of having a 'list' of activities ranked in priority order. In practice, prioritisation of complex workloads which are being done to achieve a wide variety of goals is a significant task in its own right. Factors to consider when prioritising are:

◆ The first question you must ask yourself is on what basis are you prioritising? If the prioritisation is for a few tasks then you may not need explicit criteria and management 'gut' reaction may be sufficient – but once prioritisation becomes complex you need to have some measure by which to form the basis of prioritisation. This may be to take on the highest 'value' tasks first, or those that deliver the most important customer requirements. Without this, prioritisation risks becoming simply a mechanism for vested interests to push their work first.

◆ The ideal prioritisation results in a list of each activity ranked against every other activity you may need to perform. As a result you can start by completing the task ranked at number one, then do that ranked at number two and so on until you have completed the whole list. It is a nice piece of theory, but prioritisation like planning is a tool, not an end in itself. Attempts to prioritise everything against everything else often consume so much time and resource as to make the prioritisation activity such a major piece of work in its own right that it does not get completed. The answer is to go for broad, simple categorisation of tasks that everyone understands. The categories I typically use are:

  – Must do, cannot slip – tasks that must be done and must be done on time. There should be only a few of these around which you build your plans. If you have a large number you are normally not prioritising critically enough.

  – Must do, can allow to slip to a limited extent – tasks that must be done, and have a target time to complete, but if they slip by a few days it will not cause major problems. Many tasks normally fall into this category.

  – Must do, time can move – tasks that must be done, but which you have significant leeway over when they are done. Such tasks do need to be done so they cannot languish forever at the bottom of your priorities. These are useful items on your plans as they give you great flexibility, but in reality there are not usually too many tasks like this.

- Optional, but important – tasks that do not absolutely need to be done, but it would be very good if they were. With normal levels of resourcing you should be able to complete these, but they may wait until the end of the project. If people are truly honest, in reality most tasks on most plans fall into this category. These are the things we really want, but the world will not stop if we do not get them.

- Optional, not critical – nice-to-haves that will only be done if there is time and resource left. We have to be realistic, normally these do not get done unless you are running a very well-resourced project.

◆ Such a categorisation allows flexible planning of activities. I avoid prioritisations along generic, undefined categories (such as ranking projects against a simple scale of priority 1, 2 or 3). These systems often add as much confusion as help. Ask yourself, what does priority '1' mean? What you will find with systems like this is that 90% of activities end up as priority 1, which really means you have not done any prioritisation.

◆ Having made a priority list, be prepared for a reasonable degree of volatility and to respond to escalation requests. If activities can be escalated you should agree who has final say over priorities. Within a project it should be the project manager or possibly the project sponsor. If it is part of a wider prioritisation activity you may need to set up a senior steering committee to own the priorities. Senior managers should support it – after all a key part of being a senior manager is making decisions about resource allocation – in other words prioritisation. If anyone does want to change a priority the mindset to make sure everyone has is that anything can be prioritised higher, but something else must come lower. Pretending this is not true is kidding yourself.

◆ Make sure the prioritisation is explicit; ensure everyone is working to the same list. If you do not do this you cannot assume everyone will intuitively work to the same set of priorities, it simply will not happen. There is no point in one half of a project team doing half a task, if the other half of the project team is working on half of a different task. We all prioritise intuitively all the time, and sometimes even subconsciously, but the result is often that we do the easiest tasks first rather than those of highest priority.

◆ Be ruthless in applying priorities once they are agreed. There is always too much to do. Do not be surprised when people say they will not do a task because it is too low priority – this is not a problem, this is the system working. Alternatively, do not be surprised if people keep working on low priority activities ignoring the priority list because of personal interest. This needs to be rooted out and normally a bit of management direction will stop this, but at extreme should result in disciplinary activity. (That sounds harsh but I have worked in many organisations where specialists like engineers love to tinker on their own pet interests at the cost of not doing what is an organisation's priority work.) The only valid exception to this rule is that people can work on lower priority work if it is the only work relevant to their skill set. For example, if you are a C++ programmer and the only project requiring C++ skills is a low priority one then this is obviously the one you must work on. This type of detail implication of prioritisation can make resource planning and scheduling very complex.

◆ Do not confuse how urgent a task is with how important it is. Some very important tasks can wait – some minor tasks must be done now. Be careful though that your set of urgent tasks never ends and so important tasks never get started – sooner rather than later you will need to do the important tasks even if this means dropping a less important but urgent task. This makes setting priorities intellectually harder, but you do need to be aware of the difference.

◆ Agree what you do with low priority tasks. Do they literally wait until all higher priority tasks are complete, or will some of them move up the priority list over time?

◆ Consider the time–cost–quality–scope trade-off when setting priorities. You do not have to perform each activity to the same level of quality or depth so you can get through your list more quickly if you flex on these points. Some tasks have a high priority to be completed in a minimal sense, but completing them to the maximum possible scope is not so important.

Good prioritisation is hard work, needs some critical thinking through, and challenges many people's views – if you find it easy it probably means you are not being aggressive enough. It means letting go of things we may really want. It also means making tough decisions. But when prioritisation is done well it can make you significantly more efficient and effective.

> **Do not confuse how urgent a task is with how important it is**

Skill 13 – Use of project lifecycles

Competent project managers understand and use various project lifecycles. I define a lifecycle as a structured definition of the sequential flow of a project through some standard stages. These lifecycles tend to vary either from industry to industry or by the type of project, but the basic principles that underlie them are the same. What you must be able to do is:

◆ Understand the principles of different lifecycles and apply them as appropriate.

◆ Be able to use the correct language on lifecycles for the context you are working in.

◆ Vary the lifecycle to suit the nature of the project you are running.

The advantage of utilising a standard lifecycle is that it enables you to 'quick start' your planning taking previous examples of approaches used. There are, for example, in many organisations standard checklists of activities to do within different phases of a project. I am opposed to the rigid use of checklists as every project is different, but I am very keen on them as a tool to help the project manager think through what needs to be done. Lifecycles also provide a good language set to communicate to your stakeholder group and project team members about the shape and progress of the project. For example, telling someone the title of specific activities you are performing this week may not enlighten them much on project progress, but saying you are in the testing phase, or doing requirements capture may help them understand better.

The classic lifecycle for projects has different terms in different situations, but taking the example of the software development project it is typically:

◆ **Project initiation** – which covers the activities I described in Chapters 3 and 5.

◆ **Requirements analysis and capture** – the detailed analysis of your customer's needs and the conversion of these into a documented requirements specification.

◆ **Feasibility** – a review of the requirements to determine how long the project will take and how much it will cost, and potentially whether it is possible. (This is discussed below.)

◆ **Solutions design** – designing the solution to the requirements.

◆ **Solutions build** – developing and building the solution.

◆ **Implementation** – taking the developed solution and implementing it within the environment it will operate in.

◆ **Test** – formally testing the solution. This may cover technical testing, operational testing, as well as acceptance with the customer.

◆ **Handover** – handing over the solution to the customer. This typically has a period of more focused support and ensures that users can utilise the deliverables while the project team is still available to help them with any problems that may arise.

◆ **Project closure** – includes finishing off any outstanding activities, reviewing the results to learn from the experience for the next project and releasing resources.

For each project the length and complexity of each of these stages is completely dependent on its objectives and the context in which it exists. One of the skills of a good project manager is to consider what lifecycle is required in different situations. Five specific situations in which different lifecycles help are:

1 When requirements cannot be clarified or are unstable – as the customer does not have a full vision of them.

2 Where the problem is fully understood but there is no known solution to it.

3 Where there is significant risk or uncertainty about a project and it is not possible to plan accurately. Alternatively, you can plan but your customer requires more information before committing to the project.

4 Where the impact of the solution being incorrect or not working properly is very high.

5 Where you need benefits and impact quickly even though the overall project is large.

I discuss each of these in turn.

The solution to uncertain, unstable or continuously evolving requirements can be simply to spend a huge amount of time capturing the requirements. This can work, but usually it is frustrating, expensive and can be demoralising. An alternative is to consider developing *prototypes*. This is common in the software development industry. A set of requirements is quickly captured without worrying too much whether they are complete or fully accepted by the customer. A prototype is built to expand on a concept, and to provide a basis to flesh out further requirements. It is often easier to change and expand an existing prototype, than to visualise it completely in your head. Some software is effectively now developed as a continuous line of prototypes, with each iteration improving on the previous version. While no version is perfect it gives the customer a solution quickly, which can then be improved upon. A development lifecycle can then rapidly iterate between requirements capture and development several times.

When a customer understands a problem, but has no solution to it, it is obviously not effective to start to try to deliver a solution. It may be obvious, but it is what is often proposed. Rather than doing this split the project into two high level stages. The first is a *solutions analysis phase*. This is really a project in its own right, the deliverable from which is a solutions concept, and potentially a more detailed design for it. Such a project typically has a lifecycle such as:

◆ **Problem analysis** – gaining a full understanding of the problem with the aim of being able to simply and comprehensively define it.

◆ **Solutions generation** – developing a set of possible solutions to the problem. There is normally many ways to solve any problem.

◆ **Selection criteria development** – developing a set of criteria to choose a solution against.

◆ **Solutions selection** – choosing the solution against the chosen criteria.

Where time is pressing a solutions analysis phase can often be efficiently and effectively run as a series of workshops. The second phase of the project, to implement the selected solution, can be run along a more standard lifecycle as described at the start of this section.

Another reason for keeping the solutions selection and the solution implementation phases of the project separate is that it is not until the solution has been chosen that it is possible to determine confidently how long the implementation will take, nor how much it will cost.

Where there is significant risk or the customer wants to know more before committing to a project, a *feasibility phase* can be put into the lifecycle. During feasibility essentially more time is spent in deepening understanding of the project, developing more detailed plans, and potentially doing some testing to see if the solution is actually possible. Many projects do not have a formal feasibility phase, or when it is covered the feasibility is used primarily as a planning and scoping exercise. For higher risk projects I always insist on a formal feasibility stage with an explicit decision at the end as to whether to continue with the project.

Performing a feasibility study is essentially a risk management step – with it you can:

◆ Reduce uncertainty in the plans.

◆ Identify specific risks that need to be managed.

◆ Clarify where you need contingency plans.

◆ Build a project plan accordingly.

You will have to do these activities anyway when you do your planning, whether or not it is explicitly called feasibility. The advantage of doing a feasibility study is that it makes this process explicit and at the end of it you can put a clear decision point for your customer to decide on the project, having much fuller information on the degree of risk and resulting time and resource requirements. You can also then build any necessary contingency plans into your schedule and resource estimates. By priming your customer up front that you will be coming to a decision point like this at the end of the feasibility phase where estimates and approach need to be revisited you manage expectations better. Feasibilities never give absolute certainty, but they do reduce risk. The length and depth of the feasibility is a function of how risky the situation is or how much appetite for risk your customer has, hence the lower the risk and the higher the level of risk your customer is willing to take, the shorter the feasibility can be.

Where the impact of the solution being incorrect or not working properly is very high then you should look at the *testing lifecycle* you have implemented. Testing may be a short and simple activity, but where essential testing has a complex lifecycle of its own. Preparing for testing can start very early on in a project. A typical testing lifecycle may be:

◆ Development of test acceptance criteria – what needs to happen for the solution to pass the tests. An example of acceptance criteria for software may be that the software has to pass 100% of the mandatory tests, 90% of the optional tests and have fewer than ten minor bugs in it.

◆ Development of detailed test scripts – defining the detailed actions that will happen in the test.

◆ Optionally – factory acceptance tests (FAT), and site acceptance tests (SAT) when you have equipment or supplies being produced in a third party location.

◆ Unit test – testing each component of the solution separately.

◆ Integration test – testing all the components of the solution together.

◆ User acceptance test – getting users to use the solution and checking that they accept it meets their needs.

◆ Operational testing – a final phase when the solution is integrated into the wider environment to see that it can, in practice, work with all other activities required.

At each of the test phases a solution can fail which means further development work is required. Additionally, for projects involving things like the launch of a new product it is usually sensible to include a trial phase. Trialling of products is a skill that marketing professionals have developed detailed expertise in. In essence, in this phase the product is actually taken out to prospective customers who can trial it. In this way you gain feedback as to product acceptability. Potentially this can include charging a customer for the product to understand pricing acceptance and sensitivities.

Finally, where you have a need for benefits or impact quickly from what is a very large project consider breaking the project down into many smaller *phases*. Each phase is a complete project in its own right. Alternatively, plan regular milestones on the project, at which point you should be delivering something that has external value to the customers. This often seems quite hard – but with some creative thinking is normally achievable in practice. Analyse the development process to identify partial deliverables of use to the customer and brainstorming 'quick wins' can form the basis of this approach. Customers often will not trust, usually based on good experience, the mega-project that delivers nothing of value to them for eighteen months. They will be far happier with a series of incremental value adding deliverables at regular intervals. It develops trust with your customer group if you can do this, and returns value to the business you are operating in more quickly. These interim deliverables do not need to be huge, but must explicitly be valued by the customer.

What more can you learn?

I have presented a broad body of knowledge you can build up to enhance your ability to deliver projects. Good project managers are constantly expanding their skills and learning from experience. This is beneficial, but in enhancing your knowledge do not loose sight of common sense and judgement, the bedrocks of project management.

> **Good project managers are constantly expanding their skills**

To learn you must be open to learning and be honest with yourself when things have gone wrong – or could have gone better. This personal honesty and ability to understand what has happened, not always to look for external reasons but to question yourself about what you could have done differently, lies at the bottom of true personal growth.

If you do want to expand your skills think in terms of the following categories to seek knowledge, training and exposure to:

◆ The human and 'soft' skills identified specifically in this book.

◆ Enhanced technical project management skills beyond those in this chapter. Your skills need to be sufficient for the complexity and scale of projects you are running. If you are running larger and larger programmes then it is worth looking at more in-depth training in areas such as risk management, estimating and powerful approaches such as the critical chain method. (Remember the lesson from the start of this chapter though – keep the processes you implement as simple as you can for the scale of project you are running.)

◆ Supporting skills. There are a host of supporting skills which will enhance your ability to work as a project manager. Included in this I place financial awareness, business case development, negotiation and presentation skills.

◆ Tools. Understand the full capabilities of the software tools available and what specific processes and algorithms they implement.

◆ Contextual knowledge. Certain industries require significant contextual knowledge. As I discussed in Chapter 9 you do not need to be an expert in all the areas you are managing, but you do have to be able to understand the concepts and use the language and jargon of the industry you are working in.

If you want to read more about project management, especially the mechanics, I recommend three particular texts to look at.

One of the most influential thinkers in this area in the past few years is Eliyahu Goldratt, for example in:

◆ *Critical Chain*, Eliyahu M. Goldratt, North River Press Publishing Corporation.

A couple of general project management texts which I think cover the mechanics of project management quite comprehensively. The contents overlap and it is a matter of personal taste as to which you prefer:

◆ *Project Workout*, Robert Buttrick, FT Prentice Hall.

◆ *Practical Project Management, Tips, Tactics and Tools*, Harvey A. Levine, John Wiley.

My final advice is to develop trust in your own judgement. As I have stressed on many occasions in this book every situation is different. If the specific situation you are working in has unique characteristics and needs alternative approaches – trust yourself, decide an approach, use it, and learn from the results.

11

Knowing when to say 'no'

HAVING SPENT THE PREVIOUS TEN CHAPTERS outlining some hints, tips, lessons and general advice on how to get into the master class of project management it may seem odd to be approaching the end of the book with a chapter on when you should avoid a project altogether. But some things are just not meant to happen. No matter how well the work is planned, how well structured the team is, or how inspirational the sponsor some projects are just never going to come to a successful conclusion. As a project manager these are the times to keep your head low and avoid the work, or speak up firmly against it – for project management is about ensuring delivery, not about pointless heroics against unassailable odds.

When things are not going to happen it is best to avoid them, or better still, and perhaps more constructively, ensure they are killed off before they get anywhere. There is no shame in constructively stopping bad ideas, or ensuring that unimplementable good ideas are killed off. No matter how well you do it, you will not get to be a great or successful project manager spending your whole life brilliantly failing to deliver impossible projects. A useful skill is therefore knowing when to say 'no', and equally important how to say 'no'. This final chapter looks at those tell tale signs that should make you at least think of whether the project is a flier or should be grounded for good.

When do you actually need a project manager?

Key lesson

Just because someone thinks they need a project manager it neither means they really do, nor does it mean it is actually the best use of your time.

Before having a discussion about when projects should not be recommended to proceed it is worth reflecting on the situations in which you actually do not need a project manager in the first place. Is it, in fact, your problem to solve? Project managers get asked to do all sorts of work, some of which is not really an appropriate use of their skills or time. This classically happens with inhouse project management teams within companies who get a reputation as reliable sets of hands to sort things out. My argument is that unless those 'things' are really projects, and relevant prioritised projects, a project manager is not really the best person to solve the issue or be put in charge of the work. Before accepting project work it is worth considering:

◆ **Is this the best use of the project manager?** Project management is a skill set in short supply in many situations, project managers should therefore be used on the highest priority projects only. It is worth reviewing whether you put the other possible projects you could be working on in comparison to the one on offer would any of the others be more important?

◆ **Does this project manager have the right sort of skills?** A specific project manager may be a great project manager, but may have no relevant experience in the subject being delivered. As discussed earlier, an IT project manager would probably be a high risk option for managing the delivery of a major road construction programme!

◆ **Is this really a project-based activity?** Project managers often give people a feeling of comfort that someone is managing the work, especially if no-one else has that direct responsibility. If it is not a project though this is not a good use of project manager skills. A typical example of misuse of project managers I have regularly seen is for fault and complaint resolution. Organisations start getting faults from customers, or complaints, and the nature of the resolution crosses many departmental boundaries. They have no formal fault and complaint mechanisms – or they are not working properly. The only people who regularly work across departmental boundaries are project managers, hence the logic is 'let's use a project manager to resolve the issues'. These cross-departmental 'business as usual' activities often get pushed in the project manager's way. If as a project manager you accept this type of work do so because you feel it is important and not because you are really working as a project manager.

Knowing the danger signals

Key lesson

There are many clear indications when a project is likely to fail – look for these and assess whether you are able to manage the risks or not.

If you have got through the first section let us assume the activity you are working on is legitimately a project you should be managing. Is it still sensible to accept the work? There are a number of danger signals that should make your ears prick up and start your mental risk management process firing. There are no absolute rules or algorithm that can be applied to find out deterministically whether these factors are so bad as to kill the project off, or simply that they are factors that need to be managed through your risk management approach. The only way to really tell is to use your judgement – don't rely on gut feel as it can be wrong, but use it to trigger more analysis and don't ignore it all together as it normally has some reason for being there.

Don't rely on gut feel as it can be wrong

In no priority or order of importance, the danger signs I look for are:

◆ **No energy** – the team and the sponsor seem apathetic towards the end goal. No matter how important something is, if no-one cares it is unlikely to be successfully completed.

◆ **No real drive or sponsorship** – the project seems a low priority after-thought to the sponsor. Any significant project either using a large amount of resources or resulting in a significant change on a company needs senior sponsorship and support throughout the project. Alarm bells should ring if the main sponsor treats the role of being sponsor like an honorary degree – as a symbol of seniority rather than having to do anything on the project.

◆ **No willingness to free up the right resources** – how many times have I seen senior managers, on one hand, excitedly banging on about how important a project is, only to be giving, a few minutes later, reasons why good people, or money cannot be allocated! If it is important the resources need to be freed up, if they are not – then the project is not important! It really is that simple. Of course, managers must prioritise their demands, but if your project is so low priority that you cannot get access to the right resources suggest it is put on hold until the resources are available.

◆ **Overly demanding customers with unreasonable expectations** – check out your customers expectations at the beginning of the project. If they expect to achieve significantly more than you think is possible, or do it in less time or with fewer resources, then you need to challenge them. It is worth understanding the rational for their beliefs as sometimes there can be new and innovative ways of doing things that achieve substantially more than traditional methods. Also, a challenge is often a good thing, and some managers will challenge simply to test how robust the thinking and planning behind the project are. But there are limits. More often than not the driver for unreasonable expectations is simply that the customer needs a huge amount and only has limited resources. I'm afraid that in this situation you need to get your head clearly accepting the fact that just because they want a miracle does not mean it will happen (even if you don't put it quite so bluntly to your customer!). Try to manage expectations to a more sensible place.

◆ **Customers with fixed ideas and a lack of listening skills** – customers regularly have ideas and views about how a project should be run. Your role as the project manager includes determining how to deliver the project. In doing this listen to your customers – sometimes their ideas can be helpful and provide creative help to you as the project manager. On other occasions they can be wrong or unworkable. If poor ideas come from customers who are rigidly fixated on them, or who seem incapable of listening to your input then tread carefully.

◆ **Conflicting goals** – or too many goals. An example could be to achieve a cost saving by reducing staff numbers and at the same time improve staff morale. As a project manager you not only need to understand the goals, but also need to have belief that they are achievable. At the very least conflicting goals need to be challenged, and if you cannot remove the conflict at least try to have the goals prioritised. In the example stated, ask the customer which is more important, the cost saving or the staff morale? You need to know which one is more important in case the conflict between the goals becomes real and it is not possible to achieve both. If you cannot do this you are dealing with an unreasonable customer.

◆ **Conflicting customers** – many projects do not have a single customer but a group of people who act as a sponsoring board. If this team seems to want very different things from the project and spend more time arguing between themselves than helping the project to progress this is a bad sign. If the conflict is because of differing opinions and it can be worked through then that is fine. If the conflict is because the project will impact vested interests you will need to find powerful support.

◆ **Poor understanding of requirements** – to deliver a customer must understand what he wants. It is perfectly acceptable for the requirements to be hazy if the customer is willing to invest in real analysis of requirements, or in activities such as prototyping which can drive out a better understanding of needs. However, if the poor understanding of requirements is combined with a 'just get on and do it' attitude then there is a significant risk of failure to deliver against expectations.

◆ **Lack of flexibility to plan** – you will not be able to estimate how long a project will take and how much it will cost until you have scoped and planned the work (and even then it still remains an estimate subject to risk). In many situations customers have real or perceived constraints on time and cost – the project must be complete in six months or less, it cannot cost more than £250k. This is the real world and as a project manager you must learn to work within these types of constraints, however, you are not a miracle worker. Working within such constraints is only possible if they are reasonable or you have the opportunity to flex scope and deliverable quality.

◆ **Not enough time to test** – the project's customer accepts the need to develop things but will not accept time for steps like testing that are there to ensure the quality of the output. Without testing the end results will often be very flaky. Testing time, as it usually sits at the end of a project, often gets compressed as a way of shortening delivery times. Also, it is not always intuitively obvious why you need testing. If you have an engineering background the need for testing is so inbuilt as to be unquestioned. If your customer has a background like accounting or marketing to them it is not so obvious. (For example, when an accountant or marketer has done some work it may be discussed or checked by their line manager, but it is not normally formally tested.) It is not only technical testing that is critical – user acceptance testing and operational readiness testing are critical tasks. They may think 'if you developed it properly in the first place why do you need to test'. If you cannot convince them then the project is likely to be very problematic.

◆ **Too many parallel activities and too short a time for key tasks** – timescales on projects are often shortened for a variety of reasons. A method of coping with this is to take sequential activities and try to do them in parallel. There is nothing wrong with parallel tasks, and all plans will have some degree of parallel working. Although it depends on the specific situation, in general, the more parallel tasking you have the more complex and risky management becomes. Where a plan is compressed so that more and more tasks become parallel and finishing tasks such as testing and training become shortened then risk increases, sometimes dramatically. It also means you must have more resource available at any point in time.

◆ **High risk with tight deadlines and no contingency plans** – high risk can be handled by a good project manager. In fact, some great project managers thrive running high risk projects. But if it is combined with tight and fixed deadlines, limited budgets and no contingency possible you should really think through whether this lack of opportunity to manoeuvre is not simply magnifying the risk to unmanageable proportions.

◆ **Unknown technology or solutions for a demanding high throughput situation** – applying new or novel technology always has some risk, but it needs to be done sometimes or else we would never implement anything new. The track record for delivering technology projects to time and budget is poor. However, the combination of completely novel technology and a mission and time critical project is particularly dangerous. We can all think of projects on which it has worked (the NASA moon shots, for example) but there are hundreds more examples where it has turned out disastrously wrong. Unless new technology offers significant benefits stick with the tried and tested or use it first in a situation which is not mission critical.

No single issue here need sound the death knell for a project, but any can be and a combination of them should really make you concerned. In the end this will have to come down to a judgement based on your experience – and if you are not sure, talk it through with a more experienced colleague. The best, and most highly sought-after project managers are the ones who can handle high risk projects that exhibit these characteristics, but much of their skill is not that they can perform miracles that you cannot, it is at least partially due to the fact that they are good at removing the risks, and will convince sponsors to change something so that some of the characteristics in the above list are no longer exhibited by the project.

Constructively killing projects off

Key lesson

It is far better to kill off bad ideas, or impractical good ideas than try to run an impossible project.

You have assessed a project as having very high risk with limited chance of success or limited chance that the benefits will be achieved. So what can you do in this situation? Essentially there are two options you can consider:

1   Seek to change some features of the projects to move it from the walking dead to simply a project with risks. It is unlikely you will ever be able to change such a project to a low risk one without it changing so much as to have little in common with the original concept. But you may be able to change it into an achievable project, if you can then all well and good. If not, you need to consider the next option.

2 Kill it off. Stopping work that is never going to complete should not be seen as a defeat or negative. We should positively encourage the killing off of bad ideas. We cannot avoid bad ideas, as it is a simple truth that if you allow creativity some of the resulting ideas will be no good. Strong organisations have two main strengths: firstly, they generate lots of ideas, and, secondly, they ruthlessly kill off the ones that will not work and only focus on a few good ideas.

In some organisations or some project management processes there are formal mechanisms for filtering out the weaker or riskier projects in the first place. The whole point of doing activities such as concept reviews and feasibility studies is not only to manage risk by scoping out the work more and to understand what must be done to deliver it, but also to stop some of the projects. If you have a concept review and feasibility process in your organisation and every single project is passed through you are almost certainly not being critical enough (or possibly not creative enough). Stopping poorly thought through, inappropriate or impractical ideas is a successful application of a filtering process and not a failure.

It is worth preparing yourself for some bad feeling coming back to you if you do kill off a project in mid-flight. No matter how suicidal a project was and no matter how sensible it was to stop it there may be members of the project team who have put in significant effort getting it to the state it was in. In fact, on very high risk projects people often work insanely hard because of the challenge of overcoming the problems or because they get emotionally attached to the work. These people will feel at least a degree of disappointment when the project is stopped. Don't be hard on them – this is human nature and these are the people with the right attitude to getting work delivered, it's just that it was wrongly placed this time. You may need to work with these people again so it is worth trying to manage feelings with sensitivity. I have seen major morale problems occurring in teams when a project has been killed. I clearly remember one specific situation – everyone logically agreed with the project being stopped, but people had put in extra effort trying to get the project to work, and their emotions really felt the disappointment of stopping it. One person even resigned soon afterwards.

The other group which may exhibit bad feelings comprises those with significant vested interests in the project coming off for one reason or another. Two things to realise here are that strong interests can make people blind to risk and having an absolute need for a project can remove any concern about risk, even if it is seen. Manage people who wanted or needed the project with care. Be clear in your mind that wants and needs do not make the impossible possible.

Just say 'no'

Key lesson

If you can, walk away from impossible projects. Gallantly failing to deliver is still failure.

If you do get to the point of needing to kill a project off, my tips are:

◆ Do not assume that everyone understands why you think the project is a bad idea. It may be completely obvious to you, but simply stating it is a bad idea or that it is obvious it is a bad idea will just irritate people, especially those who came up with the idea in the first place. You will need to explain it to people in a way that they understand.

◆ Structure a clear and brief presentation of why the project is a bad idea. Try to find at least some positives for the project so that you do not come across as just a negative sort of person. Put these into the language of your customer. Avoid or explain complex technical or specialist technology. Specialist reasons which cannot be explained to a non-specialist audience smack of a lack of desire to do a project rather than a lack of ability.

◆ Include constructive comments on how the project could be made feasible form your viewpoint. (You are doing this partially to provide a real alternative, but also partially to show that you are not inflexible or unreasonable. In this case, even if you know your alternatives will be unacceptable, it is worth including them in your response.)

◆ Prepare yourself to push against someone who may have emotional attachment to the idea. Emotion is a great thing when driving for success, but it can be very difficult when someone is attached to what is fundamentally unachievable. Do not assume they will always argue rationally or will not be willing to indulge in political tricks.

◆ Do not get emotionally involved – argue rationally from simple facts. If you are arguing from emotion you may, of course, be wrong and it will tend to come across in your communications.

◆ Listen and be open to counter-arguments and analyse them properly, but avoid making so many compromises that the project is pointless even if it now becomes achievable.

◆ Let the final choice be your customer's, give her the advice she needs to make a rational decision. If she understands the risk, but still wants to proceed this is her legitimate right. You may also legitimately question whether the project risk may reflect on you and become a personal risk to your own reputation. No-one succeeds by failing.

◆ Should the decision not be in your favour decide on the degree of personal risk and, if it is higher than you want, back out of the project (if possible).

So what do you do in the worst case … if you get to this part of the chapter, let's assume you have done these things. You have assessed the project and it is a disaster waiting to happen; your constructive approach to killing the project has failed. Someone still wants to move it on, and that someone is going to see it happens. All your judgement and assessments continue to tell you it will be a failure. You have tried to get the work changed or stopped. You have used all your communication skills to say why it is a bad idea.

But no-one is listening to you.

This is the time to pack your bags and say 'no'. You are the professional in these matters and if your customer or sponsor is not going to listen to this they probably will not listen to anything else you say which will make your working relationship difficult. I know you cannot always do it, but you will be amazed at the power of simply standing up and moving away from someone having said something like 'well, I have given my advice to the best of my professional ability, and I respect the fact that you wish to ignore it. Good luck and I honestly hope that I am wrong.'

> Do not get emotionally involved – argue rationally from simple facts

Thank them politely for the opportunity, say 'no' and leave. You owe it to yourself. I am not saying everyone will like you, or many people will thank you, but that is not always what being a consistently successful professional project manager is all about.

12

Closing thoughts

THIS BOOK HAS AIMED TO LAY OUT GUIDANCE for project managers on how to make that step from being a basic project manager to having advanced skills. It is intended to sit alongside any other formal knowledge and training you have had in project management mechanics.

The irony is that most of the things in this book are intuitively obvious and far simpler to implement than many advanced project management processes. That does not mean you should ignore them. When you go and see a great speaker present you will often find that when you analyse what he or she has said those brilliant points rang true and added tremendous value mainly because they were easy to understand and self-evidently true. It is no different for project managers, as project management at heart is an applied rather than abstract discipline.

I absolutely agree with the sticklers for good project management process. You should go away and learn your project management processes, but learn the practical rather than theoretical way of using them, after all project management is a practical subject as opposed to a theoretical one. But if you want to be really good, the processes are not enough – on top of these you need to apply your common sense and use of the skills referenced in this book. Build up your experience in using the lessons here so they become automatic and intuitive.

Project management can be a boom-to-bust business. When businesses are thriving they hoover up huge numbers of project managers. When business is in a downturn and costs are being looked at then project managers are an obvious target. It can be hard working in a profession that tends to be first in and first out, especially in situations where firms often find the only way to cut costs is to stop projects – and the only way to stop projects is to fire the project managers. Don't despair, however, as the irony is that the very best project managers remain in demand even in the most vicious downturn. Even cost cutting projects require project managers! In the boom times being a great project manager will drive your success, and in the downturns it will help to maintain your success.

The standards of project management will keep on rising as the occupation continues to become more professional. The days when people became project managers simply because they had nothing else to do are coming to an end. The challenge for you as a professional project manager is therefore to learn the lessons and to continue to improve.

Do observe other project managers. I have learnt many great lessons from watching other project managers, some of whom have never had a day's formal project management training in their lives. Seek out good project managers and try to work alongside them, or try to work for them as part of a bigger programme and learn their lessons. Learn from yourself as well – when you find a technique that works well, remember it and apply it again.

Every time a project completes do perform a review of it and think about what went well and what went badly. If it all went wrong, work out why, and be honest with yourself if it was your own fault. Work out what you would do differently next time. You must at least be truthful with yourself – so don't hide behind the fact that there were too many changes, too many risks, too few resources. What did you do about it? – you were the project manager! All great project managers have made mistakes at one time or other, but they have survived and learnt from the experience.

Good luck.

Quick reference guide – summary contents

This section provides a quick reference summary to the core contents of the book. It is intended as a rapid *aide-mémoire* which you can call on in your everyday application of the lessons from the book. If you need more detail do refer to the original chapter.

Chapter 1 – Some basics

Key lesson

You must understand and be able to define the key terms used within your project. This must include a clear definition of your role as the project manager, a definition of the customer, and a common understanding of success for your project.

A **project** is essentially a way of working, a way of organising people, and a way to manage tasks. It is a style of coordinating and managing work. What differentiates it from other styles of management is that it is totally focused on a specific outcome, and when this outcome is achieved the project ceases to be necessary and the project is stopped. A project starts at a defined point of time, ends at a specific point in time, and is complete when the outcome (normally as agreed at the beginning of the project, and normally defined in terms of specific tangible deliverables) is complete. It typically has some limited amount of resources, most commonly money and people's time, to deliver the outcome. When the outcome is delivered something will have changed. Although different projects may have some common features, each project is unique, with a specific one-off set of activities.

Project management is a formal approach to managing projects. It is made up of a defined set of processes, tools and methods.

A **project manager** is someone who is accountable for the delivery of a project (or a specific component of a project if working as part of a hierarchy of project managers).

You must be able to define your role in any specific project. A good way to do this is to be able to identify which components of the project plan and which set of deliverables you are accountable for.

Projects are done for **customers**, where a customer is someone who has any of the following three characteristics:

1 She will legitimately put requirements upon the project.

2 She will enjoy the benefits of the project once it is complete.

3 She has a formal role in judging the success of a project once it is complete.

Success in a project can be measured against three criteria:

1 Deliver the deliverables.

2 Achievement of associated benefits.

3 Customer satisfaction.

Chapter 2 – Listening and talking

Key lesson

Think about, plan and execute your communications with care, effort and impact. Your communications must be based on an understanding of your customer that goes beyond the requirements specification and sharing periodic reports. Your communications with the project team must go beyond sharing the project plan and having sporadic updates.

Communication skills are the core differentiator between average and great project managers. If you need to focus on enhancing your skills in any area – then start by working on your communication skills. Many points about communication can seem self-evident or obvious – they are still important. Start by thinking about who you must listen and talk to – this is your 'audience'.

Key lesson

Identify and assess your audience's information needs. Identify who is your customer and plan your interaction with them.

Your 'audience' can be split into three broad categories:

1 People directly involved in the project – this can be the project team, but will also include suppliers and other third parties responsible for delivery and delivery-related activities.

2 Customers of the project – the person or group of people for whom a project is being delivered. The customer can be broken down into several distinct categories:

   – The sponsor.

   – The financer.

   – The beneficiary.

   – The end user.

   – The end customer.

   The project manager has to:

   – Identify who the customers are.

   – Determine what information is relevant to them.

   – Determine what is the best timing, media and approach to use in passing this information.

   – Determine what you need in return from the customer.

3 Other stakeholders – a broad group that may include anyone else impacted by, or able to impact the outcome of the project. As far as the stakeholders are concerned the project manager needs to:

   – Identify who the stakeholders are.

   – Assess their relevance to the project.

   – Target those with significant impact on the project's success.

   – Target those significantly impacted by the project's outcome.

Key lesson

There is much more to understanding your customers needs than is written in the requirement specification. As project manager you must understand all the requirements at a high level, and specifically understand fully the scope of the project. Real understanding requires a constant two-way dialogue.

There are several things the project manager always needs to know before she can say she understands what the customer wants. They are:

◆ The scope of the project.

◆ The measures of success.

◆ The detailed requirements.

There are six key lessons for the project manager when it comes to understanding customer needs:

1 Make assumptions explicit – minimise the number of assumptions and if you must assume get the assumptions clear and shared.

2 Understand the scope – and make sure you can write down the answers and express them in words meaningful both to you and your customer.

3 Make sure you understand the customer requirements and how they relate to the project you are running. Expect differences of opinion and put in place some mechanism for resolving them. The test for you is:

– Do you have an overall grasp on the customer requirements, and how they relate together to give the overall customer solution?

– Do you understand why the customer has included these require-ments?

– Do you understand how these requirements will translate into blocks of work that the project will deliver?

– Do you understand how these blocks of work hang together?

– Can you visualise and explain this?

The answer to all of these questions must be 'yes'. This is not a demand that you understand and memorise each and every line of the requirements specification, and each and every line of every plan within your project. It is a demand though that you have a logical understanding of how it all comes together and when you look at every major activity within the project you know why it is being done and what the impact of it failing is. Without this knowledge you cannot plan, manage or deliver the project. If you are on a project and you cannot answer 'yes' to each of these questions – do some more work so you can answer 'yes' (or find someone else to run it).

4   Keep checking your understanding. Being sure last week is not the same as being sure today.

5   Customer needs go beyond the requirements specification – you must also understand how your customer wants to work with you.

6   It's not your project – remember you are working for your customer!

Key lesson

Talk, talk and talk again – the weekly report will not do it all. Practise and learn the seventeen communication skills to ensure you communicate fully and continuously with your customer and project team.

The basic mechanism for a project manager to communicate via is usually some form of regular reporting be it weekly or monthly (and in some cases daily or quarterly). Also, there are seventeen additional communication capabilities required of project managers. They are:

Lessons 1–4: Your planning and approach to communications

1   Plan your schedule of communications.

2   Accept regular reporting as part of the job.

3   Use formal presentations appropriately.

4   Use informal communications spontaneously and continuously.

Lessons 5–13: The style and method of communications

5 Use your audience's specialist language where appropriate.

6 Avoid too much project management jargon.

7 Clarify what you mean by risks.

8 Present complex information in a clear way.

9 Tailor communications to the audience.

10 Effectively communicate with senior audiences.

11 Do not rely on e-mails.

12 Be specific.

13 Present key factual information in whole messages at discrete time intervals.

Lessons 14–17: Rules to underpin all communications

14 Tell the truth.

15 Maintain only one version of the truth.

16 Obsessively manage expectations.

17 Communicate to deliver (don't deliver to communicate).

Chapter 3 – What actually is your project?

Key lesson

The foundation on which all good projects are built is a clear understanding of the scope. Without it a project manager will struggle to deliver successfully.

Scope is the foundation stone upon which all further project management activities are performed. The scope defines what is in and what is out of the project. Before you understand the scope you must not start to develop your project in any detail. Do not rush into developing solutions until you understand the scope.

Key lesson

The scope of a project can best be understood by going through a set of structured questions with your customer.

A good set of scoping questions are:

1 What is the overall objective of the project?

2 What are the deliverables?

   – Are there are deliverables required by the project which it is explicitly not responsible for?

   – Are you working to deliver a finite set of deliverables or provide some business capability?

   – Are you working to deliver a set of independent deliverables or an integrated end-to-end solution?

   – How will the quality of deliverables be determined?

3 Are you working to implement a specific solution, or to solve a problem?

   – Are you responsible for the delivery of deliverables or for achieving the business benefits?

4 How is the customer going to measure success at the end of the project?

5 What from the customer's viewpoint can flex?

   – Do you want predictability or speed?

6 Are there any other constraints on the project?

   – Are there any currently known issues, risks or opportunities?

   – Are there any external considerations?

7 How does your customer want to work with you?

   – How will decisions be made on the project?

   – How high is the project in your customer's overall priorities?

   – Can your sponsor allocate all the resources the project requires or do other stakeholders need to be involved?

   – Who can legitimately put requirements upon the project?

8 Are there any implicit requirements, assumptions or needs that the customer has that are not defined in the scope or requirements documents?

Chapter 4 – Some key traits

There are three key personality traits required by project managers:

1 A sense of ownership for what they do.

2 Good judgement.

3 The ability to be creative.

Key lesson

To be the most successful project manager you must feel and externally display a sense of complete ownership for the project and its outcome.

Key lesson

Each and every project is different and a project manager needs to adapt to each one. Although tools and processes will help, the basis for this adaptation must be the project manager's judgement.

Fifteen sample areas where a project manager regularly needs to apply judgement are:

1 What is in scope? Ensuring the scope is broad enough to achieve value, yet narrow enough to be achievable.

2 What should be in the plan? Making your plan detailed enough to achieve what you need to achieve with it, and yet to be manageable.

3 Which bits of project management process to apply and which to ignore? If you try to apply every project manager discipline in every situation you will spend your whole life managing and nothing will actually be delivered.

4 When to escalate? Finding the balance between escalating too soon and too late.

5 When to get into the detail and when to skim?

6 When to do and when to delegate?

7 Who can you trust in your project team?

8 What is an acceptable level of risk? The things to think about when assessing whether the level of risk is acceptable are:

 – Do you fully understand the risk or is it just the tip of an iceberg?

 – Are the risks independent issues or are they interrelated and cumulative?

 – Have you got a way around this risk – can it be reduced, can you mitigate it happening, or do you have a contingency plan should it happen? (Is the plan viable and are there resources to implement it?)

 – How risk-averse or risk-favouring is the organisation you are working in?

 – How critical is it that the project is delivered – if the risk derails the project will that have a significant impact on your customer or will they cope easily?

 – How good is your project team? A strong team is usually better able to handle and resolve risks.

9 What is an acceptable level of parallel activity? The questions you need to ask yourself are:

 – Do you have sufficient resources to do the work in parallel?

 – Are any of the tasks now in parallel logically only possible sequentially?

 – What is the impact on testing and training?

 – Can you as the project manager actually manage this?

10 What is an acceptable level of change? The key things to do are:

 – Ensure there is a robust change control process.

 – Develop an ability to explain the impact of change unemotionally.

 – Determine how important the change is.

 – Determine what the impact of the change on the project is.

- Assess how the project team handling it.

11 When should you enforce the change management process?

12 When is it reasonable to progress based on an assumption?

- What is the impact of not making an assumption? (Will your work be delayed, cost added, etc.?).

- What is the risk of making an assumption? (How likely is it that it will be wrong, and what will the impact be if it is)?

- How easy/difficult would it be to confirm the assumption you want to make?

13 How many levels of project management organisation do you need? One simple way of looking at it is how many people do you have managing work as opposed to doing work? If your number of managers is not a small percentage (less than 25%, perhaps as low as 10%) of the doers then you have too many layers of management. I have seen projects where 40–50% of the team seem to be managing rather than delivering – this is too high. Countering this – if you have significantly less than a 10% management overhead you probably have too few managers.

14 When to consider broader stakeholder groups?

15 When is the project complete?

Key lesson

Never be creative with your customer's requirements, but always look for creative ways to deliver those requirements.

Creativity has its roots in many places. In practice the main sources of creativity are:

◆ Yourself and the project team.

◆ Other people.

◆ Formal processes.

Chapter 5 – Getting your project started

Key lesson

The way you plan and resource your project will set the framework and constraints within which you will operate through the project. Take the time and effort to do it properly.

The following points should be considered in planning:

1   What your plan is for:
    - Forming a view of what tasks there are in a project and from this how long it will take and from this be able to derive what resources will be required.

    - Explaining to senior managers and other stakeholders how a project will be delivered.

    - Enabling people involved in the project to be allocated to work and for them to understand how their work fits within the project.

2   Therefore you should consider in every situation you are using a plan:
    - The level of detail required in this situation.

    - The presentation format.

    - The degree of 'specificity' – for example, is it generic about resources and resource type, or is it specific and names a particular individual?

3   The basic planning process is:
    - Build a work breakdown structure.

    - Add the lengths of time each task will take.

    - Build in the dependencies between the tasks.

    - Determine the resource types and quantities you need to meet this plan.

    - Add in your resource availability.

4   The factors to consider in building your plan are:
    - Who helps you develop the plan?

- Milestones.
- How many plans?
- The level of detail in your plan.
- Task size.
- The types of dependencies.
- How much parallel activity will you allow?

Key lesson

Be prepared to change your plan – the measure of success is not an unchanging plan, but meeting the end goals within the reality of continuous change.

The following points should be considered in resourcing:

1 The key questions resourcing will resolve are:

   - Where are you going to get resources from?
   - How are the people allocated to the project going to interact with the organisation in which they work?
   - How are you going to organise the project team members within the project?

2 The basic points to resource allocation are:

   - To determine from the plan what skills you require, and how many people with those skills you need for how long.
   - To work with resource owners (generally line managers), to get the necessary people allocated to the project.
   - To aggregate resources to understand points of over and under usage.
   - To reiterate the plan taking account of the actual resources available, which may be different from those you originally requested. You may reiterate between planning and resourcing several times. (In fact, to some extent this is a continuous interplay for the life of the project.)

3 The organisation of the project team. Take account of:

- – Size of project.
- – Stage of a project.
- – Complexity of the work.
- – Type of staffing.
- – Relationship to end users.

It's not just people we have to resource a project with! The following points should be considered with regard to budgeting:

What you must budget for:

◆ Items the project must buy as components of deliverables.

◆ Items the project must pay for as they are required to do the work in the project.

◆ External resource costs – contractors and consultants.

◆ Internal resource costs – staff from your own organisation.

Key lesson

Having contingency built into a plan is essential and is not a sign of poor project management. The critical factor is how much contingency, and how you allocate and manage this. This should be related to the degree of risk of your specific project.

The following points should be considered with regard to contingency:

The basic process for including contingency in your plan is:

◆ Avoid building contingency into every activity.

◆ Hold your contingency pot centrally.

◆ Manage people to hit the plan – but release contingency when required.

◆ Manage and monitor your contingency pot. If it is disappearing faster than progress on the project you have a problem looming.

The following points should be considered with regard to mobilisation. Mobilisation is to:

◆ Energise and align the project team. If it is a large project team this may take some considerable effort (see also Chapter 8).

◆ To ensure the broader stakeholder community is supportive of the project and ready for it (or you have activities planned to overcome resistance where necessary).

◆ To ensure project team members understand the objectives of their involvement, the specific work tasks that have been allocated to them, and how they fit within the overall plan.

Key lesson

Project management theory often defines the ideal environment to set up and run a project in. In practice, not all ideal environmental conditions will be achieved and as a project manager you must learn to deliver in sub-optimal situations managing a variety of constraints and compromises.

When you have to work within constraints:

◆ See the constraint as a constructive challenge.

◆ Start by assessing what the impact of the constraint is.

◆ Then review your approach to your project.

◆ Look at the project lifecycle you are implementing and see if additional stages need to be added.

◆ Are there mitigating actions you can take?

◆ Talk to your customer and explore options.

◆ In doing this, present them with options.

◆ Make an explicit decision on how you will manage this constraint.

◆ Having decided which path you are taking, re-plan the project accordingly and communicate the changes.

Chapter 6 – Personal styles

Key lesson

There is no right interpersonal style for a project manager – successful project managers have a variety of styles. But there are certain approaches to avoid, and some key attributes of style to develop.

Key lesson

Certain interpersonal styles will limit your success as a project manager.

Styles to avoid:

1 Bully boys.
2 Process nuts, compulsive planners, and detail obsessives.
3 The Teflon man.
4 The panicking manager.

Key lesson

Choose the personal style that best develops your personal brand. Build the attributes of good style to help you succeed.

What are the attributes of personal style that have the largest impact on people's perception of you? There are eleven factors:

1 Having empathy with your customer.
2 Displaying both management and leadership skills.
3 The ability to handle stress.

4 Respect for people.

5 Dynamism and positivism.

6 Networking skills.

7 Political sensitivity.

8 Having sufficient presence.

9 A sense of humour.

10 Being sensitive to your environment.

11 Adapting your style to the situation.

Chapter 7 – Managing your project

Key lesson

To manage projects a project manager must understand what she should be managing, have a mechanism to provide information to understand when management action is required, and finally implement action when the information tells her it is necessary.

Key lesson

The degree of difficulty in managing project is closely related to how well you have set the foundations (in terms of expectations, scope, plan and resources) in place.

1 What should you manage?

- – The time the project is taking to deliver.
- – The resources you are using to deliver.
- – The quality of the work done.
- – The scope.

    – Your customer's expectations.

2 How do you know to take management action?

    – Formal progress reporting and progress monitoring:

        – Progress reports and other formal inputs from the project team.

        – Ongoing planning and monitoring.

        – Budget and spend.

        – Project team meetings.

    – Use and assessment of outputs from project management tools, e.g.:

        – Risk management.

        – Issue management.

        – Assumption management.

        – Change control.

    – Quality control and quality audits of deliverables.

    – Informal day-to-day conversations and communications.

    – Direct feedback from the customer.

3 How should you manage?

    – Change the way the team are working.

    – Change resources on a project.

    – Change the scope of a project.

    – Add tasks to the plan.

    – Change the plan or approach.

    – Change the quality.

    – Escalate to senior managers to make decisions.

    – Terminate the project.

Key lesson

The success of a project manager depends on an understanding of what can be managed and sources of information to trigger management action. The measure of success is only dependent on the taking of the action and its result.

> ## Key lesson
>
> Change control provides a mechanism for a project manager to respond to changes in a project's scope and requirements in a controlled fashion. It is essential to successful project management to have a robust change control process supported by ongoing expectation setting.

Change control and management

◆ Capture and log any changes that are proposed.

◆ Understand and assess the change.

◆ Determine viable options for responding to the change.

◆ Discuss with the sponsor and agree whether to accept the change, and if so which approach to take to it.

◆ Adapt your plans accordingly.

Decision making

The key points about decision making are that it is a constant trade-off between:

◆ How critical is the decision and what is the impact if it is wrong?

◆ How critical is the decision and what is the impact if you take too much time to make it? (The most difficult to make being those that must be made quickly, but which also need lots of information and have a big impact if wrong.)

◆ Understanding who can and who should make the decision. Can you do it? Do you need an expert specialist? Is it something for your sponsor to decide?

◆ What is the culture of your organisation? Some company's value considered decision making, others value speed and pace over accuracy.

Chapter 8 – The team

Key lesson

One of the main tasks for a project manager is to manage and motivate the project team to deliver all that is required for the project. Pure project management process and methodologies will not achieve this – a project manager above all else is a people manager.

To get the best from the project team the project manager must follow sixteen key people management tasks.

Getting the basics right – right people, right skills, right tasks (management tasks 1–4)

1 Ensure the project team has the right capabilities and skills – managing any gap between the abilities of the project team and the needs of the project as a risk.

2 Go for quality rather than quantity. When in doubt always go for fewer, better people – they will be easier to manage and will produce more.

3 Ensure all team members have clear roles and defined objectives. Everyone on the team should therefore know:

- What their role is and what the tasks are that they are expected to perform. This should be defined clearly and succinctly.

- Who on the project is allowed to allocate them work, and who they will be working with.

- Who they need to interact and work with to complete their tasks.

- How much time they are expected to spend on the project (both in terms of duration and percentage of time in this period to be made available to the project).

- What are the measures of success for their task.

- Why they were chosen. Even if it is true, avoid telling people that they are on the project because they were the only person available as it is not very motivating!

4 Manage poor performance, give people a chance, but do not hesitate to throw people off the project team if they are adding unnecessary or unmanageable risk.

Motivating and building the team (management tasks 5–9)

5 Align personal objectives and motivation with the needs of the project – even without direct line authority over team members.

6 Actively work to build the team.

7 Align personal development needs and opportunities for team members with project activities.

8 If possible ensure project team members have a home to go back to once the project is complete.

9 Be aware of team dynamics and team politics.

Project team management challenges (management tasks 10–14)

10 Try to get the project team working in close physical proximity, and manage the communications channels. Where it is not possible to make people work in close proximity make sure that communications chains are robust, and that people communicate in the most 'intimate' ways possible. By this I mean ideally face-to-face, next via video conference, then by phone and, finally, by e-mail (and e-mail should be seen very much as the poorest way to communicate).

11 Do not forget your physically remote and geographically diverse staff.

12 Learn to manage part-time staff – not all resources will be full time, dedicated to your project.

13 Learn to manage upwards.

14 Learn to manage specialists who are not dedicated to the project. Ensure the specific specialist in question has actually set aside time for your task; fully understands the implication of being late; has a clear understanding of the quality required and the degree of risk acceptable to the project; and finally that they understand you are an important client who needs to be satisfied.

The broader context (management tasks 15–16)

15 Don't forget the wider organisation – manage your relationship and communications with them.

16 Plan for the end of the project and disbanding the project team.

Chapter 9 – The limits of knowledge

There are two traps project managers sometimes fall into. The first is to try and apply generic project management skills to the situation in which a specialist is required. The second is to try and do things that are best done by other people.

Key lesson

Complex projects are best managed to success by people skilled in project management. Project management is largely a generic approach to managing projects – but being a project manager is not a completely generic skill that can be applied to any project in any situation. To be successful, project managers need to understand and be able to use the language, concepts and ideas which are used within the context of the project they are managing.

If you are a project manager and are having to consider whether you are competent to manage a project in any specific situation, ask yourself:

1 Are you comfortable managing this scale of project?

2 Are you able to operate within the organisation this project is for? Do you broadly understand any specialist language and terminology they use?

3 Can you plan, direct and control the various components of the project assuming the necessary specialists are available to do the work?

4 Can you assess the quality of deliverables?

5 Can you challenge specialists competently?

6 Will the customer accept you?

If the answer to all six of these is 'yes', then you have enough specialist skills to manage the project.

> ## Key lesson
>
> Project managers must respect the need for a range of specialist disciplines on their project, and must fight for all the resources the project needs. Being a project manager on a large project is a full-time job, and even if the project manager has the skills to do other tasks he must focus his time and energy on managing the project and not doing other project tasks.

There are seven regular culprit areas that project managers often try to do themselves when they are usually better off using a specialist expert in the area. The culprits are:

1 Business analysis and requirements capture.

2 Change management. The three key uses of this term are:

 - Project change management – legitimately part of a project manager's role.

 - Operational change management – typically the responsibility of an operational manager, but needs to be understood by the project manager.

 - People change management – to be done by specialists in change management.

3 Systems integration and testing.

4 Supplier negotiations.

5 Contract and legal issues.

6 Project office.

7 Communications. Projects that have been set up to drive things such as large organisational change activities often need much wider communication – for example, to thousands of staff impacted across a company. This type of communication is more akin to a marketing, journalistic or PR skill set than straightforward communications by a project manager to customers or team members.

Having looked at some areas which are close to the project manager's heart, but critically not his responsibility in all but the simplest project, what actually should he do about these?

1 Get a basic level of competence in all of these areas – not to complete complex tasks in each area but so you can actively and fully interact with professionals in each of these disciplines and so you can manage them.

2 Learn when and how to engage people in each of these areas.

3 Learn to use their language and concepts so you can manage and challenge them without doing their job.

4 If you do engage them make sure your project sponsor understands why it is not your task and what the specialist brings.

Ask yourself four questions if you are unsure whether to pick up a task or not:

1 Do you understand the task well enough to be able to fully scope out what needs to be done?

2 Do you have the knowledge and experience to complete the tasks to the quality required and without exposing the project to unnecessary risk?

3 Is the input of a professional in this area optional?

4 Do you have the time to do this work without jeopardising your project management responsibilities?

Only if you can answer 'yes' to all four of these questions should you do it.

Chapter 10 – The mechanics of project management

Key lesson

Project management methodologies contain a rich set of approaches and tools, yet project managers frequently only apply a few of these. Do not forget the other components which on complex and risky projects will be very useful. Successful project managers have a very broad toolkit which they make use of regularly.

Excluded because they are covered elsewhere in the book, or are not relevant to the book:

1 Planning (Chapter 5).

2 Project change control procedures (Chapter 7).

3 Decision making (Chapter 7).

4 Create standard forms and documents.

5 Create weekly and monthly reports to a standard format.

6 Allocate resources and manage using tools such as timesheets and time recording systems.

7 Use common project management software.

Key lesson

Good project managers accept that each and every project is different, and they therefore adapt their approach accordingly – choosing which parts of the project manager's toolkit to apply in which situations – and applying them in the simplest fashion commensurate with the complexity and scale of the project.

Thirteen skills to ensure you understand and apply as required are:

Skills 1–7: The core project management mechanics

1 Management of assumptions:
   - Document them.
   - Challenge them.
   - Asses them.
   - Give them an owner.
   - Set target dates to resolve them by.
   - Be prepared.
   - Remove critical ones.

2 Sign off – do it.

3 Management of external dependencies:

- Ensure you understand what project or piece of work is delivering the dependency, and who is responsible for ensuring it is being delivered?
- Try to see if you can remove the dependency.
- Ensure somebody somewhere is responsible for delivering the dependency.
- Get periodic updates on progress.
- Probe the progress reports to give confidence that they are accurate.

4 The time–cost–quality–scope trade-off – understand it fully and apply it in day-to-day decision making.

5 Basic risk and issue management.

- Use a phased project approach that enables you to understand and manage risk. Performing a feasibility study is essentially a risk management step – with it you can:
  - reduce uncertainty in the plans;
  - identify specific risks that need to be managed;
  - clarify where you need contingency plans;
  - build a project plan accordingly.
- Ensure your project has a robust risk management approach, and regularly identify and review the risks that you have.
- Assess these risks to see if any of them result in a significant chance of something occurring with a significant impact on the project. If this is true you need to do something about the risk.
- Plan what you can do about the risk. This essentially falls into four categories:
  - Maintain a watching brief.
  - Mitigate against the risk.
  - Mitigate against the impact of the risk.
  - Have a contingency plan.

6 Contingency planning and triggers:

- The key points to think through with respect to contingency plans are:

    - What triggers your contingency plan?

    - Do you have the resources to implement the contingency plan?

    - Does it actually reduce risk?

    - What can you de-scope if the choice is not delivering?

7 Using escalation effectively.

Skills 8–13: Supporting mechanics

8 Benefits realisation:

- Define well-estimated benefits at the start of the project.

- Ensure it is possible to measure these benefits.

- Assign resources and responsibility for measuring the benefits.

- Set expectations about how much benefit will be achieved during the lifetime of the project and agree with the sponsor how benefits will be tracked after the project has been completed.

9 Stakeholder analysis:

- High impact, high support.

- High impact, low support.

- Low impact, high support.

- Low impact, low support.

10 Use of project office:

- Do you understand what you may want the project office to do?

- Will this make you more efficient or effective?

- Who has access to the project office resource?

- Does everyone else understand what it does?

11 Administration and management of meetings.

12 Prioritisation:

- On what basis are you prioritising? You need to have some measure by which to form the basis of prioritisation.

- Go for broad, simple categorisation of tasks that everyone understands, such as:

    - Must do, cannot slip.

    - Must do, can allow to slip to a limited extent.

    - Must do, time can move.

    - Optional, but important.

    - Optional, not critical.

- Be prepared for a reasonable degree of volatility and to respond to escalation requests.

- Make sure the prioritisation is explicit.

- Be ruthless in applying priorities once they are agreed.

- Do not confuse how urgent a task is with how important it is.

- Agree what you do with low priority tasks.

- Consider the time–cost–quality–scope trade-off when setting priorities.

13 Use of project lifecycles:

- Understand the principles of different lifecycles and apply them as appropriate.

- Be able to use the correct language on lifecycles for the context you are working in.

- Vary the lifecycle to suit the type of problem you are trying to resolve.

Chapter 11 – Knowing when to say 'no'

Project management is about ensuring delivery, not about pointless heroics against unassailable odds. When things are not going to happen it is best to avoid them, or better still, ensure they are killed off before they get anywhere. No matter how well you do it, you will not get to be a great or successful project manager spending your whole life brilliantly failing to deliver impossible projects. A useful skill is therefore knowing when to say 'no', and equally important how to say 'no'.

Key lesson

Just because someone thinks they need a project manager it neither means they really do, nor does it mean it is actually the best use of your time.

Before accepting project work it is worth considering:

◆ Is this the best use of the project manager?

◆ Does this project manager have the right sort of skills?

◆ Is this really a project-based activity?

Key lesson

There are many clear indications when a project is likely to fail – look for these and assess whether you are able to manage the risks or not.

Danger signs to look for are:

1 No energy.
2 No real drive or sponsorship.
3 No willingness to free up the right resources.
4 Overly demanding customers with unreasonable expectations.
5 Conflicting goals.
6 Conflicting customers.
7 Poor understanding of requirements or scope.
8 Not enough time to test.
9 Too many parallel activities and too short a time for testing or training in the plan.
10 High risk with tight deadlines and no contingency plans.

11 Unknown technology or solutions for a demanding high throughput situation.

Key lesson

It is far better to kill off bad ideas, or impractical good ideas than try to run an impossible project.

Key lesson

If you can, walk away from impossible projects. Gallantly failing to deliver is still failure.

Index